Praise for AMERICA'S GREAT STORM

"I'll never forget reporting from the Mississippi Gulf Coast the morning after Hurricane Katrina. It was overwhelming to see where I grew up virtually wiped away by our country's worst natural disaster. Those impacted by America's Great Storm needed food, water, shelter, and above all we needed leadership to see us through this difficult time. I'm grateful that Haley Barbour showed us and now shares with us in this book what it truly takes to be a leader, perhaps the most valuable lesson being that leadership is about focusing on the people and not the process."
—ROBIN ROBERTS, co-anchor of ABC's *Good Morning America*

"Governor Haley Barbour's personal account of how he responded to the Hurricane Katrina disaster is a study in effective leadership. Required reading for all those interested in learning how one leader of one state can make a difference in the lives of thousands. A Mississippi and national hero."
—KENNETH R. FEINBERG, administrator of the September 11 Victim Compensation Fund and other compensation programs

"Haley Barbour, the best public official to deal with Katrina, is the best at telling its story. He was a can-do leader when Mississippi needed to have one and the country needed to see one. I've often said that Haley gives the best political briefing in the country. With *America's Great Storm*, he shows himself just as sharp sizing up an historic disaster and how his state boldly addressed it. He's right that it did wonders for the image of Mississippi."
—CHRIS MATTHEWS, host of MSNBC's *Hardball*

"Governor Barbour has been a tremendous advocate for smart emergency management. As director of Florida's Emergency Management Division, I witnessed firsthand his commitment to putting survivors first. During the response to Katrina, he cut red tape and supported our work to get resources into the hands of those who needed them most by helping us treat Mississippi counties like Florida counties. Working across state lines helped us save lives and helped Mississippi recover from this disaster more quickly."
—WILLIAM CRAIG FUGATE, former director of Florida's Emergency Management Division

"Hurricane Katrina revealed the character of America's leaders in its rawest form. Too many were tragically overmatched by the great flood's force and fury. But Haley Barbour stood alone, equal to the challenge before him in a way that lifted his state and inspired a nation. On this somber anniversary, we are fortunate to get this recounting of the Mississippi governor moving through those gripping times with strength and certainty. Like Barbour himself, this story is nothing less than inspiring."
—JOE SCARBOROUGH, former Florida congressman and host of MSNBC's *Morning Joe*

AMERICA'S GREAT STORM

LEADING THROUGH HURRICANE KATRINA

HALEY BARBOUR

With Jere Nash

FOREWORD BY RICKY MATHEWS

University Press of Mississippi
Jackson

www.upress.state.ms.us

The University Press of Mississippi is a member of the Association
of American University Presses.

First printing 2015

∞

Library of Congress Cataloging-in-Publication Data

Barbour, Haley, 1947–
America's great storm : leading through Hurricane Katrina /
Haley Barbour, with Jere Nash ; foreword by Ricky Mathews.
pages cm
Includes bibliographical references and index.
ISBN 978-1-4968-0506-5 (cloth : alk. paper) — ISBN 978-1-4968-0507-2 (ebook)
1. Barbour, Haley, 1947–   2. Hurricane Katrina, 2005.   3. Governors—Mississippi.
4. Political leadership—Mississippi.   5. Emergency management—Mississippi.
6. Disaster relief—Mississippi.   I. Title.
HV636 2005. M7 B37 2015
976.2'064092—dc23
2015011841

British Library Cataloging-in-Publication Data available

To my wife, Marsha Dickson Barbour, the heroine of the story of our recovery from Katrina who became to those on the Mississippi Gulf Coast the face that showed their state cared and was trying to do all it could to help them.

To the nearly one million volunteers who came to the Gulf Coast and South Mississippi and gave their time, energy, and hearts to people they didn't know before the storm, and to the faith-based, charitable, and governmental groups who helped organize and direct so many of these volunteers.

To my late mother, LeFlore Johnson Barbour, who raised my two brothers and me and from whom I learned the bases of many of the lessons that helped get the people of Mississippi through this catastrophe.

To Anthony J. Topazi, president of Mississippi Power, who set the standard for leadership in the worst natural disaster in American history.

And, finally, to the courageous people of Mississippi whose strength and character allowed them to overcome the devastation of America's Great Storm.

Contents

CONTENTS

Foreword

"**O**UR TSUNAMI." That was the *Sun Herald* headline on August 30, 2005, the day after Hurricane Katrina wiped the Mississippi Gulf Coast off of the face of the earth.

At the time of Katrina, I was president and publisher of the *Sun Herald*, South Mississippi's dominant newspaper. I grew up in Gulfport, and to serve as publisher of the newspaper that covers the wonderfully diverse set of coastal communities that make up that region was an honor—and an obligation. Our former publisher and my mentor, Roland Weeks, hammered into me a deep appreciation and understanding for the important role a newspaper plays in society to not only help keep democracy viable but to contribute toward the quality of life of those it serves.

The devastation created by the largest storm surge ever recorded in United States history was mind-boggling. And heartbreaking. Yet it quickly became apparent that if there were to be a path out of the catastrophe and toward recovery and rebuilding, it would be defined and led by one man: Haley Barbour, then Governor of the State of Mississippi.

Haley, as he prefers to be called, will go down in history as the gold standard for how a chief executive should lead when the previously unthinkable becomes the undeniable reality. After Katrina, Haley was a man on a mission. We have never seen anyone like him. And if a man is measured by his ability to respond to the worst of times, we may live our whole lives without seeing another elected leader called by such a challenge and answering in such a way.

In important ways, Haley was made for this moment. His accent and folksy mannerisms comfort those who need reassurance that he knows where he comes from. For those in the region, this provides an instant connection with those who must believe and trust him. For those beyond the South, the Haley style is disarming, perhaps even an invitation to underestimate him—which serves him well in complicated negotiations to advance the goals of Mississippi's communities in need. It's a temporary advantage, though, because anyone who has seen Haley in action comes to respect his extraordinary capacities as a leader and thinker.

Behind that friendly, confident exterior is a man with a mind like a steel trap. There's a driven man who is often five steps ahead of most of us. There's a leader who has an extraordinary ability to inspire others. And as political insiders across the ideological spectrum can attest, Haley's understanding of the levers of power—and, as a result, his access to those levers—are unparalleled.

At his core, Haley Barbour is a policy wonk. He understands the complicated and sometimes tepid waters of policy and seems to enjoy the process of extracting the best of not-so-promising ideas. And standing behind him and supporting him is an amazing woman in Marsha Barbour, who has a heart bigger than the State of Mississippi. Marsha was truly touched and driven. She not only became Haley's eyes, ears, and heart on the ground but was in many ways the face that said "Somebody cares and is doing everything possible to help." She poured everything into trying to understand the needs, and she left nothing on the table. I saw it with my own eyes. Over the weeks and months, I wondered how she kept going. Like those of us who lived and worked in ground zero, I believe she felt she literally had no choice. It was her destiny to help as many people as possible.

At the core of my newspaper's mission was a call to public service journalism, a determination to make a real difference in the communities served by the *Sun Herald.* Watching my team at the newspaper come together in the wake of the storm, in spite of so many of them losing friends and family and all worldly possessions, was something to behold. All employees committed themselves to telling the story of Katrina. And the *Sun Herald* editorial board wrote an unprecedented number of editorials focused on finding help and solutions and celebrating the volunteers who came from far and wide to help us. For our work, the *Sun Herald* was awarded a Pulitzer Prize Gold Medal for Public Service, which we dedicated to the people of South Mississippi.

At an editorial board meeting with Haley Barbour a few months after Hurricane Katrina, we covered the full spectrum of recovery efforts happening across the Mississippi Coast. A question was raised about a specific infrastructure project in Waveland, Mississippi. Off of the top of his head, Haley dove deep into the facts of that project, recalling numbers and details. I remember thinking how impressive it was watching Haley's mind in action. His ability to process and discuss massive amounts of information from memory was truly impressive. It was a demonstration of the strengths disguised by his down-home style and a comfort to those of us who realized how much of South Mississippi's future was invested in this man's considerable gifts.

As you will read in the pages to follow, Haley's mission was to help Mississippi not only recover much of what the storm blew away but also build back better and stronger than ever. He told us there would be a recovery period that would last for years. In order to recover, we had to rebuild. And the process of rebuilding would open opportunities to raise the bar for safety and quality of life—provided, he told us, we invested the passion, determination, and commitment those tasks required.

There were literally thousands of people who were brought together by the work of the Governor's Commission on Recovery, Rebuilding, and Renewal through the various meetings, committee efforts, and public forums. The effort showed that the cities and counties that make up coastal Mississippi could set their differences aside while finding common cause. And it revealed the character of the people and incredible passion they had for their towns and neighborhoods, many of which no longer physically existed. We all came to appreciate that buildings did not make a community. People did. Once that fact was understood, the unprecedented rebuilding effort began. And it was Haley who brought us all together.

There were debates and battles and moments of great success along the way. Some I was part of. Some I watched. But no matter what side of the debates you were on, Haley always had an appreciation for the need to move forward together. South Mississippi, he told us over and over, was in control of its own destiny. He encouraged debate and innovation. And while he had patience most of the time, he knew when to apply pressure. He realized that before people could start the process to rebuild their lives, the entire infrastructure would have to be rebuilt: schools, roads, bridges, sewage systems, water systems, town centers, city halls, police and fire stations, the nonprofit community, and homes. The sense of urgency was always front and center.

It seems surreal to me now, ten years after the storm, as I sit in New Orleans as publisher of *The Times-Picayune* and recall the political dimensions of the post-Katrina efforts that seemed to pit Louisiana against Mississippi. But for those of us in the trenches of the recovery, including Haley, there was a strong appreciation that, for the Mississippi coast to come back strong, New Orleans and the Louisiana coast had to come back strong as well. We were all in this together.

In the pages that follow, you'll go on Haley's Katrina recovery journey. You will read about incredible volunteer leaders like Jim Barksdale, Anthony Topazi, George Schloegel, and hundreds more like them. You'll read about the roles played by President George W. Bush, Senators Trent Lott and Thad Cochran, Congressman Gene Taylor, Mississippi Speaker of the House William "Billy" McCoy, and many other elected leaders.

You'll see how amazing things can happen when all levels of government strive to work together after a disaster. And while the high cost of construction and insurance, a challenging economy, and other factors impacted coastal Mississippi's recovery efforts every step of the way over the past ten years, we have arrived at a better place as a result of the leadership of Haley Barbour.

This book shows you why.

Ricky R. Mathews, President NOLA Media Group

Acknowledgments

THIS BOOK WOULD NOT HAVE BEEN POSSIBLE without the forty-seven men and women who not only agreed to be interviewed for several hours at a time but have since read through various drafts of the manuscripts, double checking our narrative and offering edits and improvements. They are listed in the sources, and while they earned my everlasting gratitude and admiration for their public service in the days and months following Katrina, I am honored they agreed to participate in this memoir.

Keeping track of my writing, all my hand-scribbled notes, and the editing process as this book came together was handled perfectly by Zoe Louise Jackman, my assistant in Washington, and by Jenny Berryhill, my assistant in Jackson. They were critical to getting this done, for we could never have met our deadlines without them.

The interviews were transcribed by Molly Eaton and Carrie McDill of Bond & Benoist Court Reporting, and by Terri Whitmire Henderson and Jana McNair, all in record time and all flawless.

David Warrington spent weeks on end reading through microfilmed newspapers at the Mississippi Department of Archives and History, getting us copies of relevant articles and editorials, and tracking down obscure references whenever we needed corroboration for a story or anecdote.

Susan Watkins and Lida Gibson organized thousands of photographs we used to choose the few that made their way into the book, and they tracked down the credits we needed. Like Zoe and Jenny, they accomplished these tasks in record time. Susan also coordinated our process for having the people we interviewed review the chapter drafts. To say this required attention to detail is an understatement.

I am grateful that Leila Salisbury and her staff at the University Press of Mississippi agreed to take me on as a project. Because we were late getting started and because we wanted the book out in time for the tenth anniversary, I believe it is safe to say we offered them a challenge. That the book is in your hands is a testament to their professionalism and their ability to rise to the challenge.

Last but certainly not least, I sincerely thank Jere Nash, my co-author, for the super job he did in organizing, interviewing, writing, editing, and Lord knows what else to get this done. Without Jere, and left to my own devices, this book would probably have never happened. He has been a great, indispensable partner.

America's Great Storm

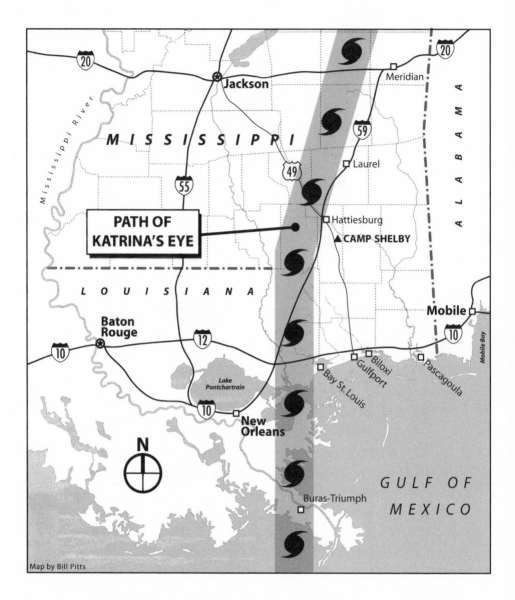

Map by Bill Pitts

Introduction

O N AUGUST 25, 2005, as Hurricane Katrina crossed Florida as a Category 1 storm, I called Gov. Jeb Bush to offer the assistance of Mississippi's National Guard, as I had several times previously when his state was hit with five serious hurricanes during 2004–5. Little did I know or expect that four days later that same hurricane would visit my state as America's Great Storm, the worst natural disaster in our nation's history.

This book is my personal account of the twelve months that followed Katrina's destructive path over our Gulf Coast and through the southern half of Mississippi. It is not an all-inclusive narrative or a comprehensive history of that period—the books by James Patterson Smith, Douglas Brinkley, and others largely achieve that goal—but more a memoir of the experiences of the fellow who was providentially placed at the head of the effort to prepare for the devastating storm with its massive destruction, then the frantic search and rescue, and on to the cleanup, recovery, rebuilding, and renewal of more than half of my state. That being said, much of what I write about is covered by neither Smith nor Brinkley. I also wanted to share lessons in leadership I learned from this megadisaster, lessons that I believe apply to almost any major crisis.

Our recovery from Katrina is the story of strong, resilient, self-reliant people who were knocked flat but then got back on their feet, hitched up their britches, and went to work helping themselves and helping their neighbors. My mother taught Wiley and Jeppie, my two older brothers, and me that crises tend to bring out the best in people, and although there were, of course, exceptions in the weeks and months following Katrina's drive across Mississippi, I saw Mama's observation demonstrated over and over and over again.

Because the news media focused much of their initial coverage on looters and those who failed to protect lives and property in Louisiana, many Mississippians were angry when their horrendous losses were ignored or, at best, underreported. I reminded them, "The news media doesn't like to cover airplanes that land safely."

Nevertheless, as time went on, Americans began to notice the way in which Mississippians met head-on the challenges of recovery. I have come to believe that the response of the people of Mississippi to Katrina's destruction did more to improve the image of our state than anything that has happened in my lifetime. Not only were neighbors helping and, quite honestly, making sacrifices for each other, but first responders and other government employees performed their jobs magnificently in the critical first hours and days of search and rescue and security—and for the weeks, months, and years that followed. An oft-cited example of that fidelity is the Waveland Police Department's response after the storm slammed that small town of about 6,700. Waveland is the western-most incorporated municipality on the Mississippi Gulf Coast and, thus, the closest to the path of the storm's eye. It was totally submerged under a twenty-eight-foot storm surge, plus waves of six or eight feet on top.

The plan for the twenty-six members of the Waveland Police Department was to ride out the hurricane in their headquarters and, after it passed, to engage in search and rescue and reestablish security throughout the community. Of course, the storm surge went far over the top of the building, with the officers escaping out of the windows and doors into the deluge. Despite winds of more than one hundred miles per hour, several formed a "human chain" by holding on to a bush near the headquarters while others were washed completely beyond the city limits. Nevertheless, by eight o'clock that night, despite knowing their own homes were destroyed, all of Waveland's police officers were back on duty. The valor of these sworn officers was just one of many such stories about those who engaged in the effort to save lives, protect property, and clean up from the utter obliteration. Remembering those heroes is another reason I wanted to write this book.

I also address head-on the question of the performance in Mississippi of Federal Emergency Management Agency (FEMA). Did things go wrong? Did some people or systems fail? Sure they did. But the key was the way in which we responded to those failures.

My account begins in the days leading up to landfall, when we had made plans based on the worst hurricane Mississippi had ever experienced—Camille, in the summer of 1969, considered the "gold standard": one of three U.S. hurricanes to have come ashore as a Category 5 with winds approaching 190 mph. Mississippians could not conceive of anything worse. Katrina proved us wrong, and I explain the reasons for that and how it defined our response.

As I stared down at the Coast from a helicopter the morning after, it looked as if the hand of God had wiped away a seventy-mile stretch of coastal communities, in some places erasing everything for blocks away from the beach, in other places for miles inland. Obliterated were multiple infrastructures from electrical to communications, to schools, to roads and bridges, to water and sewer lines. After the storm, some sixty thousand homes were destroyed or left uninhabitable along the Gulf Coast, with thousands more throughout the rest of the state.

Restoring schools, reclaiming jobs, and rebuilding houses defined our recovery strategy—if we could accomplish those three goals, then I had faith the Gulf Coast and South Mississippi would come back better than ever. How we met those goals consumes much of the book's narrative.

A lesson of Katrina is the critical importance of preparation, especially self-preparation for families and businesses in dealing with a disaster. Even if the plan you established in your preparation can't be executed as practiced, having a plan will help you deal with the disaster more effectively. You have to help yourself and your business because no government is or ever should be big enough to take care of every problem for every family or company all the time, even during a disaster.

A key to our ability to recover as quickly as we did came not only from preparation and from the character of the people affected but also from the uniform acceptance that someone had to be in charge. With three coastal counties and eleven incorporated municipal governments, it would have been easy to have had competition for control by and among the local officials. Believe me, unlike in the business world where everyone recognizes that the CEO is in charge, in the political world that is not a given. Despite the fact that I am a Republican and only the second GOP governor since 1876, and that many of the local officials were Democrats, it was universally accepted that the only "someone" who could be in charge was the Governor.

That recognition was critical in the early days after Katrina, but it was also very important in dealing with the federal government and in working out long-term plans. My team and I certainly didn't make the right decision every time, but local officials, legislators, and private citizens and businesses felt they were being heard and their disagreements were being considered.

A lesson from this disaster is you must make decisions, and I believe that is applicable to leadership in any crisis. You can't dither, but you must also be willing to reconsider those decisions in the subsequent face of evidence that things are not working as expected or that a better solution is available. I did that on several occasions after Katrina, and my team made many adjustments to improve outcomes.

This brings me to another reason I wanted to write this book—to use this year's tenth anniversary to recognize all the help Mississippi received from the federal government, from other state governments, from hundreds and hundreds of businesses, churches, and nonprofit organizations, and from hundreds of thousands of individuals who gave in ways large and small that lifted our spirits day in and day out.

While the failure of FEMA's logistical system received the most attention and the response of the Bush Administration was roundly criticized, the federal government actually did a whole lot more right than wrong, certainly in my state. From the planning and preparation in which the Mississippi Emergency Management Administration teamed up with its sister federal agency in a unified command to the disaster assistance program it provided during months of cleanup and years of rebuilding, the federal government was a good, faithful partner. Not perfect but, as you will see, ultimately very generous.

Perhaps the most unnoticed assistance was all the help from our sister states. Despite the fact that Mobile, Alabama, still had several feet of water in downtown areas, Gov. Bob Riley sent two companies of his National Guard Military Police into Mississippi the night the storm hit. Hundreds of Florida law enforcement officers served on the Mississippi Gulf Coast for weeks after landfall. When they returned home, they left behind a number of their patrol cars to replace those of our local law enforcement agencies that were inundated and made unusable by Katrina's storm surge. My wife, Marsha, speaks to this day of North Carolina One, a portable hospital that the Tarheel State sent to Hancock County and set up in a shopping center parking lot. Hancock General Hospital was severely damaged, and North Carolina One and its fabulous team of doctors and nurses saw dozens of people every day.

In all, forty-six states sent people or resources.

The support from the private sector was equally indispensable to our recovery. It came as no surprise to me that the worst natural disaster in American history elicited the greatest outpouring of philanthropy and volunteerism in American history. Even though private charities like the Red Cross were also overwhelmed at first, volunteers were essential to every phase of response, recovery, rebuilding, and renewal.

During the first five years nearly one million volunteers came to the Coast and South Mississippi to help, and that number includes only those whose names and addresses were captured by the volunteer organizations that helped organize and direct them.

These volunteers, mostly from faith-based groups, made great contributions early on, manning shelters and food stations, cleaning up debris. But they continued to play major roles in rebuilding. Habitat for Humanity was a critical organization that brought in large numbers of volunteers for several years. AmeriCorps, a government-supported organization, brought scores of college-aged workers who did yeoman's service, particularly in debris removal, home repair, and building both public facilities and private dwellings.

My most vivid recollection of the volunteer miracle happened repeatedly. Literally hundreds of times over several years, as I would be with groups of volunteers, one or more of them would tell me, "Governor, your citizens are so grateful. But I actually feel like I've gotten more out of this than all the good I've done for the people I came here to help." That is a powerful statement about the goodness of the American people. It reminded me of my mother's lesson about a catastrophe's bringing out the best in most people. It speaks volumes about how great it is to live in America.

You will also read about the incredible efforts of some of Mississippi's finest corporate citizens as examples of the exceptionally effective response, ingenuity, and generosity of the private sector. The state's electric utilities, Entergy and Mississippi Power, restored power in record time, and Hancock Bank developed ingenious ways to get money back into circulation when data networks and ATMs couldn't operate. When the absence of fuel threatened to shut down generators and emergency vehicles, Chevron's refinery on the Coast opened its facilities to anyone who could bring a car or a tanker to its plant in Pascagoula. Other companies, large and small, were incredibly generous, good citizens.

Giving the volunteers, faith-based organizations, charities, and business donors the credit they deserve and expressing the genuine gratitude Mississippians feel for them is one of my main reasons for writing this book. The vast majority came to help people and communities they didn't know existed on August 29, 2005.

I devote one entire chapter to a behind-the-scenes account of our successful effort to convince Congress and the White House to support our rebuilding efforts with billions of dollars in special disaster appropriations, grants, and tax incentives. Another chapter describes the courageous move by our Legislature to authorize onshore casino gaming in order to bring back more than fourteen thousand jobs in that industry. I spend the good part of a chapter telling the story of how we reopened every public school in Mississippi before any public school in New Orleans could receive students.

State employees ultimately managed more than twenty-five billion dollars in federal disaster assistance funds, often under federal programs with which they were unfamiliar before the storm hit. And some of those programs are still going on ten years later. They were well-run, effective efforts that later served as models for special disaster relief following Superstorm Sandy in 2012. I can't thank them enough.

If a moral of Katrina is that the leader needs a lot of help from great helpers, I cannot end this introduction without recognizing my wife, Marsha. This is not some matrimonial tip of the hat to my spouse; on the Coast, Marsha became the face of the recovery effort, the face that assured those in and returning to the coastal communities that the state cared and was going all out to help. Arriving with a convoy of Highway Patrol and National Guard, Marsha got to the Coast the night the storm hit, the evening before I did. She was on the Coast seventy of the first ninety days after Katrina's landfall.

As you will learn from this book, Marsha saw as her mission helping people who were the neediest before the storm and knew the least about how to get help. From the first week she saw and learned a lot that she used to help me and our team, state and federal, do a better job assisting families at the grassroots level with their recovery, rebuilding, and renewal.

When all was said and done, the folks on the line providing assistance and the people they were helping all loved Marsha, for all the right reasons.

This story of renewal is a powerful American story filled with strong, courageous people. It is also a tale of well-intentioned efforts that failed and of persevering heroes from the public and private sectors who wouldn't accept those failures, who righted the ship and in the process revived communities by giving citizens the wherewithal to overcome the destruction caused by the worst natural disaster in American history.

It is a wonderful story. I hope I have done it justice.

CHAPTER 1

Before Landfall

For Mississippians in the summer of 2005, Hurricane Camille was our definition of the worst natural disaster possible. When it came across the Mississippi Gulf Coast on August 17, 1969, Camille became one of only three Category 5 hurricanes to hit the United States. Its 190-mph winds left near-total destruction along its path.

A few days after Camille hit, I drove a Yazoo City dump truck to the Coast. My oldest brother, Jeppie, was mayor of Yazoo City, Mississippi, our hometown, and he recruited me to drive one of three city dump trucks filled, in my case, with bedding, mattresses, box springs, pillows and sheets, for people who had lost their homes. Once on the Coast, our little convoy crossed the CSX railroad, the bed of which is elevated several feet above natural ground on a berm that has the effect of a levee several blocks inland from the Gulf of Mexico and the Mississippi Sound. Though the roadway had been cleared to both sides of the street, there were enormous piles of debris—wood, shingles, refrigerators, tree limbs, and much more—that had been caught by the levee as the winds had roared through. I could not believe my eyes, much less imagine how anything would ever be worse than what I was seeing. Thirty-six years later, I was proven wrong.

The Beginning

Hurricane Katrina began as a tropical wave off the west coast of Africa on August 11, merged with what was left of a tropical depression around the Leeward Islands on August 18, and was first noticed by satellites on August 22 when it was just east of the Turks and Caicos Islands near Cuba. It became an official tropical depression when the National Hurricane Center assigned it number 12 the next day, when it was about 175 miles southeast of the Bahamas.

Robert Latham, Mike Womack, and their colleagues at the Mississippi Emergency Management Agency (MEMA) took note and published their first report describing the gathering storm on Tuesday, August 23. Gen. Harold Cross and his command staff of the Mississippi National Guard began to track the storm's path, putting their operational plans into action, and reaching out to adjutant generals in other states to let them know he might need some backup. Anthony Topazi, Bobby Kerley, and their team at Mississippi Power Company, the electric utility serving the Coast, southeast, and east-central Mississippi, started making contact with companies across the country, putting them on notice that crews might be needed. Ricky Mathews and his staff at the Biloxi *Sun Herald*, the longest active newspaper on the Coast, had conversations with their corporate headquarters about publishing the newspaper in the days following landfall if they lost power in Biloxi. Butch Brown and his project managers at the Mississippi Department of Transportation held their first group of meetings to allocate employees to the Coast. Similar conversations were taking place among many other state and local officials as well as business leaders across the Coast.

With hundreds of plans being put in place, a process was unfolding that I didn't even know to appreciate until I became Governor. What I came to learn was that emergency management agencies, utilities, and major corporations spend months and countless man hours getting ready for hurricanes, planning for all kinds of contingencies, thinking through different scenarios, and actually rehearsing those plans. They would all plan for a worst case, and that worst case was Camille. No one ever considered the possibility that Mississippi could sustain damages worse than those from Camille.

Thanks to a combination of weather-related phenomena, the system got itself organized and became a tropical storm on August 24 around the central Bahamas, when it was named Katrina by the National Hurricane Center. The same day, I returned from a three-week economic development trip to Asia.

Atmospheric conditions caused the storm to strengthen into hurricane status and move westward, where it hit the southeastern coast of Florida on Thursday, August 25, and then traveled out into the warm waters of the Gulf of Mexico. The same day MEMA held its first executive planning meeting in preparation for a possible Katrina landfall. Thursday morning's *Sun Herald* reported that "meteorologists believe the storm could take a turn to the north and possibly hit the Florida Panhandle by Monday afternoon, but the cone of error extends from southeastern Louisiana to South Carolina."

By this time, Bill Carwile, Bob Fenton, and others, knowing that hurricane trajectories were difficult to predict this far out, were headed to Mississippi from the Federal Emergency Management Agency (FEMA) headquarters in Washington and from other locations around the country. Carwile's title was federal coordinating officer and as such was Mississippi's top liaison to FEMA; Fenton was his operations chief. As it turned out, this core group of FEMA officials had a dedication to their job and a commitment to the people of Mississippi that would be of singular importance to our rescue and recovery efforts in the days, weeks, and months following landfall.

As the storm gathered strength, trying to decide which way it would head, I cancelled a Southern Governor's Association trip to Georgia on Friday after talking with Latham about Katrina's latest movements. At his request, I issued an executive order declaring a state of emergency and a separate executive order authorizing the mobilization of the National Guard. MEMA activated its State Emergency Operations Center in Jackson and its State Emergency Response Team for deployment to Camp Shelby, just south of Hattiesburg and more than halfway to the Coast from Jackson, and sent county liaisons to the six coastal counties (three actually on the Coast and the three just above them). A National Guard element with vehicles capable of high-water rescue was also prepositioned at each of the three coastal county emergency operation centers. The emergency order authorized MEMA to incur costs and deploy state assets that would have to be covered with a legislative appropriation or federal reimbursement after the fact. And until General Cross received the order directed at the Guard, he was limited in his ability to use all of the soldiers, equipment, and logistical support available to his command.

General Cross and his team had planned for many types of disasters, thinking through how many soldiers and support staff would be needed to do search and rescue, distribute supplies, and handle security as well as where they would be stationed before landfall, how they would travel, and the logistics needed to support that kind of operation. Responding to a Camille-type calamity, a worst-case scenario, would require a force of about 3,200 people, and Cross knew he could put that many in position, in spite of the more than 3,000 who were on active duty in Iraq or Afghanistan. With an enlistment of some 10,000 men and women, Mississippi's Guard was one of the largest in the country and was seeing plenty of action in the Middle East. As a consequence, General Cross made the point of telling me that our soldiers had become highly trained and had been given loads of experience overseas in the years following 9/11. They would soon be called upon to put that training to work in their home state like never before.

These declarations, conversations, and movements had ripple effects throughout state and local government, especially as we approached what would have been a big summer tourism weekend on the Gulf Coast. Local emergency officials convened meetings in their hometowns and connected with MEMA. Government employees, emergency staff, and volunteers were assembled to make preparations. Supplies were checked, vehicles were topped with fuel and moved to high ground, generators were tested, water and food were stored, and logistical manuals were pulled off the shelves. Thousands of details were worked through. As a number of emergency officials had told me, you cannot ramp up the process too often or people will become immune to calls for action.

Just a month earlier, Hurricane Dennis had threatened the Coast, forcing us to call for evacuations. At the last minute Dennis veered east and made landfall over the western Florida Panhandle near Navarre Beach. The previous year we had followed four major hurricanes, with Ivan hitting Gulf Shores, Alabama, in early September with 120-mph winds. Three other major hurricanes—Jeanne, Frances, and Charley—had hit parts of southern and eastern Florida.

Latham and I recognized the need for caution, but we also recognized people needed time to prepare, store supplies, and, if needed, to evacuate. Quite frankly, I never did want to take any chances.

As Friday turned from morning to afternoon, meteorologists began to tell us of shifts in Katrina's flow and a change of direction. Mississippi was now probably in play. Latham told the media that the National Hurricane Center had adjusted the hurricane's projected path to the west and "as of now, landfall would be west of the Mississippi-Alabama state line in Jackson County." Based on the latest measurements, Latham estimated tropical storm winds should reach the Coast about three o'clock Monday morning, and Katrina would be at least Category 3 and possibly a 4. The question now was whether to order evacuations.

City and county officials agreed to meet on Saturday to make final decisions about evacuations. We thought waiting on the evacuation orders was worth the extra time primarily because Gulf Coast residents suffered from "hurricane fatigue"—that is, they had become weary of leaving without anything really happening, as Latham admitted to a *Sun Herald* reporter later that day: "Based on a survey conducted after Dennis, it appeared the general public is very tired and weary of evacuations. We are worried many people will not evacuate."

That being said, as we were going to bed Friday night, the National Hurricane Center was predicting Hurricane Katrina would strike the town of Buras-Triumph, Louisiana, sixty-six miles southeast of New Orleans. That put Mississippi to the northeast of the hurricane's eye, which we all knew contained the most powerful winds.

At the time, ten years ago, my question was: how strong would the winds be? We now know that wind speed, as used to determine the category ranking of a hurricane, can be very deceiving. We didn't think about factoring in the size of the storm surge and the amount of rain a hurricane would bring with it, nor did we consider the breadth of the storm. Katrina was fundamentally different from Camille: while the winds in Camille were stronger; Katrina's storm surge was much greater, the amount of rain was much greater, and the sheer size was much greater. That's why Camille turned out to be such a poor benchmark.

Saturday, August 27, 2005

Overnight, the computers got a better fix on Katrina—her winds extended 280 miles across (or about 140 miles from the center), and the storm appeared to be headed straight for us. To put that in perspective, the length of the Mississippi shoreline is about seventy miles. The headline in the *Sun Herald* was "Fear the Worst" and, as Latham told the newspaper, "I don't think the scenario could be any worse for us." Saturday morning's *Clarion-Ledger*, the largest-circulation newspaper in the state, published in Jackson, delivered a similar message to a statewide audience: "This is a tremendously dangerous storm. Everyone needs to prepare to evacuate in the coastal counties." Latham headed to the Coast to meet personally with local officials and advise them to order mandatory evacuations.

Although I had the legal authority to order mandatory evacuations, governors have traditionally allowed local governments to issue evacuation orders so as to improve the chances for compliance. On the Coast, these decisions are made by local emergency officials, including mayors and county supervisors, acting in concert with MEMA and other state agencies. More recently, the Mississippi Gaming Commission has been an integral component of that decision making process too. In addition to the prospect of "crying wolf" too often, evacuations exact a toll that all of us had to consider. Businesses shut down. Wages and revenue are lost. People have to leave and find housing elsewhere. Shelters have to open north of the Coast.

But as the day wore on, I was fully prepared to exert my executive authority and order evacuations if the local officials had not intervened. Regardless of where the storm might make landfall, the sheer size of Katrina meant we were in for a rough ride. I was on the phone all day, talking with local officials, checking in with MEMA, urging business leaders to support the call for evacuations. A local businessman's response was typical of what I was hearing: "They're trying to make us evacuate Zone B, and it's never flooded." "We've got to err on the side of safety," I would say. "Well, we just don't need to be doing this," is typically what I would hear back.

Mississippi Power's Bobby Kerley remembered on Saturday:

> Our weather specialist came to see Anthony and me and told us, "This one was going to be the worst that he had ever seen, including worse than Camille. Bobby, you live two blocks from the beach. The water's going to be 20 feet at your house." I said, "Ain't no way. When Camille came ashore, it didn't get within a block of my house." "I'm telling you," he said, "This one's going to be the worst."

Saturday was a long day, pushing everyone to understand the seriousness of the coming storm and the need to leave the Coast. As the day wore on, the National Hurricane Center began to predict a direct hit on New Orleans, though the hurricane warning extended from Morgan City, Louisiana, to the Alabama–Florida border.

Slowly, though, we were making progress. The Mississippi Gaming Commission ordered all casinos to shut down and evacuate as of five o'clock Saturday afternoon, and we urged the officials in Hancock,

Harrison, and Jackson Counties to order mandatory evacuations for all the flood-prone areas. As New Orleans officials began to issue evacuation orders, the Louisiana–Mississippi traffic contraflow agreement went into effect at four o'clock that Saturday afternoon, enforcing northbound one-way traffic in all lanes for vehicles exiting greater New Orleans and Louisiana's surrounding areas on interstates 55 and 59.

By Saturday churches were opening as shelters, meetings on the Coast were being cancelled, folks from the Coast and from New Orleans were finding their way to places in Mississippi, colleges in Jackson began taking in students from New Orleans, and hotels were filling up.

As some point during the day, we had a FEMA-initiated call with people from all over the southern region, checking plans, ordering supplies, and seeing where we could share personnel depending on where Katrina finally made landfall. As I discuss in more detail later, one of the problems with FEMA or at least those who were running the day-to-day at the national FEMA headquarters—was not that they were inattentive; they just failed to execute their logistical operation. Like all of us, they would ultimately become completely overwhelmed by the magnitude of the damage and the near-total breakdown of their supply system. But in the days leading up to landfall, MEMA had placed our water, ice, food, tarps, and other supply orders with FEMA, indicating what we thought we would need. FEMA had contracts with a number of vendors to supply these provisions in the days leading up to an emergency, and we all assumed what we ordered and needed would be available. We also assumed we could reach everyone quickly after landfall and that the damage would be primarily limited to the coastal counties. All of these assumptions turned out to be far too optimistic.

As for the calls we were making during the day, Latham and his team would stay in touch with state agency personnel and local emergency officials. I would call local sheriffs, mayors, supervisors, and business owners, backing up the message Latham was delivering but also gaining valuable information about activities on the ground.

Let me pause just for a moment and say a word about MEMA.

As a state agency, MEMA has a very small staff whose role is to plan for emergencies, to use the resources of other state agencies to respond to those emergencies, and to coordinate our emergency response with local officials and FEMA. FEMA is organized in much the same way; it does planning and training and acts as a cash register to pay for supplies and services. Once the governor issues the emergency declaration, MEMA can incur expenses, and it can also require other state agencies to send personnel to its emergency operations center and to respond to requests for assistance from the MEMA director. The idea is to put all of state government under one roof during times of natural disasters or other emergencies. What I came to realize and really appreciate is that all of those people engage in training exercises almost year-round. Those exercises range from tornadoes to terrorist attacks to a failure at the Grand Gulf Nuclear facility. They don't walk through the door and ask, "What do I do now?"

That being said, Robert Latham and Bill Carwile, FEMA's coordinating officer for Mississippi in this emergency, put something into place that had never been done before. They created a joint state and federal command group, merging the MEMA and FEMA operations into one coordinated operation, a unified command as they called it. As Latham said, "We look to see if the state can do it; if the state can't do it, then we look to see if the federal government can do it or we go get the assets from the private sector." This decision—alone among the states affected by Katrina—contributed greatly to our response-and-recovery effort.

General Cross spent Saturday getting his soldiers and logistical support in place and identifying the guardsmen he was going to call up, where they would be stationed, what tasks they would perform, how he would get water and food for them, where they would sleep, and how they would be transported. The folks at Mississippi Power Company were reaching out to utilities throughout the country, lining up additional crews who would be needed to clear right-of-ways and reinstall the electric lines. We talked several times, comparing notes, making sure they were coordinated with MEMA. The Department of Transportation staff were already deployed, handling the logistics associated with the contraflow decision and getting ready to clear the debris from and repair damaged roadways after landfall.

As Saturday evening approached, Hancock and Jackson Counties had ordered evacuations for all low-lying areas, and while we were waiting for Harrison County to make its voluntary evacuation mandatory, which it subsequently did, we began to worry that people were still not taking the Katrina threat seriously. Latham was calling from the Coast, telling me he was touring the coastal counties, meeting with local officials and emergency officials and was worried that people didn't realize this was going to be serious, especially when he saw families on the beaches Saturday afternoon. Hurricane fatigue was clearly a problem, and a dangerous one.

At some point that night, while we were thinking about ways to make people understand the need to leave, the Governor's Mansion switchboard operator found me and told me I had a call from Max Mayfield, head of the National Hurricane Center. I knew Latham thought well of Dr. Mayfield and his staff and had a good relationship with him. The operator patched him through and after sharing his perspective—that Katrina was a deadly storm of immense strength—his first question was as thoughtful as it was timely. He said, "Governor, what can I do to help? This is going to be a Camille-like storm." For Mississippians, Camille was the gold standard. A hurricane could not be worse. "If you want to help," I told him, "you need to get the news media to start saying the storm is going to be like Camille. Because down here, we know what that means."

Dr. Mayfield did just that; the media started calling Katrina a hurricane like Camille within the hour, and our Sunday evacuation could not have been better. The headline in Sunday's *Sun Herald* summed it up: "Fearing the Worst: Category 5; All Are Urged to Evacuate as Soon as Possible," while another article indicated "between 250,000 and 300,000 people are expected to leave the coast."

Sunday, August 28, 2005

While Miami is home to the National Hurricane Center, Keesler Air Force Base in Biloxi is home to the "Hurricane Hunters," the planes that fly into the heart of hurricanes each year, and Hancock County is home to the Naval Oceanographic Office and the National Oceanic and Atmospheric Administration (NOAA), the agency that maintains hundreds of buoys throughout the Gulf of Mexico. From all the data being gathered from all these sources, it became clear on Sunday that we were looking at a monster storm. The wind field continued to expand with tropical storm–force winds extending out to about 230 miles from the center and hurricane-force winds extending out to about 125 miles from the center. A National Hurricane Center bulletin that afternoon warned of coastal storm surge flooding of eighteen to twenty-two feet above normal tide levels . . . locally as high as twenty-eight feet. One of the buoys, located in the Gulf of Mexico about 50 miles east of the mouth of the Mississippi River, reported a frightening peak wave height of fifty-five feet, which equaled the highest ever measured by a NOAA buoy.

Based on the data we were getting, the possible storm surge was out of relationship with the wind, and we were beginning to understand we were seeing something new and different. At this point, I no longer had to call and shake anyone up. Everyone cooperated, and they did it aggressively. People were beginning to grasp the significance of the storm. The call I had with Capt. Albert Santa Cruz, one of my Highway Patrol leaders on the Coast who had ridden out Camille with his family more than thirty-five years ago, was typical. He told me, "Governor, I think we're going to get it."

Transportation officials were telling us the roads were full of traffic and moving steadily. My wife, Marsha, had shared my concern about insufficient evacuation, and she flew down to the Coast Sunday by helicopter with Commissioner of Public Safety George Phillips to encourage people to leave and to make the rounds with the Highway Patrol leadership team. Around lunchtime all of us in the region had a videoconference call with President Bush. Max Mayfield told the group he "had no good news." Our Mississippi team had a number of meetings, and nearly everyone on the Coast was getting ready. I had a separate call with President Bush, letting him know we would be calling on him after landfall, and I asked him to issue an emergency declaration for Mississippi now, which he did.

And at this point, I knew it was important for me to be visible but to stay out of the way. State agency heads I had appointed knew they had the authority to make plans and take action, and the unified FEMA/MEMA command had created the framework for a working partnership. Sometime that afternoon I took a tour of the entire MEMA Emergency Operations Center, thanking everyone for what I knew would be long hours to come, giving them a pat on the back. We were starting to get more and more federal officials into the building, more military guys, and more people from different agencies. It was clear everyone was both worried about the storm but proud of the teamwork and the preparation. In maintaining a presence at MEMA and making hourly calls to officials and business and community leaders on the Coast, I wanted them to know the Governor had their backs.

We were also putting into place procedures we had learned from other states and other hurricanes. For example, Florida had hosted our MEMA team on several occasions, impressing on them the need for a clear, consistent message, one that was coordinated and agreed with messages from county and municipal emergency operation centers. Latham had also realized MEMA did not have a good, broad base of statewide search-and-rescue teams. In the months leading up to hurricane season, he and his staff began to identify teams in fire departments across the state—a fire truck with three or four firemen on it—small groups that could go door to door. MEMA deployed nineteen of those teams in the days leading up to Katrina.

Bobby Kerley told me what his company had learned from Hurricane Ivan the year before: "We thought we had a great plan in place before Ivan. Standards we used then were that there would be hotel rooms in place. But there were no hotel rooms, so we learned we had to be self-contained, have tents, trailers with portable air conditioning. Completely changed our plans. It saved us in our restoration efforts associated with Katrina."

By this time the National Guard and MEMA had established forward operations at Camp Shelby below Hattiesburg. The Highway Patrol had prepositioned more than one hundred officers at its regional headquarters in Hattiesburg too, while the Department of Transportation had created a headquarters operation at its regional facility in Hattiesburg with some emergency equipment and personnel at its site in northern Harrison County. On the north side of Biloxi Bay in that county was also the site of Mississippi Power's Plant Watson, which would serve as their emergency operations center, or so they thought.

When Marsha got back from the Coast on Sunday, she said she had been invited to go Monday to Hattiesburg and Camp Shelby by Commissioner Phillips to visit the Highway Patrol and National Guard prepositioned there. She wanted to make the rounds to thank the hundreds of National Guard personnel, Highway Patrol officers, and other emergency responders who were scheduled to go down U.S. Highway 49 to Gulfport in a convoy as soon as the hurricane cleared Hattiesburg or lost its strength, whichever came earlier. Then they would deploy across the Coast, according to the plan.

Little did I know, Marsha would be embarking on a memorable adventure that resulted in months of dedicated service that made her a fixture in the recovery in the hearts and minds of victims, elected officials, and the men and women on the line for MEMA, FEMA, and other first responders. She was in the right place at the right time from the very first day.

As the night progressed, it no longer seemed to matter where Katrina's eye was located, or its category ranking, or the rain and storm surge it would soon bring to our Gulf Coast. What was becoming clearer and clearer with each passing minute was the sense that only nineteen months into my service as Mississippi's governor, we would soon confront nature at its most destructive.

CHAPTER 2

Landfall, Monday, August 29, 2005

A s Sunday turned into Monday, Katrina's wind speed dropped from what had been a Category 5 hurricane to a high Category 3. Given a normal hurricane, that would be welcome news. But Katrina was anything but normal. By five o'clock Monday morning, the breadth of the storm ranged over four hundred miles of the Gulf of Mexico; indeed, when the northernmost edge of Katrina came ashore in the Gulf South, trailing bands of this monster storm were still in the Caribbean Sea! The high winds combined with an extraordinarily wide storm to churn up so much water that peak waves measured as high as fifty-five feet. By the time the sun sneaked over the horizon, much of that water was headed straight for South Mississippi.

For hundreds of first responders as well as the state and federal agency officials primed to move into the area, there was no demarcation from Sunday to Monday. Most of them didn't spend the night at home but instead were positioned in key locations, waiting for the storm to pass so they could take action. Tens of thousands of individuals and families had evacuated areas that were, at the time, viewed as prone to flooding and had sought overnight housing they were hoping was merely temporary. By Sunday night, there were close to sixty shelters, including the Mississippi Coliseum in Jackson, open and housing more than 7,600 individuals and families. The problem, of course, was that Katrina would push millions of gallons of water into areas that had never before flooded, wreaking havoc in neighborhoods and communities that never did evacuate.

Even though I felt very good about the people we had in place to respond to the storm and the planning we had accomplished to anticipate the effects of the storm, none of us expected or even imagined the level of destruction Katrina would leave behind when it finally exited Mississippi early Monday evening.

The eye of Katrina hit the Mississippi–Louisiana line at the mouth of the Pearl River about ten o'clock Monday morning, which meant the most dangerous part of the hurricane—the right front quadrant—covered the entire Mississippi Gulf Coast and more. Prior to making landfall in Mississippi, Katrina's 125-mph winds had been battering the Coast for several hours, though by the time the actual eye reached Hancock County, the wind speed was down a little because of the Louisiana coastline it had overrun. Nevertheless, the winds brought four to ten inches of rain. The eye pushed a storm surge ahead of it that reached a height of twenty-six to thirty feet, plus the waves on top, from Waveland to Long Beach and up to twenty-two feet along the rest of the Gulf Coast. The surge crossed Interstate 10 in many locations, which meant water from the Gulf and from the bays traveled, in some cases, ten or more miles inland—far past any land that was considered vulnerable to hurricane flooding, and thus deep into large areas that had not been evacuated.

Even though Katrina weakened as its eye hit land, its reach was so large and its movement so strong that it remained a Category 1 hurricane until reaching north of Meridian, 150 miles north of the Gulf Coast, later in the afternoon. Once on land, of course, we had the added danger of tornadoes. A total of forty-three reported tornadoes were spawned by Katrina throughout the southeast, including eleven in Mississippi, several of which hit the population centers in Jones and Lauderdale Counties.

Besides the unexpectedly large storm surge, it was Katrina's continued strength over the southern half of our state that distinguished it from other hurricanes. The strong winds not only delayed our state's first responders from getting to the Coast, until after Katrina had moved north of Hattiesburg, Camp Shelby, and other staging points, but it left many roads and highways impassable.

In the hours that Katrina's wind, rain, and surge destroyed or damaged everything in its path, the examples of individual heroism I could cite here run well into the hundreds. James Patterson Smith and Douglas Brinkley have each written books that recount many of those individual acts. Others are described by the numerous print and broadcast reporters who covered Mississippi from all over the world, while many more are captured in the special Katrina oral history collection at the University of Southern Mississippi.

I doubt we'll ever know how many lives were saved by the hundreds of sacrifices and heroic acts by hospital staffs, emergency operations personnel, first responders, law enforcement officers, and private citizens. In the days and weeks following landfall, as I toured the devastated areas, I had a chance to meet many of those heroes and hear their stories first hand. Their dedication and bravery, and their commitment to the Gulf Coast and South Mississippi, were more often than not the reason people all over the country came to help, and in the corners and offices of the U.S. Capitol, the reason members of Congress voted for unprecedented funding for our recovery.

An ever-present reminder of the extent of the flooding can be found in one of Mary Mahoney's dining rooms. An iconic restaurant in Biloxi, located in an eighteenth-century French house on an elevated area less than one hundred yards from the coastline, Mary Mahoney's keeps a framed indicator of the high-water mark above one of its fireplace mantles. If you can imagine yourself seated at one of the tables on that fateful Monday morning, you would have ended up completely underwater with at least another foot of water on top of you, and this at a restaurant some fifty miles east of the eye of the storm. Bobby

Mahoney, the restaurant's owner and son of the late Mary Mahoney, rode out the storm in the upstairs dining room of the restaurant.

Early Assessments

My first report from the Coast Monday morning was not a good one. Anthony Topazi was able to get through to me mid-morning and indicated the damage was much worse than anyone anticipated. In fact he said the Mississippi Power emergency operations center had flooded, and all of their emergency crew were in the process of moving. We all knew that if Mississippi Power's emergency center was flooding, that meant water was coming inland several miles. The early reports were so bad that later on Monday President Bush issued an emergency declaration for the state and affirmed that the entire state was a major disaster area. These declarations meant a variety of FEMA funding sources would be available to individuals and businesses throughout the state as soon as the storm passed.

In many ways, Monday was the most frustrating day of the 365 days this book covers. Communications systems went down. Power was disabled everywhere. Many of our first responders couldn't travel south until the storm—still a Category 1 hurricane through south and parts of central Mississippi—passed them by. For the first responders already on the Coast, the roads and bridges were so damaged that moving around was virtually impossible. The winds remained too strong to allow even helicopters to view the damage before nightfall shut down visibility. Debris blocked roads that weren't destroyed or damaged.

Even though we had little information to report by mid-afternoon, I went ahead and called a press conference so reporters would have a forum to ask questions, raise issues, and generally offer everyone a chance to exchange information. I came to believe that having a daily press conference was important for people to receive the latest updates on rescue and recovery efforts and for them to hear from the Governor and other state agency leaders. The impact of Katrina was so over-whelming and affected so much of our state that I felt our citizens needed to know that all of us in state government were working day and night to help them. I also wanted to send a signal early that our law enforcement personnel would have zero tolerance for looters. As I told one reporter, "Looting is the equivalent of grave robbing."

That first afternoon I had no idea what lay ahead of us or how bad the damage would turn out to be, but much of the advice I had been given made good sense to me—it was important that people knew someone was in charge of the overall rescue and recovery effort, and they needed to know who that was. And, for better or for worse, that was me. People needed to have someone and some office to contact, and that should be the Governor's Office. Over the next twelve months, I worked to make sure we were visible, open, truthful, accountable, and able to respond to the needs of our people.

Because affected people need to see you and know you are trying, I wanted to get to the Coast on Monday afternoon. But with Katrina's winds still affecting such a huge swath of our state, the Federal Aviation Administration had banned all flights to the area, so my staff spent most of the afternoon and evening making plans for a Tuesday morning trip. Robert Latham would go down with me on Tuesday morning while Gen. Harold Cross had started to work his way down by land after our press conference. We knew from our contacts in Florida, the Coast Guard, the National Guard, and from spotty conversations with local emergency personnel, that rescue efforts were underway on the Coast and throughout South Mississippi, but as an example of the severity of Katrina, it was not until late afternoon that winds had died down enough south of Camp Shelby to allow our main prepositioned Highway Patrol, National Guard, and Department of Transportation units to begin their drive down.

And it was on that drive down that my wife Marsha began her own personal journey. Early Monday morning she had gone to Camp Shelby to meet with the troops and other first responders to let them know how much we all were counting on them. As the hurricane passed Hattiesburg, though, it became clear there was no getting back to Jackson due to the conditions of the roads. Besides, everyone was headed south to get organized for the recovery. However, getting to the Coast that evening was more arduous than anyone imagined. Debris covered the sixty miles the convoy had to travel, and only limited equipment and chain saws were available to the crews from MDOT who led the way and were able to clear one lane for traffic; what would have been an hour's drive took more than seven hours. As I learned later, Marsha hitched a ride with George Phillips, then our commissioner of public safety. For most days until at least Thanksgiving, she would be on the Coast helping with relief efforts, a story you will hear more about in the next chapter.

And while this seems the best place in the book to summarize the extent of the destruction, I remember well visitors to the Coast—whether volunteers, elected officials, and even law enforcement or military—expressing astonishment at what they saw. A photo in a magazine or television footage simply could not capture the scale or degree of devastation; it had to be seen to be believed.

On President Bush's third trip to the Coast after the storm, nearly two weeks after Katrina had slammed into Mississippi, a Secret Service agent introduced himself to Marsha and me as we were waiting for Air Force One to arrive. He said he had not been to the Coast since the storm, and he was anxious to see the area because several other agents had told him he wouldn't believe what he saw. Soon the plane arrived and the president came down the steps and invited Marsha and me to ride with him. Later, after the motorcade drove several miles through Hancock County and arrived at St. Stanislaus School in Bay St. Louis, it happened that this same agent opened the car door for Marsha and me. As we were waiting for the president to get out, I noticed the agent had tears in his eyes. He looked at me and said, "Now I get it."

What Katrina Left Behind

While I think it important to provide a summary of Katrina's destruction, these statistics do little to convey an understanding of what individuals in the affected areas had to endure in the days, months, and in some cases years that followed the hurricane's landfall.

Even though we wouldn't realize the extent of the damage for several months, we now know that Hurricane Katrina was the most destructive natural disaster in American history, as measured by property destruction—$108 billion—and the third deadliest—1,833 people lost their lives. It was the costliest disaster in the history of the global insurance industry. The hurricane's wind and water damaged more than 90,000 square miles of the southeastern part of the country, and forced the evacuation of more than 1.1 million people. More than half of Mississippi was declared a federal disaster area. Overnight, the unemployment rate effectively doubled in most of the affected areas. The storm devastated the regional power infrastructure, causing 2.5 million power outages; crippled thirty-eight 911 call centers; and knocked out more than 3 million customer phone lines. Katrina battered the offshore energy business and forced the evacuation of more than three-quarters of the 819 oil and gas platforms in the Gulf, temporarily reducing, according to some estimates, the energy output of the United States by a fifth.

The storm created all manner of health and environmental hazards, including standing water, oil pollution, sewage, household and industrial chemical spills, and both human and animal remains. The storm surge struck 466 facilities that handle large amounts of dangerous chemicals, 31 hazardous waste sites, and 16 Superfund toxic waste sites, 3 of which flooded. The surge destroyed or compromised 170 drinking-water facilities and dozens of wastewater treatment facilities.

In Mississippi, 238 people died, of whom nearly one-third were not on the Coast. There were at least 17,600 storm-related injuries, and 216,000 individuals were displaced. Over 4,800 people were rescued in the days following landfall. Well over 60,000 housing units were destroyed, and another 160,000 were damaged. At the peak of our relief efforts months later, more than 97,000 Mississippians had lived in more than 35,000 travel trailers or mobile homes. Over the full course of the recovery, almost 47,000 families lived in some form of temporary housing at one time or another, most for months and many for years. Five years out, more than 486,000 claims had been paid by insurance companies totaling nearly $12 billion. Of that amount, $8.7 billion was paid into the six coastal counties alone (that is, the three counties directly on the Coast—Jackson, Harrison, and Hancock—and the three immediately north of them—George, Stone, and Pearl River).

The town of Waveland in Hancock County was left with no habitable structures; the downtowns of Bay St. Louis, Pass Christian, Long Beach, and Gulfport were largely destroyed, and much of East Biloxi was obliterated. The bridges connecting Harrison County with Hancock County to the west and with Jackson County to the east were washed away. The four-lane east–west highway along the beachfront—U.S. Highway 90—was largely destroyed; parts of Interstate 10 and Interstate 110 were washed away; and all the major north–south highways throughout South Mississippi were impassable due to debris and timber, as were virtually all of the county roads. Water and sewer systems were either destroyed or compromised because of the inflow of salt water and debris. Systems further north with the ability to operate could not because of a lack of electricity for the lift pumps. As one South Mississippi mayor described it, "The water came in, blew off manhole covers, then receded and caused a vacuum, sucking gators and DVD players and lots and lots of sand into water and sewer pipes. You couldn't have backed a truck up to a manhole cover and dumped it in more effectively." Even areas presumed to be flood-proof, like the Hancock County community of Diamondhead, built after Camille and about ten miles north of the coastline, sustained major flood damage.

Virtually the entire state was without electrical power by Monday evening; the number of metered outages was greater than 900,000.

Major components of our economy came to a standstill. The poultry industry learned Tuesday morning that more than 3 million chickens had been destroyed. Crops on prime agricultural land, much of it on the verge of delivering its harvest, were destroyed. Millions of trees, the backbone of our timber industry in South Mississippi, were uprooted or snapped off and left on the ground. The gaming industry along the Coast, which directly employed 14,000 Mississippians at the time of landfall and thousands more indirectly, was in shambles. By the time the waters receded, the hurricane had left behind about 47 million cubic yards of debris across 28,000 square miles, or roughly 60 percent of the state. Tuesday morning's *Clarion-Ledger* quoted Joe Spraggins, the Harrison County emergency management director, as saying, "Right now, downtown [Gulfport] looks like Nagasaki."

The extent of the destruction, that entire neighborhoods, schools, and shopping centers were leveled—not just damaged but wiped away, and the breadth of the destruction, that more than half our state was hard hit, combined to create an environment that could have overwhelmed our recovery efforts. Systems we all take for granted no longer existed.

The loss of power for an extended time meant gas station pumps, for example, didn't work, so rescue vehicles couldn't find fuel, and there was no gas available to run generators. The absence of electricity meant grocery stores all over South Mississippi would soon lose anything requiring refrigeration. Even something as simple as going to an ATM to get cash was brought to a standstill because of the lack of power.

Broken sewers meant bathrooms didn't work; broken and contaminated water lines meant there was no safe water to drink or cook with. Emergency responders couldn't move around because roads and bridges had been destroyed or were covered with debris three to six feet deep, and, like many others, responders had no place to sleep. On top of that they were dealing with their own losses.

Our local hospitals were confronted with massive demand, though many suffered major damage; they had only generators to deliver power, and the generators required fuel. Banking, health care and government computer networks and data bases were down or destroyed, so it was futile for almost any business to try to access data to complete virtually any transaction. And Katrina hit two days before the end of the month, which meant thousands of hourly and salaried workers were expecting a paycheck. Or, as the *Clarion-Ledger* quoted the Hinds County emergency director, Larry Fisher, on Tuesday morning, "It's not like people can get up [today] and go to work like any normal day." In fact, it would be many months before any of us enjoyed a normal work day.

I knew none of this Monday evening, and nothing could prepare me for what I would see from a helicopter Tuesday morning.

CHAPTER 3

The Four Days after Landfall

Search and Rescue

Monday and Tuesday

Throughout Monday evening and into Tuesday morning, I knew the storm damage was much worse than any of us had feared: electric power was off in virtually all parts of the state; while the number of fatalities was unknown, many had been confirmed and many more reports were coming in; few people had working phones, many cell towers were down and the remainder had no power on which to operate; and Marsha was somewhere on the Coast, bivouacked with the National Guard and Highway Patrol advanced deployment. All of this made me anxious to get to the Coast first thing Tuesday morning.

More ominous, I had heard numerous accounts of bodies floating in the coastal waters. When I was able to reach General Cross late that evening, I told him to make his own reconnaissance early Tuesday morning and let me know. Thankfully, he reported after a very early helicopter ride Tuesday morning he had seen none.

Although we had at one point planned to go down by helicopter, that changed when the Mississippi National Guard cleared one of the runways at the Gulfport airport, where a unit of our Army National

Guard's Aviation Wing is located. The flight from Jackson to Gulfport is about thirty minutes, and I was able to discuss logistical issues with Charlie Williams, my chief of staff, while in flight. Halfway to Gulfport, though, the FAA air traffic controller told Richard Kaldon, our head pilot, they were not allowing any landings at Gulfport because of the damage. Even though Kaldon explained that the Guard had cleared a runway for "the Governor" to land, the air traffic controller persisted and ordered us to turn around. I asked Kaldon to tell the controller to check with his supervisor and tell him we were going to call Marion Blakey, the head of the Federal Aviation Administration and a Mississippian I had known from my days with the Reagan Administration, to get clearance. A few minutes later, we were cleared to land, though I seriously doubt the controller or his supervisor ever called Washington.

Once on the ground I met quickly with Guard and Highway Patrol leaders as well as MEMA and FEMA staff. Also waiting for me was Marsha. She had been up all night and had completed her own helicopter survey of the area earlier that morning. When I asked her to join me, she said she couldn't; the enormity of the destruction was too much to witness again. She told me she would wait for me to return and that I would soon understand what she meant.

The airport is almost due north of downtown Gulfport, so we first flew over the central business district. While most of the buildings were still standing, the bottom two or three floors had clearly been washed through, with layers of debris covering the streets, sidewalks, and parking lots. The Port of Gulfport is just south of downtown and extends six thousand feet out into the Gulf. Port buildings were simply obliterated, wiped away. The Copa Casino, on a large barge tied up in the port, had torn away from its moorings and been carried by the water up into the parking lot used for containers, several hundred feet north of its previous berth. Worse, every ship container on the parking area just north of the west pier had simply floated away; some hit downtown buildings while others were swept in an arc to the northwest because of the counter clockwise rotation of the winds, landing on houses, cars, and churches as far as six or eight miles away. Strewn throughout the area were thousands of blue packages, which turned out to be bags filled with frozen chickens that had been stored in a refrigerated freezer warehouse on the port's east pier. The warehouse was totally destroyed, and for several days an unpleasant and near-constant reminder of Katrina was the smell of rotting chickens.

As we flew west, staying at five hundred feet or lower, we saw where residential areas near the beach had been wiped away. What had been blocks and blocks of homes were simply no longer there, giving rise to the verb "slabbed." To say that a house was "slabbed" meant nothing was left but the concrete slab.

Early on I noticed that everywhere I looked the ground appeared gray. There was only this one color, no matter the direction. I couldn't see a road surface, a parking lot, or a lawn. And then I realized I was looking at debris, a virtual cover on the geographical area over which we were flying. The storm surge had knocked down and torn up so much that what had once been the structures sitting on those slabs had been ripped to shreds, leaving the earth and every other ground-level surface covered in debris, waist high or head high or in some places twenty or thirty feet high and consisting of automobiles, refrigerators, washing machines, roofing, siding, furniture, bricks, bedding, rugs, clothes, and incredible amounts of trees, sand, grass, and flowers. As far as I could see, it was all that singular color gray.

People who had lived on the Coast all their lives were disoriented; they couldn't find where their homes had been, for landmarks were gone and streets were covered in three or more feet of this debris. The ramifications for recovery then became very clear; we couldn't even begin to start rebuilding until the debris was removed.

We continued to follow the coastline to the west, toward Pass Christian. On the north side of the highway, as one approaches the mouth of the Bay of St. Louis, there is a ridge of higher ground, referred to as Scenic Drive. Scenic Drive is a tiny part of the town, and north of it the elevations drop quickly to just above sea level. The effect from a helicopter that morning was to see that most of the large houses on Scenic Drive were damaged but still standing. As we flew by on our way to the mouth of the bay, it gave me false hope that this area wasn't as badly damaged as those areas we had previously flown over.

The hope was not long lasting. Expecting to see the U.S. Highway 90 bridge and the CSX railroad bridge as we crossed the mouth of the bay, I saw nothing but the upright concrete pilings left from the highway bridge. Every single section of road surface and the entire railroad bridge had been lifted up and dropped into the bay. If the force of water had done that to concrete bridges, I couldn't imagine what we were about to see in the low-lying areas of Hancock County, the area hit by the eye of the storm.

Neighborhoods throughout the eastern part of the county were gone, though downtown Bay St. Louis appeared less damaged because of its higher elevation. But further west we came to Waveland, where we couldn't see one intact structure left in what had been a town of some 6,700 people plus many second homes. It was breathtaking and heartbreaking. The storm surge at Waveland was thirty feet or more, plus six to eight foot waves on top. Finally we got to Pearlington, the village on the banks of the Pearl River on the Mississippi side, where we likewise found nothing left.

From the helicopter we all saw a very prominent feature in a curve of the river. As we got closer, I realized it was a mound of floating debris that the winds and storm surge had pounded up into the bend. What had once been several hundred homes and businesses were now pieces of lumber, timber, shingles, windows, siding, furniture, and personal effects floating in the water.

As we flew back to the east, the layout of the debris served as a telltale sign that the storm surge had actually crossed Interstate 10 several miles inland. Veering back to the south to examine the communities around the bay, the near absence of what had been thriving neighborhoods was nothing short of stunning. As Katrina pushed this massive amount of water through the area, the effect was to raise the Bay of

St. Louis to the level of the Gulf. It inundated everything, creating a powerful north to south surge that rose increasingly for hours, pounding the bayside towns as it rose and again for a like number of hours as it receded. This is the area where Congressman Gene Taylor's home had been wiped away. I was seeing with my own eyes utter obliteration of areas that Camille had hardly damaged at all!

We then headed back east along Highway 90. What once had been billions of dollars of development of casino barges moored to huge hotels along the highway was now only flooded buildings and casinos either left on the highway or so badly damaged it would make no sense to repair them. Ten years later, it is hard to describe the sight of a 2,000-ton casino barge resting in the middle of the highway. Perhaps speechless comes close. And this was more than fifty miles from the eye of the storm. Crossing the mouth of Biloxi Bay and heading east to Jackson County, I expected to see the long bridge connecting Biloxi with Ocean Springs on the other side of the bay. Instead, all I saw were the upright support structures. There was no bridge, just fingers of concrete sticking out of the water.

Ocean Springs, Gautier, and the western beach neighborhoods of Jackson County had all endured a storm surge that exceeded twenty feet. Even Pascagoula, the easternmost city on the Coast and some seventy miles from the eye of the storm, had storm surges of more than twenty feet. The huge shipyard of Ingalls Shipbuilding, Mississippi's largest private employer with some 13,000 workers and builder of surface combatants for the U.S. Navy and large cutters for the Coast Guard, soon came into view: it had been inundated. My mind flashed to the idea of the Coast without Ingalls and the critical private-sector companies that drove the economy and were supplied and served by hundreds of smaller enterprises across the Coast. Giving the private sector as much support as we could give them was going to be critical to reviving our economy.

Just after we turned east again beyond Ingalls, I got the pilot to slow down and reduce altitude. I had heard that Senator Trent Lott's antebellum home in Pascagoula had been destroyed and wanted to see for myself. Although the house sat at nineteen feet above sea level and the eye of the hurricane had come ashore more than seventy miles away, his house was indeed gone. There may have been some part of the foundation still there, but the beautiful old house was wiped away, like tens of thousands of other people's homes. Having sat on the front porch of that old house and visited with Trent, I had a lump in my throat, but not the first or the last one of that day.

We turned west and flew back to the base, where we landed nearly two hours after we started. Bert Case, the senior television newscaster in the state and based in Jackson, walked up to me on the tarmac after I stepped down from the chopper. Bert had tears in his eyes; he put his arm around my shoulders, and we both cried.

I tried to compartmentalize my thoughts into short-term, mid-term, and long-term. The first was pretty obvious: maintain and ramp up search and rescue as time was running out for any survivors; get as much help as fast as possible for not just search and rescue but for security; get food and water for the survivors; try to keep residents from returning before we could help take care of them and to make security easier; and, as bad as it was, make the public aware of the situation in an accurate way but also give them confidence.

As quickly as possible, I wanted people to believe their communities would come back and would again be great places to live. To start that kind of thinking, you have to show people in a relatively short period of time that families would have housing, parents would have jobs, and kids would have schools reasonably quickly. Achieving those mid-term goals also required unprecedented help from many sources: federal, other states, volunteers, charities, and the private sector, beyond whose philanthropy we needed its investments and jobs.

My long-term goal was to convince not only pre-storm community residents but the world that Mississippi was serious; we would come back better than ever.

Once I got my game face back on after embracing Marsha and quietly sharing our helicopter experiences, we had a meeting of department heads and our unified command at the facility at the Gulfport airport. Afterward I called President Bush and described the devastation, explained it was not just a coastal calamity but horrific damage for some two hundred miles north, with many fatalities and lots of people unaccounted for. He promised unprecedented federal support for the unprecedented disaster and said he'd do everything he possibly could. The FEMA logistical failure was not fully evident then, so I didn't mention any deficiencies, I just thanked him for what he said. I also mentioned the help his brother Jeb was giving us.

Jeb Bush was Governor of Florida, and his emergency management director was Craig Fugate. As it became clear Katrina was headed for our state, Robert Latham, Fugate, and their counterpart in Alabama had worked out an agreement that Florida would assemble a major contingent of first responders, pass through Alabama, and be ready to move into the Gulf Coast via Interstate 10 on Monday as soon as weather would allow. Having been in Mississippi during training exercises, Fugate was familiar with the coast terrain and had arranged for a number of search-and-rescue teams to be on the ground as soon as possible after landfall. Coming from the east, behind the hurricane, meant Florida's teams would make it to the Coast before our contingent would arrive from Hattiesburg. As a result, Florida first responders saved lives early on.

But Florida then went beyond the call of duty when Fugate began to get requests from Bill Carwile for the kind of basic supplies FEMA was unable to deliver, an ominous sign for the days to come. Late on Wednesday night, Fugate remembered getting a call from his operations chief, telling him that if they didn't start ordering the supplies that Carwile was requesting, they would never have them in time for the dire situation our Coast was becoming. Not knowing whether FEMA would ever reimburse his state for the costs he was about to incur, Fugate gave the go-ahead and sent a memo to Governor Bush and his senior staff that night explaining his decision. The next morning, Governor Bush called and asked him to attend a meeting with his budget staff, who, as Fugate recalled, "were pretty upset and worried about getting paid by FEMA."

Bush called me and wanted to know if we would go to bat for Florida with FEMA. By this time I had only been in the trenches with Bill Carwile and his crew for a few days, but I knew they were with me a hundred percent, which I told Jeb. But then he said something else, that Craig wanted permission to adopt the three Gulf Coast counties, to count them as if they were Florida counties, to give them the resources they needed to stabilize and support the work on the ground. As Fugate told Latham later that day, "we are treating a request from one of these Mississippi counties as if it is coming from a Florida county. We are not going to wait and get clearance. We will give you what you need. The paperwork will have to catch up."

Florida set up a command center at the Stennis facility in north Hancock County, and by the end of 2005, more than six thousand public workers and private contractors from Florida had contributed time along the Gulf Coast. It was truly a gift.

Florida first responders were just one of many groups who worked throughout Monday night and into the week rescuing people. The Coast Guard was a magnificent partner, with thousands of survivors being picked up by their helicopters, of which some 1,900 were in Mississippi, sometimes by young "Coasties" hanging on lines from the choppers to reach the stranded. Despite the valiant efforts of all these first responders, as I got off my helicopter after the flyover, if someone had told me our state would have only 238 fatalities from Katrina, I'd have considered him or her an overly optimistic Pollyanna.

After the department head meeting, our team knew the main priorities and focused on them. In fairness, I doubt they needed me to tell them to focus on priorities, and they were already pushing as hard as possible to check every structure, every mound of debris, every vehicle, not to mention the streams, bays, and sloughs.

As we met, search-and-rescue teams were going through every neighborhood in an orderly fashion, inspecting every structure, searching for survivors or bodies. They would spray paint the structure to show that it had been searched and, if it were the case, the number of bodies inside. The coroner would follow. And looters be damned. Our tolerance for looting was zero. Don't confuse this, however, with not recognizing there were many merchants who were giving away food and other products that were about to be spoiled. In repeated instances store owners invited people in off the street to give away products, and I applauded them then and now.

Before leaving the Coast I went by the Harrison County Emergency Operations Center to meet with local officials from Gulfport and Harrison County. The center had been relocated because of the storm surge, but it was functioning by the time I got there in the middle of the day. The man in charge was Col. Joe Spraggins, who had been hired to replace the retiring director. Spraggins's first official day on the payroll was, unbelievably, August 29.

What I have since learned, and what I remain grateful for to this day, is the way many of our emergency management leaders had been connected to each other in the years leading up to Katrina. Spraggins had spent thirty-four years in the National Guard, had known and worked for Harold Cross, and when he retired to take the Harrison County emergency post, he was the commander of the Guard air base there in Gulfport. Robert Latham and his top deputy, Mike Womack, both had Guard backgrounds and knew General Cross. Bill Carwile served his country in the Army before joining FEMA and knew many of my Mississippi team through shared training exercises and regional meetings. There are similar examples all over South Mississippi, and I am convinced that, as tough and as nerve-wracking as the challenges Katrina gave us were, one reason we were able to overcome those challenges was because of the respect and familiarity leaders had with one another.

Like many other local officials we interviewed for this book—Biloxi mayor A. J. Holloway, Long Beach mayor Billy Skellie, and Bay St. Louis mayor Eddie Favre—Spraggins and others from the emergency operations center were out in the community as soon as the eye had passed, looking for survivors and attempting to size up something they never expected to see during their lifetimes. There are literally hundreds of stories like the one Spraggins told us, of coming across a five-year-old boy who was looking for his parents and grandparents. His apartment complex was nothing but rubble. The boy told Spraggins he had been holding on to his father but had lost him in the water. Later that day, they found the remains of the boy's grandparents and father. But then Spraggins remembered the Sunday night, when the coroner, Gary Hargrove, called to say they had located the boy's mother and brother recovering in Mobile, where they had been sent by other first responders.

By the time I talked with Spraggins on Tuesday, he was already organizing teams of officials to tackle the various tasks confronting them—logistics, legal, operations, finances, rescue, and communications. Emergency operation centers in all the counties affected by the storm were doing the same thing, all tied together by a similar arrangement that MEMA and FEMA were establishing. I always knew when I could reach any of these men and women because almost all of them had briefings at six o'clock every morning, seven days a week, for weeks on end.

After a briefing by Spraggins and his team, I walked out the front door and noticed several large trucks inscribed on their sides with "Ohio One Urban Search and Rescue." I went over to thank them and learned these first responders had driven overnight and all morning from Ohio and were getting their instructions about where to deploy. Like the Florida law enforcement officers, these Ohio professionals were in the vanguard of what would be a spectacular sharing of resources by our sister states, like the Rhode Island Search and Rescue Team, whose photograph, autographed by all the members, I later hung in my Governor's Office, and the Indiana Conservation Officers, who brought their own boats to search for survivors or bodies in the many rivers, bayous, and bays above the Coast.

After visiting with the Ohio One team, I was walking to the car when I saw another group of men getting out of two pickup trucks. I went over to speak to them as they were starting to reach into the beds of the pickups, loaded with chain saws, axes, and other such tools.

They were Mennonites from North Carolina who had also driven overnight to help people clean up the trees and limbs from their property. This was a mission of service from their church. They would go to people's houses and ask if they could help them by clearing their debris away; then they'd get after it, working tirelessly until they finished and neatly stacked the wood by the street. Only then would they move on to the next home, volunteering to help people they didn't know and never would—all out of service to their faith.

Through the various agreements our National Guard and MEMA had with their peers in other states, more than twenty-five thousand professionals from forty-six states assisted Mississippi during the recovery process, and before it was over so did nearly a million volunteers like those Mennonite men. What a statement about our country!

MEMA's Robert Latham and FEMA's Bill Carwile were establishing mobile command centers, creating satellite communication links to Jackson and Washington and among sites throughout the stricken area. Latham and Cross were among the leaders who created a system of runners to manually deliver messages to officials and workers along the Gulf Coast where there was no power and no telecommunications systems. I later learned from General Cross that two weeks prior to landfall he and his company commanders had conducted a training exercise at Shiloh National Battlefield Park, learning, as Cross said, "that the time-honored principals of warfare don't change," one of those being that in "the fog of war," you may have to communicate with someone three thousand yards away by runner, just like they did in the Civil War. And, sure enough, it was runners moving in and around South Mississippi who formed the backbone of our communications system for the first week or more.

At this point, everyone assumed FEMA had water, ice, food, and supplies on the way, so Latham and Carwile began establishing distribution points for relief operations, creating procedures to allocate resources, coordinating with local officials, and continuing search-and-rescue efforts. General Cross issued the order to activate all the other National Guard troops that had not already been activated, and

he called the National Guard Bureau in Washington to activate agreements with other states to add more guardsmen to our effort. By the
end of Tuesday, more than 4,500 soldiers and airmen were working
in Mississippi. Within four days, we had more than 15,000 guardsmen
in the state.

Before I left, someone handed me a copy of Tuesday's Biloxi *Sun
Herald.* I didn't understand how Ricky Mathews, the publisher, was
able to get the paper out a day after landfall, but I later learned he had
made arrangements with a sister Knight Ridder paper in Columbus,
Georgia. Ricky and his staff had spent Monday night using a satellite
phone to transmit copy to Georgia. The newspaper there printed
twenty thousand copies of the *Sun Herald* and trucked them five hours
to the Gulf Coast on Tuesday. This routine lasted more than two weeks
and allowed the *Sun Herald* to never miss a day of publication of a
print newspaper.

There was a lot to get organized and assigned after I got back, but
one of the first things I did was conduct a news briefing for all the
local, state, and national media. We considered it critical to keep
the public as well-informed as possible as often as possible, so I had
at least one news briefing a day. My attitude was and is that in a crisis
a well-informed and engaged citizenry is essential to a full recovery.
Managing a disaster or crisis is not like a war or competitive business
battle, where it is important to keep "the other side" from knowing
certain things. In this case there was no "other side," from my point
of view, so I put all the cards on the table face up. Being open with the
press was key to that.

During the question-and-answer period, I remember two questions
and my answers vividly: Bert Case, who made the trip and the helicopter flyover, asked what was my biggest concern after surveying the
scene? I told him, "How many more bodies will we find under all that
debris." The second question came from a national reporter, who said
in New Orleans the government (city government, I assumed) was
taking away all guns from all citizens. He wanted to know if I'd do that
in Mississippi. I told him law-abiding citizens need their firearms to

protect lives and property, so we would not take away people's guns here. Then I added, "In Mississippi, people who shoot looters won't be prosecuted." That got a rise out of some people, but as I have commented about that statement for the last ten years, "We didn't have much looting." Plus, nobody shot a looter.

After the news conference, I returned a call from Michael Brown, the head of FEMA. I raised the issue of FEMA's capacity to fulfill our order for emergency supplies in the needed quantities. Brown was pleasant and tried to reassure me by saying FEMA had been through all these Florida hurricanes and knew what to expect and how to handle it. I told him, "I don't think you've ever seen anything like this. We're talking nuclear devastation." Brown gave me little confidence we could expect what we needed.

My visit to the Coast also made clear that the Red Cross was having a hard time fulfilling its mission as well. Of course, neither they nor any other charitable group had ever faced a megadisaster like Katrina. But as with FEMA, we had to learn how to do some "workarounds." In particular, we had to improvise when the Red Cross couldn't get to hard-hit areas like East Biloxi and all of Hancock County.

In a disaster of this magnitude, it is the things we all take for granted that, when not available, have the potential to not only affect morale but also prevent recovery. Take the simple case of cash money. ATMs didn't work because they had either been flooded or, for those that were not, there was no electricity to power them. On top of that, the major banks along the Coast had been badly damaged, along with everything else. Hancock Bank CEO George Schloegel remembered walking a mile to his company's headquarters in downtown Gulfport on Tuesday only to find a "twenty-million-dollar, fifteen-story building decimated; roof gone, soaked all the way through; water everywhere, computers knocked out." Not only did Schloegel and his employees have their own personal lives to get back together and then to rebuild, but their business was critical to our recovery. People needed money, payroll checks had to be paid, and loans had to be processed. But none of that could happen in a disaster situation, nor

could merchants accept credit cards with no power and no functioning computer networks.

So Schloegel and his team did something I heard about a day or so
later. They found a few mobile homes, placed them in key locations
along the Coast where people had gathered, and started giving out
money. And when I say "giving out money," that's what they did. This
is how George described it:

> We didn't have any records. So, if we knew you, because you're a cus-
> tomer, fine. If not, it didn't matter. We created a system of IOUs on
> blank pieces of paper. People would sign the IOU and we would give
> them cash, $500 or $1,000, some reasonable amount. And even if we
> didn't know you, we'd at least give you $200. Within a few weeks we
> had given out about $3.5 million, all based on promises written on
> blank pieces of paper. The bank examiners expressed concern about
> potential credit losses, but we assured them we could cover any risk.
> We had enough capital in our bank to sustain the loss, but we didn't
> think we were gambling. We knew the people on the Coast and it
> was the right thing to do. By Christmas time, things were slowly get-
> ting back to normal, and people started coming back, paying off the
> IOU loans. We got back all but about $300,000. And we picked up
> more than ten thousand new accounts.

One of the many logistical challenges confronting Schloegel was
where to get the cash. At first, he later told me, they pulled the cash
from flooded out ATMs and organized teams to make use of washing machines powered by generators to clean all the mud off, while a
separate team ironed dry the newly laundered money. But that
wouldn't be enough in the long term, so, Schloegel told me, "We had
a management trainee, a big burly football player, in Atlanta, home
of our Federal Reserve Bank. So we gave him the bank's address, told
him to fill up his car with gas, buy some extra plastic cans and fill
them up, because once you leave Atlanta, you are non-stop all the way
to Gulfport. And he brought us $30 million, in the trunk of his car."

By Tuesday evening, the Mississippi Department of Transportation had cleared the interstate and highways going north and south, and we solved what was becoming a critical problem, which was lack of fuel. Service stations were not operating, which meant fuel was not coming into the area; on the other hand, the growing number of rescue vehicles needed gas, as did all of the generators in use throughout South Mississippi. But for the fact that Chevron has a major refinery near Pascagoula on the Coast and the willingness on the part of its manager, Roland Kell, to make gasoline and diesel fuel available to anyone who could get to the plant, I don't know how we would have managed during that first couple of weeks.

Wednesday

Early Wednesday morning CNN sent a satellite truck to the Governor's Mansion for a remote interview with Miles O'Brien, one of their veteran reporters. Rather early in the interview, O'Brien asked three times why I was not being more critical of FEMA, intimating it was because of politics. My mother taught me to "praise in public and criticize in private," so I would answer to the effect that "the FEMA people were trying hard; Katrina was an unprecedented disaster; and they were doing more right than wrong," all of which was true, particularly of the FEMA team in our state, who were really good. O'Brien wouldn't take that for an answer, so on his third try I responded, "Miles, we can have an interview or an argument. That's up to you, but I'm up for either one." He let it go. Notwithstanding the dustups that I had with Miles and other journalists—more often than not about FEMA—Mississippi was treated fairly by virtually all reporters, and several, including Joe Scarborough, Robin Roberts, Shepard Smith, and Kathleen Koch, were generous in making sure we were able to tell our story to a broader national audience.

As the day wore on, though, the FEMA logistical system of delivering supplies was clearly not working. To their credit, the FEMA people on the ground in Mississippi had already begun circumventing it, not out of disloyalty but to help the people they were here to help. And to their credit, the FEMA bureaucracy in Washington gave Bill Carwile this flexibility because they knew the system was broken. As Robert Latham told us in an interview, "What was so unique about Bill is he had been in the military, and he was used to making decisions. When it was obvious to Bill that the federal system was collapsing, he just started issuing contracts himself. He was back and forth with D.C. saying 'look if y'all can't do this, I'll get a contract with someone who can.' He just started doing stuff because it was the right thing to do."

At one point during the day, Robert and Bill made their first drive over to Hancock County, where they found the Hancock County Emergency Operations Center building with a collapsed roof. Robert remembered the scene:

> Coming in on Highway 603, there was a house sitting in the middle of the road, power lines down and debris everywhere. At the emergency center they are operating out of a tent. Congressman Gene Taylor introduced me to the local funeral director, who was very upset, crying. He told us his morgue was full, that he had no place to put the bodies they were finding. Just as we are hearing this story, a guy drove up in a nice shiny refrigerated eighteen-wheeler. When he stopped to ask for directions, I instead asked him if that was his truck. He said he had just delivered a load of ice to Stennis and he was headed back to get another load. I looked at Bill and said "Can I buy that truck?" and Bill responded with "Yeah, we'll figure it out." So, after negotiating with the truck driver, we bought the refrigerated trailer for $25,000 and gave it to the funeral director as his new morgue.

By Wednesday afternoon the situation on the Coast was becoming untenable. People were stranded, had no transportation, fresh water, food, or other basic supplies, and FEMA was nowhere. Bob Fenton, Bill Carwile's deputy, warned Washington that "if we get no more than the quantities in your report tomorrow, we will have serious riots." Even though Florida and others were already circumventing FEMA's system and providing us some help, it just wasn't sufficient.

At this point, General Cross dispatched helicopters to fly along the interstates north of the Coast to determine if FEMA trucks were en route. And, sure enough, the pilots found none. Cross had already released much of the Guard's store of ready-to-eat meal packets and water, so not only were rations running thin for the general population but likewise for the guardsmen and other first responders. By mid-afternoon Cross had had several conversations with officers at the Pentagon, pleading for water and food. The Pentagon kept putting him off and calling back, wanting more updates.

Finally, Cross had lost his patience and ended up on a conference call with a number of generals and colonels at U.S. Northcom, the Pentagon's chain of command for natural disasters. Cross said, "By tonight, you send me military air transports loaded with body bags or food and water. The choice is yours." As Cross remembers it, "There was a long silence, and they terminated the call. In about 15 minutes, one of the officers called back, 'General, when you mentioned body bags or food and water, all kind of alarm bells went off up here. Tonight, two C-5 transports will be flying into Gulfport loaded with water and food.'"

Cross told me the first planes arrived around ten o'clock that night. What followed he has described as probably the largest airlift of supplies within the continental United States. In the meantime, he had to find a way to get the supplies distributed, so he organized a fleet of sixty helicopters and ordered them to fuel up overnight and start flying out of the Gulfport airport first thing Thursday morning. The National Guard team ended up running fifteen to eighteen sorties per day per helicopter. Since there were sixty helicopters in our fleet, that would equate to about a thousand sorties per day for four days. More than 1.7 million ready-to-eat food packages and 2 million gallons of water were delivered. As Cross said in an interview for this book, "It was the most intense operation I have seen tactically in the military, with the airlifters constantly coming in and the helicopters going out and back. There were probably fifteen transport planes coming in every six hours."

In between the phone calls and press briefings, I had four meetings that set the stage for a lot of great work down the road. Senator Thad Cochran came by the Governor's Mansion after doing his own tour of South Mississippi and promised to help in any way possible. His work on our behalf is described in chapter 7.

In an earlier call with Jeb Bush, Jeb had recommended creating an independent fund to collect and then spend the millions of charitable dollars that were already coming our way. It just so happened that an old college friend and former Director of Development for the Mississippi Band of Choctaw Indians, William Richardson, had called Charlie Williams the day before and offered to help. We took advantage of his offer, and when he came by the Mansion I asked him to organize the Mississippi Hurricane Recovery Fund. In less than four days, Richardson had a letter from the IRS giving the fund tax-exempt status, a board of five bankers from across the state, and an accounting system up and running. Over the three-year life of the fund, serving as a volunteer, Richardson processed more than $36 million from more than nine thousand contributors.

By this time it became clear we had to establish a call center to handle the thousands of inquiries we were getting from people who needed help and from people who wanted to offer help. My staff got in touch with Marsha Meeks Kelly, the director of our state's office of volunteer service, which coordinated the AmeriCorps program in the state. Within two days she and my staff had acquired space in a donated building in Jackson and recruited a bank of volunteers to staff a growing number of phone lines. Kelly's work with the phone bank will be described in more detail in the next chapter.

The fourth meeting set up the internal staff system for operations and focused on the three big mid-term goals of jobs, housing, and schools. My chief of staff, Charlie Williams, would continue to focus on all things non-Katrina. We still had the normal responsibilities of state government. We couldn't ignore those, and Charlie would over-see staff and administration work in those areas.

Paul Hurst, my chief counsel, and Jim Perry, my policy director, would divide responsibility for managing the staff and administrative work on the things related to Katrina. Jim would be responsible for financial arrangements, including design and passage of a federal spe-cial disaster assistance package, and he would staff the Barksdale Commission and our federal lobbying efforts.

Paul would manage the implementation of all our response-and-recovery activities. He was in charge of people, whether staff, my administration, or outside support groups such as MEMA, the departments, and other state agencies connected to our relief operation.

At this meeting I emphasized that my strategy for rebuilding the coastal communities depended on getting residents to return and stay. That meant we had to achieve three critical short- to mid-term goals: get people a place to live; get people employment; and get schools for their kids to attend. People wouldn't return and stay without a job, a home, and their kids in schools. We had to achieve these goals in a way that gave people hope and, ultimately, confidence that their com-munities would come back better than before and would be great places for their families to live and learn, to work and worship. Both Paul and Jim did fabulous jobs. Both are great leaders with good judg-ment but are also excellent, detail-oriented managers.

While I spent several hours in meetings and on the phone trying to help manage these and many other problems, I saved part of Wednesday to go to Laurel, which, despite being nearly ninety miles inland, took a pounding.

Besides hurricane-force winds, Laurel and Jones County, of which Laurel is the largest city, were hit by tornadoes thrown off by Katrina, killing several people. It was important for me to visit Laurel and other noncoastal towns to demonstrate that the Governor's Office, as well as FEMA and the other federal and state agencies, would focus on all of South Mississippi, not just the Coast. The Laurel I saw that Wednesday bore little similarity to that beautiful one-time timber center, which was loaded with hundreds of huge, old hardwoods despite being in the middle of the Piney Woods area of the state.

I drove around the town with state senator Stacey Pickering, who represented part of the county and is a first cousin to then Congressman Chip Pickering. There was a great deal of wind damage, mostly caused by falling trees that crushed homes and buildings.

Two huge, locally owned industries at that time were Sanderson Farms, one of the nation's major producers of chicken, and Howard Industries, one of the largest manufacturers of transformers in the country. While Howard Industries suffered damage, the greater risk was for Sanderson Farms—not so much because of damage to its processing plants but because without electricity, the farmers who raised the chickens Sanderson processed had no air conditioning. In late August, the heat can kill chickens in large numbers. In fact, several million chickens died in Katrina's wake because of the storm damage as well as lack of electricity and fuel for generators.

After Pickering's tour I went to City Hall to meet with Mayor Melvin Mack, a Democrat who had just taken office for his first term in early June. I found him cordial but concerned and focused, which was just what a town needed at a time like this. Since he didn't have the search-and-rescue issues of the Coast officials, he was already concerned about how to access federal and state funding for cleanup and rebuilding.

While I was in Laurel, I was told all the local radio stations were off the air, but a Clear Channel station was still broadcasting a signal. Clear Channel is headquartered in San Antonio, Texas, and run by the Lowry Mays family. Clear Channel's stations typically broadcast national programming and don't offer local news. With no radio station broadcasting local news, citizens had no source of information about conditions and places to go for assistance. Someone asked if I could call Clear Channel about allowing one of the local stations to broadcast news every hour using their signal. I called Mays, whom I had met over the years but certainly didn't know well. The receptionist put me on the phone with Mays's son. I made the ask, and it took him a split second to say, "Yes." The Mays's people were on the phone with the Jones County Emergency Operations Center shortly, and they handed off to the local radio station manager. Local news overrode Clear Channel's own broadcast in Laurel every hour until the electricity was back on a week or so later.

My Wednesday media briefing had a number of questions designed to get me to wallop FEMA. Yes, FEMA and the federal government let us down, especially with their logistical failures. Having said that, FEMA did a lot more right than wrong. Even as we grappled with them over silly procedures and considered some of their policy decisions wrongheaded, overall Mississippi and especially our Gulf Coast could not have come back as strongly or as quickly as it did without FEMA programs and the selfless service of some great Americans who made FEMA their second career, as was normally the case with FEMA's mid-level and senior civil servants.

Marsha held FEMA leaders like Nick Russo and Sid Melton in particularly high regard. They wanted to get the job done and were always willing to figure out a way to get it done. So I sidestepped the questions that were intended to fuel ire. Meanwhile, the *Clarion-Ledger* focused on the unthinkable devastation, which was appropriate. The level of destruction was hard to accept, to appreciate. A photograph in a magazine or a television shot simply couldn't capture it.

This is a good point in the book to tell you how blessed I was to have a sensational staff at this incredible time of crisis. They were simply as good as it gets—and not just Charlie Williams, Paul Hurst, and Jim Perry, but all of them. Great work ethic. Unwavering commitment to the state. Bright, clever, but with really good judgment. Totally trustworthy and had earned the trust of the people with whom they dealt. No politician (or any other leader, in my opinion) is better than the people around him or her. No elected official ever made it alone. I certainly never have.

Thursday

This was the day the FEMA logistics office in Washington finally admitted its failure and informed the Mississippi FEMA and MEMA teams they would only be able to provide about one-tenth of the food, ice, and water promised to Mississippi. Bill Carwile was livid but kept his composure, mostly because he and others had already taken independent measures to address the huge shortfalls. The good news was that there was starting to be a steady stream of military aircraft flying in food and water to the Coast, while volunteer and relief organizations were beginning to also make their presence felt.

On another front, Kansas City Southern Railroad announced the reopening of its "Meridian Speedway," a line from Meridian, Mississippi, to Shreveport, Louisiana. Making the reopening more significant was that it allowed Norfolk Southern to use the line and bypass its regular route through South Mississippi, which had seen many obstructions on its main line from Meridian to New Orleans, where in some parts of Mississippi there were an average of five hundred trees per mile down on the line or in the right-of-way. CSX railroad, whose bridges were out and rail lines were damaged on the Coast, also rerouted freight trains through Meridian.

In the middle of the day, I arrived in Hattiesburg for meetings with local officials, some of whom were impatient and felt that their hard-hit area wasn't getting enough attention. While about sixty miles from the Coast, the greater Hattiesburg area was slammed with 110-mph winds generating a tremendous amount of damage. And, like much of the rest of the state, it would go without electricity for more than a week. We were available to the press after the meeting, and I was frank about the situation: "The system is overloaded." I went on to be totally open by saying, "This is the worst natural disaster in the history of this country. Nobody's ever done this before. Every day we try to make a little progress. We are going to make mistakes along the way, realize things we should have done, things we shouldn't have done, and things we should have done differently. We are out there in uncharted water."

In the meantime, the White House was causing another problem. Maggie Grant, the White House liaison with governors, called to feel me out on an idea the president was considering in light of the problems in Louisiana. Maggie said President Bush was considering "federalizing" the response to Katrina. I told her I was absolutely against it for Mississippi, "Maggie, we know the terrain, the geopolitics, the history, and the relationships better than the federal government ever would. Our National Guard, working with the support of thousands of soldiers from the Guard are and would be far more effective than the Pentagon's Third Army." She called me back two more times that day, but she got the same answer every time. Moreover, I made it plain I would publicly oppose the idea if it were proposed, and I wouldn't be nice about it.

Not long after my conversation with Maggie, President Bush called, but not about federalization. He asked if I knew where the town of Collins was. I laughed out loud, "Of course, Mr. President, I know where Collins is. Why do you care about Collins?" The president told me that two huge pipelines, the Colonial and the Plantation, both run through a pumping station in Collins, and they were critical carriers of refined oil products. The absence of power had shut down the pumps, which was threatening a fuel shortage on the East Coast, one that could really hurt the economy and inconvenience millions of people. He asked if I could do anything to get their power restored. I assured him I could.

I called Anthony Topazi, president of Mississippi Power Company, and learned the Collins facility was not in Mississippi Power's service area. He said that the rural electric cooperative that served that area was most likely overwhelmed. I asked him to look into it. A couple of hours later Topazi called me back to say he would restore power that day, which he did. Because Topazi recognized the national importance of the fuel supply, he pulled workers off Mississippi Power's main priorities and got this done. He never told me if he had cleared it with the cooperative. I called the president to tell him product would be flowing through the two pipelines. He never asked me on those calls about federalizing the response to Katrina.

It was also on Thursday that Topazi, as Mississippi Power's CEO, made a pledge that inspired all of us. A local TV reporter asked him when he thought power would be restored. His response is captured in an interview that his vice president, Bobby Kerley, gave us for this book:

> By the third day we had a pretty good idea what it was going to take to get power to the working meters. We were thinking a month. Then some of our crew members came back from working in the Bay St. Louis area, big ole linemen, pretty rattled about what they had seen, telling us they had given away their own food and water to mothers and babies who had nothing, no place to sleep, nothing to drink or eat. They were telling us, you've got to go see this. So Anthony and I drove over there and what we saw changed everything: babies living under tarps, in boxes. People begging for food and water. When we got back to Gulfport, Anthony went to the TV station for an interview he had scheduled and I went back to our operations center. All we had was an old TV hooked up to a generator and rabbit ears. I had about fifty linemen in there with me, and I was trying to pump them up, keep their spirits high and they were asking me how long, how long. I was telling 'em about a month. About this time, Anthony comes on the TV and the reporter asks how long is this going to take? And he turned and looked at that camera and he said, "Now, I know there are going to be people back at the crew headquarters that may be upset with me, but we're going to get power back on by six o'clock, September 11. We've got no other choice. We've got to do whatever it takes." That was thirteen days. And I turned around and all those linemen, it was so quiet you could have heard a pin drop. I looked at them and said, "Brothers, we've got to do it." And they jumped up and started applauding. They were giving him a standing ovation. They were ready to conquer the world.

By Friday, Kerley had more than twelve thousand workers and five thousand bucket trucks and other vehicles on or coming to the Gulf Coast and South Mississippi because Topazi's commitment was not just for the Coast but for the entire Mississippi Power service area of thirty counties and more than 180,000 customers. Like so many other first responders on the Coast in those early days, Topazi's commitment could only have been made real because of Roland Kell and the Chevron refinery in Pascagoula, which made gas available to all of their vehicles.

The biggest topic at the press briefing on Thursday was President Bush's visit to the Coast on Friday. Questions about FEMA's problems continued, and I continued to avoid them. It was clear by then, however, that Bush and his presidency were being hurt by the problems with the Katrina response. Historically, Republicans are viewed by the public as better managers than Democrats. Katrina was seriously undermining that long-held perception. The president would add fuel to the fire in Mobile the next day.

Friday

President Bush flew to Mobile, Alabama, where I met him at the Coast Guard station. The president, Alabama governor Bob Riley, and I walked around the hangar where we met and thanked crews of Coast Guard helicopters, many of whom had flown into the Mississippi Gulf Coast beginning Monday to help with search and rescue. They were real heroes who took great risks to rescue people.

Later we walked to Marine One to fly to Keesler Air Force Base in Biloxi. FEMA chief Michael Brown was traveling with the president, and he asked me how the government was doing. I equivocated and gave a non-answer. Nevertheless, as we were walking with the press, President Bush said, "Good job, Brownie." This casual comment, caught by the traveling press corps, greatly compounded public perception that the president didn't even know the federal effort had problems that were obvious to everyone else.

For me the Mobile stop was also important because it gave me a chance to personally thank Bob Riley. While Katrina didn't hit Alabama nearly as hard as it hit us, there were several feet of water in areas of downtown Mobile because of storm surge. Yet Bob sent two companies of Alabama National Guard Military Police straight across the state line into Jackson County, Mississippi, Monday evening. The most valuable military assets in a civil disaster are MPs, who are trained in crowd control and policing.

As we flew the short distance from Mobile to Biloxi, President Bush mentioned federalizing the response. I told him politely but emphatically I was opposed to the idea. If Louisiana wanted it, I said, that was their business, but we didn't want it or need it. Thankfully, the president did not push it.

In a snap we landed at Keesler and motored a short distance to East Biloxi, an old, diverse, and largely low-income area of the city that had a mostly minority population and that had sustained dreadful devastation. The White House advance staff had picked a good venue to allow the media and the American people to see the utter obliteration Katrina had dealt this old community some fifty miles from where the eye had come ashore. The motorcade stopped, and the president got out to see a residential neighborhood where almost every house was destroyed.

Marsha met us there as well. The president had always liked her and had been very gracious to her. He gave her a hug, and it was an emotional moment for all three of us. Then the president was greeted by a half dozen local officials before meeting a Catholic priest who had been responsible for a mission that had sheltered homeless alcoholic men. It had housed twelve men before the storm, and the surge had killed six. Three of the survivors were there to meet President Bush. It was a memorable scene, and the president spent some time with them. Then one of the men made a profound statement that affected us all: He said, "I've wondered why God saved me, why I didn't die with the others. I've prayed about it and wrestled with it. Today I've realized He saved me so I can build back the mission."

Marsha and I then walked over and talked to a young man the president would shortly meet. He was likely in his twenties, dressed in long blue, baggy shorts and a T-shirt; he had long red hair pulled into a ponytail that hung down to the middle of his back. The "red-headed boy" was a tourist who had decided to "ride out" the storm in the predawn hours. When the storm surge swelled beyond his expectations, he climbed a tree, which he pointed out to us just a few feet away, to get above the rising water. Ultimately, he was twenty feet or so high. Amazingly, we were several blocks inland, and the waters had been twenty feet high. He described how he had found a perch in the tree where he could rest and watch objects float by. The young man said being on top of a gigantic storm surge riveted by winds approaching 150 mph was like "a NASCAR race" as objects in the water, from limbs to appliances, floated past him at high speeds. He laughed, "Zoom, zoom." Then his mood changed, for he had had a young woman in the tree with him; for hours they had held onto each other until they lost their grip, and she was pulled away by the storm. He told us he had so far failed to locate her. Obviously, the local authorities had told the advance team about the red-headed tourist, and they thought the president should listen to his story, just as he'd heard the story of the mission survivors. It floored me to hear it. The president walked over, and Marsha and I excused ourselves. We separated from the presidential party by fifty or hundred feet, to catch our breaths. President Bush spent another hour or so touring the Coast and then headed for New Orleans while I headed back to Jackson.

A tremendous amount of staff work had been accomplished in just a few days to both understand and access the federal disaster assistance programs as well as to learn what needs we had or would have that were not going to be met by the existing FEMA reimbursement policies. We were already putting in place procedures and working with local officials to ensure they had the help they needed to apply for and receive federal assistance.

A first step we took that week was to hire the Horne CPA firm to help the worst-hit city and county governments ascertain their financial conditions and their financial needs in the wake of the disaster. This was the start of an incredible journey that ended with federal auditors and inspectors praising the systems we created to ensure the integrity of our financial operations. More than once our team's programs were termed "models" by federal overseers. We expected to get unprecedented federal aid, as would be appropriate after this unprecedented catastrophe, but I was determined that our stewardship would be such that lawmakers and administrators would be proud they dealt with us so generously. The next victims of a future worst disaster in American history deserved no less.

As the week drew to a close, the single biggest reason for my optimism was the spirit and character of the people of Mississippi. These were not wealthy people with great material resources, but they were strong, resilient, self-reliant people. They had borne the brunt of the worst natural disaster in American history; they had been knocked down flat, but I believed they'd get right back up. I believed they'd help themselves and help their neighbors. That was the bulwark for my confidence.

Here are just two examples of the hundreds I could cite to demonstrate why I placed so much confidence in our people. Joe Spraggins told me about a man who walked into his office two days after the storm and introduced himself as Mike Matthews, owner of M&M Petroleum; he told Spraggins, "I'm here to help; what have you got for me to do?" When Spraggins responded that he needed fuel for emergency vehicles and generators, Matthews said, "I have no fuel, but have one or two trucks that can haul anything. I can get fuel for you out of Mobile." Incredulous, Spraggins issued the test: "How quick can you get it and what do you need?" Matthews came back, "I can start running now and all I need is a handshake." By the time Matthews came back late that evening with his first load, Gulfport Memorial Hospital had been calling, pleading for fuel; its generators were close to empty, and if they shut down, so would expensive medical equipment that would threaten the lives of a number of patients. Luckily, Matthews got back in time to refuel all of the hospital's generators, with about thirty minutes to spare!

Friday night Marsha returned to the Mansion from the Coast and told me a story I'll never forget. She was in Hancock County that afternoon in a pickup with two Bureau of Narcotics agents, Wade Parham and Sam Owens. As they were driving just above Kiln in a rural part of the county, they rounded a curve and on the left was a doublewide trailer that had been crushed by the storm. Marsha said it looked like a beer can someone had squeezed in his hand. More importantly, in the front yard were two little children and their father. Sam pulled over onto the front edge of the property, and they all got out and learned from the man this trailer had been home to his family, including their eight children. His wife and their other children were gone to look for food and supplies. The officers started to unload supplies from the pickup, and after a couple of trips the man said that was plenty for them, and he was grateful. The agents kept unloading supplies saying, "Look, we got plenty here. Let us help you." The fellow responded, "Thanks, but that's enough for us. If you really have more, take it to the little old lady across the road who's a shut-in. She needs it more than us." Wade said, "We'll take care of her, too, but here's this for your family."

The man continued to protest, "If you've got more, you need to drive down this highway about a quarter mile, and there's a gravel road that angles sharp back to the right. There are six or eight families who live down that road, and I know nobody's been there to help them."

Can you imagine? Here's a family that had nothing before the storm and lost what little they had. Yet he was concerned about his neighbors. How can you not believe in people like that? How can you not make sure you do everything you can and, in fact, more than has ever been done before to help them? My mother's belief that catastrophes bring out the best in most people was proven right time after time.

CHAPTER 4

Volunteers, Housing, and Recovery

T HE DAY AFTER MISSISSIPPI POWER COMPANY restored
electricity to its customer base on September 10, Entergy did
the same for the three hundred thousand customers in the
western half of our state served by its grid. More than five thousand
workers poured into Mississippi in the days following Katrina's
landfall to help Entergy's existing workforce achieve this modern-
day miracle.

The Mississippi Fairgrounds near downtown Jackson was the
staging area for this operation, and that's where I was early on Saturday morning, meeting and thanking many of those workers on
September 3. Very few of the ones I saw that day were from Mississippi, but the morale among them and their commitment to the hard
and dangerous task of helping our state recover lifted my spirits
immensely.

The fairgrounds is also home to the state Coliseum, which was
serving as a temporary home for hundreds of stranded Mississippians and Louisianans in addition to many of Entergy's workers. A
week after my visit that Saturday, many of the Mississippi residents
had left the Coliseum and could return home to air conditioned
houses thanks to the sacrifices of the Entergy and Mississippi Power

workers and the out-of-state workers who mastered this incredible logistical challenge.

Even though I have highlighted the work of Mississippi Power and Entergy, I don't want to leave out the similar efforts of other utility companies throughout the state, including AT&T and the many electric power associations. They also recruited hundreds of out-of-state workers to engage in the monumental cleanup and rebuilding of our electric and telecommunications infrastructure. We simply could not have embarked on any recovery plan without those utility services.

By Saturday our call center had been up and running for a couple of days and was already fielding thousands of calls over more than fifty phone lines that were staffed twenty-four hours a day for about the first month (and would remain open for nearly the next three months). After being asked to organize the center two days after the storm, Marsha Meeks Kelly, the director of the Mississippi Commission for Volunteer Service, and her small but determined staff had it open for business in two days. Not only was its phone number the one Mississippians used to obtain assistance, but the center itself became the place where folks from all around the world would call to donate goods and money as well as schedule volunteer trips to the state. By the first anniversary of the storm, Kelly's office reported that nearly 600,000 volunteers from outside Mississippi had registered with over 250 organizations and had traveled to our state to help with the recovery. That number would eventually rise to nearly 1 million.

The core of the call center operators were AmeriCorps members who came from all parts of the country, often with little more than a sleeping bag—since many of them spent night after night at the center when they weren't taking calls—but with huge hearts and boundless energy. State agency personnel, released from their regular duties, also made up a significant share of the operators.

A week or so after the center was established, I remember being notified by one of my staff members that Kelly and her team had expanded into the warehouse and distribution business. So many people were donating so many clothes, housewares, and other supplies that they needed a place to sort and distribute donated goods to various charitable help centers set up on the Coast. Next Kelly and her team turned to accepting credit card and cash donations. Early on she had no processing equipment for the cards, so the volunteers took the information by hand on legal pads—thousands of people from all over the world gave their credit card information to total strangers, all because they wanted to help Mississippians.

Kelly shared many great examples of the volunteer spirit she had under her wings, but this one needs to be included here. It was written by a volunteer from California who gave up two weeks of personal leave to work in Mississippi:

My second week at the center I was asked if I could handle a big request. The operator of a tow truck service in Pass Christian, one of the hardest hit cities, had lost everything when the hurricane hit. Johnny Hogan's wrecker service had been started by Johnny's father in 1948 and was the only work Johnny had ever known. The hurricane took his home, his business and even his beloved mother had been killed in the storm. His daughter Fay was all the family he had left and Johnny desperately wanted to get back into business so he could support himself and Fay. After hearing this story, I made it my mission to find a tow truck for Johnny. I called every chamber of commerce and transportation group in the south but everyone was tapped out. So I decided to give California organizations a try; maybe they could point me to a group that could assist. My first call was to the California Tow Truck Association. I was connected to their Executive Director, Jeff Hunter, and when I told him Johnny's story and what I was asking for, he didn't hesitate for even a second. His response: "Yes, we can make this happen." Jeff said he'd initiate a fundraising drive at once to get money for Johnny Hogan to purchase a new truck. When I got back to Los Angeles, I often thought of Johnny Hogan . . . how he was and if he'd ever get a truck to get him back to work. A couple of months later, I got my answer in the form of a phone call: "Hi, it's Jeff from the California Tow Truck Association. Are you sitting down?" I wasn't,

but I would be by the time he told me how the association had continued to fundraise for Johnny until they had enough money to buy him a
truck. They then bought a wrecker in California, loaded it onto a trailer,
and drove it to Pass Christian. When Jeff emailed me a photo of Johnny
being presented with the keys to the truck, I burst into tears. Jeff's
group had never stopped their fundraising drive, and had even been
in touch with Johnny over the months to let him know how many
people were working to get him working again. My friends at the association had given Johnny the greatest roadside assist in history.

Volunteers from the Seventh-day Adventists took on warehouse logistics and were indispensable in those early days, helping us get organized and training other volunteers. As the task grew and resources
were in great demand, the Department of Finance and Administration under the leadership of J. K. "Hoopy" Stringer and the Mississippi
Economic Council and their executive director, Blake Wilson, identified people and resources to help run the operation. Wilson's daily
and eventually weekly calls with state chambers of commerce around
the country were an incredible asset to our state during those early
months. As resources were deployed from communities around the
country, one location quickly developed into a second sorting location, and others followed. Soon thereafter UPS and FedEx took us
under their wings and provided groups of their employees to help train
the volunteers who ran the distribution centers.

After the first month, the AmeriCorps members headed south to
work, and inmates from the state correctional work facilities and a
handful of state employees managed the main operation, working
twenty-four hours a day, seven days a week, for the first four months.
One key factor to the distribution was the establishment of distribution centers on the Coast. With the help of various charities and many
churches and everyday people, the centers provided sites where people
could come get much-needed food, water, clothes, and cleaning supplies. Six to ten trailer truckloads of goods left Jackson daily for points

across the Coast until donated items could flow directly to the centers on the Coast.

The work of the denominational distribution centers greatly added to the capacity of our centers, giving greater access to basic needs in the early days and weeks following Katrina. The Episcopal Day School in Long Beach was the only Episcopal structure more or less intact along the entire Mississippi Gulf Coast; yet the bishop, The Rt. Rev. Duncan Gray III, put all his efforts and the efforts of the national church, through Episcopal Relief and Development, into Coast Episcopal School. This school became a distribution center for clothes, food, water, medical supplies, and counseling assistance known as Camp Coast Care, and it, along with three other facilities sponsored by Lutheran Episcopal Services in Mississippi, became a volunteer housing facility serving tens of thousands of volunteers who were building and rehabbing thousands of homes over the next five years.

When no medical clinics or hospitals were available in the early days, the school's gymnasium became a medical clinic. Doctors from across the state and nation came to assist those physically injured by Katrina. Tetanus shots were badly needed, in addition to more serious wound care and stress-related issues. The doctors from Duke Medical Center stand out for their determination to serve. They showed up and stayed for weeks or months until the county could reopen adequate facilities to meet the mounting needs.

One small group of volunteers was even more special to my wife, Marsha, and me. Eight U.S. Department of Commerce staff members took their two weeks of vacation and came to volunteer. One was our younger son, Reeves Barbour, who had been at Commerce for just over a year. Reeves and his colleagues manned phone banks, worked in the warehouse, and did whatever they were asked both in Jackson and on the Coast. They were no different than the rest of the nearly one million volunteers; they just wanted to help people who had been slammed by America's Great Storm. The outpouring of support we received and the individual stories Marsha Meeks Kelly told me about

Americans wanting to help Mississippi were a constant source of encouragement.

Debris Cleanup

Leaving the fairgrounds on Saturday the third, I headed over to Meridian. Despite being some 150 miles north of the coastline, the area had nevertheless suffered significant damage from Katrina's winds, which was still a Category 1 hurricane when it hit Meridian. Nearly all of the streets had been cleared by the weekend, and, like every other local government in the state, Mayor John Robert Smith and his staff were learning the intricacies of FEMA reimbursement rules.

President Bush was leaning forward to allow the affected states and their local governments the maximum possible reimbursement of costs; he and we recognized that none of these governments could begin to afford the cost of cleanup and restoration. So understanding the regulations, creating the accounting systems necessary to keep track of and report these off-budget expenditures and finding companies to do the work were quickly becoming challenges we had to overcome in order to accelerate the recovery.

Under FEMA rules, local governments had two options for debris removal: they could delegate the responsibility to FEMA or do it themselves. If FEMA were asked to perform the cleanup, the work would be assigned to the U.S. Army Corps of Engineers, who would bring in a contractor that had previously won a competitive bid contract. In our case the contractor was AshBritt Environmental, a company based in Florida. Throughout the fall and into the next year, this became a controversial issue because of complaints that local contractors and workers were being passed over in favor of out-of-state people brought in by AshBritt to perform the work.

More often than not, local governments chose the FEMA option because they didn't have the staff or systems in place to manage the contracts necessary to remove the massive amounts of debris and because—as I later learned—choosing FEMA essentially indemnified the local government from liability or "deobligation," the dreaded word used to describe subsequent (usually years later) decisions by FEMA that the local contractor had not followed certain rules, which would mean the local government would have to pay back the federal government.

I had initially suggested to local governments that they authorize local contractors to perform the debris removal because every area needed the jobs and business. As it turned out, many of those local officials were just not equipped to handle the legal and accounting paperwork necessary to get reimbursed for the cleanup. The Corps contractor, AshBritt, knew the Corps and FEMA procedures. The federal government had almost never demanded money back from Ash-Britt, so they virtually eliminated the risk of deobligation. Moreover, using AshBritt effectively indemnified the locals against that risk anyway. While AshBritt ended up hiring lots of local contractors and thousands of Mississippians, the issue of cleaning up, removing, and disposing of debris persisted well into the summer of 2006.

Housing

In addition to helping local officials manage the mammoth task of removing 47 million cubic yards of debris, we were focused on the special session, the Barksdale Commission, our request for special funding from Congress to rebuild the damaged highways and bridges, and getting students back into classes—all of which are described in subsequent chapters.

The overriding challenge in the fall months leading into the winter was housing, especially on the Gulf Coast, where more than one hundred thousand Mississippians had either lost their homes or the homes were so badly damaged that it would take months to repair them. By the second week, housing had become the critical issue, and it stayed the pivotal issue every week for the next three or four years.

Above the coastal plain were tens of thousands of wind-damaged homes, including about forty thousand that were uninhabitable. Many thousands of others had lost part or nearly all of their roofs, so there was a major push to distribute special tarpaulins to cover the damaged areas. The government-issue tarps are bright blue, and most neighborhoods in the lower two-thirds of the state had some "blue" roofs for weeks or even months before contractors could repair the shingles.

In September the hurdle was temporary housing. Under the FEMA regulations, the federal government will cover the cost of temporary housing for those whose homes (owned or rented) were left uninhabitable. For example, FEMA would put people up in hotels, if rooms were available. The problem, of course, is that Katrina was not selective in the structures it destroyed, taking out houses, hotels, schools, civic centers—virtually anything that could have been used under ordinary circumstances to temporarily house people. On top of that, there were housing demands for all of the federal employees, out-of-state construction and clean-up workers, and volunteers who had come to help.

Biloxi's Imperial Palace Casino hotel was the first to reopen. Although the lower couple of floors, including the casino, were heavily damaged by the storm surge, the owners quickly got the rooms higher up available for use. The IP, as it is known locally, primarily housed relief workers from FEMA and other agencies. At one point FEMA arranged for a cruise ship to dock at the port in Mobile, and later Pascagoula, and serve hundreds who had lost their homes. The U.S. Navy sent a hospital ship to treat patients and house them, as necessary.

With nearly a quarter of a million people whose homes were either uninhabitable or damaged throughout Mississippi, the regular FEMA temporary housing model turned out to be wildly insufficient, as everyone soon recognized. That housing model consisted of using what became known as "FEMA trailers" to serve as temporary housing. The term "trailer" is actually misleading. We think of "trailer" as referring to a mobile home, which are sixty or eighty feet long and may have two or more bedrooms. A FEMA "trailer," however, is actually a camper, typically less than four hundred square feet, the kind of trailer that you take to the lake for a weekend or maybe a week.

Even though FEMA had a few thousand trailers stockpiled in Arkansas, none had been placed and occupied in early September because the trailers required electricity. While Mississippi Power, Entergy, and the electric power associations were racing to get power restored, that date was still a few days away. Moreover, many of the proposed sites where the trailers would be set up were next to destroyed homes, and those sites would have to be prepared to receive electricity by erecting poles to hold the wiring that came in from a nearby transformer to a meter that also had to be put up. Moreover, the move by Mississippi Power to get electric service restored by September 11 to everyone who had a meter wouldn't apply to these neighborhoods for quite a while after that date. Then it dawned on all of us that a massive building campaign by FEMA was going to be required to deliver the number of trailers we were ultimately going to need, which at its peak was more than forty thousand.

While a small percentage of FEMA trailers were set up in "trailer parks" or group areas, the vast majority were located on the lot or yard where the displaced family's home had been before Katrina. Obviously this had a lot of benefits, such as the homeowners' being able to keep an eye on their property and able to conveniently work on repairing or rebuilding the damaged or destroyed structure. It also vastly reduced the number and size of temporary group areas of trailers, which could become security risks under certain circumstances.

And we were faced with other housing issues. Early in September we convened a group of FEMA experts on housing to discuss the coming need for labor housing. With the decimation on the Coast, there would be a huge demand for labor, especially construction workers, including many who would first work for some time in the debris removal operations. We knew it would take a while to clean up, transport, and dispose of the tens of millions of cubic yards of debris left behind from Katrina (we didn't know in September that it would eventually be 47 million cubic yards, or that it would take eleven months), and we knew thousands of workers would be needed for the unprecedented amount of reconstruction needed to replace or repair tens of thousands of homes and commercial buildings.

At that meeting, the "experts" were encouraging about the federal government's ability to bring in temporary housing that could be used to house laborers who did not live in the community; however, within a few days FEMA told us their lawyers said labor housing was not a permissible use of temporary housing under the federal disaster law. This was a real blow. There were already hundreds of workers, including large numbers of Hispanics, who had come to the devastated areas from all parts of the country and taken short-term jobs. They wanted and needed work, and many of them slept in tents or in cars or the beds of pickup trucks. It was still very warm in September, so the conditions for these individuals were rough. Nevertheless, they stayed and worked and helped us rebuild.

I learned quickly that the need for locals to have "hope and confidence" would occur sooner rather than later. Within the first week health care professionals—physicians, dentists, nurses, and others—began receiving recruiting contacts from hospitals and other medical facilities across the South. "Your hospital is out of service for months. . . . We heard your clinic was destroyed by Katrina. . . . We will pay all of your moving expenses, and your pay will be more than you were making before." But even though their homes had been destroyed, their health care facilities damaged, and there were yet no schools for their children to attend, it is positively remarkable how many of these heroes stayed in their communities to rebuild. And the same can be said for shipyard and refinery workers, bankers and insurance agents, school teachers and state employees. I marvel to this day at how strong, resilient, and faithful to their communities these tough Mississippians were.

Looking back ten years later, that weekend of September 9, 10, and 11 was a pivot point, when we were about to learn how to operate effectively within the FEMA public assistance network of debris removal, temporary housing, and other programs, while we were ourselves preparing to focus on the longer term: developing a plan for Congress to add needed assistance programs not contained in the federal disaster law and organizing a broad, participatory process for the leadership of the Coast and South Mississippi and the citizens at large to decide how their communities would be rebuilt and renewed.

Mississippi Rising

The outpouring of generosity reached a crescendo on Saturday, October 1, when two Mississippi natives, Sam Haskell and Lanny Griffith, each of whom had had a successful career away from the state, produced a spectacular variety show on the campus of the University of Mississippi in Oxford. Sam and Lanny are both Ole Miss alums, and Oxford is far enough from the Coast to have suffered no significant damage. This fundraising event for the Mississippi Hurricane Recovery Fund raised more than $15 million and featured some of the most celebrated entertainers in music, movies, theater, and television. Lanny came up with the name—Mississippi Rising—and recruited two companies, Wal-Mart and UnitedHealth Group, to underwrite the cost of the production. Sam used virtually every connection he had as a top executive of the William Morris Agency in California to invite more than forty celebrities, musicians, and actors to donate a day for Mississippi. Sam asked the crew that just produced the Emmy Awards on September 19 to move to Oxford and transform the Tad Smith Coliseum into a Hollywood production site. The show was broadcast live for three hours on MSNBC and featured several Mississippians, including Faith Hill, Morgan Freeman, Sela Ward, Gerald McRaney, Lance Bass, Mary Donnelly Haskell, and Mary Ann Mobley. There were also many big stars who had no relationship with the state but who wanted to help their fellow Americans, including Ray Romano, Whoopi Goldberg, Marilu Henner, Marilyn McCoo, Jason Alexander, Alison Sweeney, Pam Tillis, Macy Gray, Doris Roberts, Billy Davis Jr., and Jean Smart. B.B. King and Alan Jackson also gave videotaped performances. I'll never forget the impromptu arrival of Samuel L. Jackson, who took time off from filming in Memphis, walked on stage, looked out at everyone in the audience and said, "If anything bad ever happens to me or my family, dear God, please let it happen in Mississippi!"

Later in October a group of friends and colleagues led by Tom Boggs, head of a major D.C. law firm, put on a Katrina benefit in Washington. Although a native of Louisiana—both of his parents had represented the state in Congress—Boggs made sure Mississippi got an equal division of the proceeds, which meant several hundred thousand dollars to our recovery fund. Many of my longtime friends and colleagues in D.C. contributed generously and got their clients to do so as well. World-class Democratic lobbyists like Tony Podesta, Jim Free, John Jonas, and Joel Jankowski joined Ed Rogers, Don Fierce, Kirk Blalock, Charlie Black, and others on the Republican side in making it a success and a good time.

In December, a gala event was held in Tunica, our large gaming area just south of Memphis, and was spearheaded by Wayne Newton to raise money for Mississippi first responders, including National Guard members, who had been injured or suffered losses because of America's Great Storm.

Clinton Visit

As we got further into the fall, my office received notice that former president Bill Clinton would be visiting the Coast and was inviting me to meet with him. Even though I had been chairman of the national Republican Party during his first term in the White House, he treated Marsha and me like we were old college friends instead of his former political nemesis. President Clinton was visiting the Coast to survey the damage and make decisions about the best way the Bush-Clinton Katrina Fund—the charity he and former president George H. W. Bush had established—could support our relief efforts.

They ultimately donated more than $5 million to the Mississippi Hurricane Recovery Fund.

Marsha and I met President Clinton in a predominantly African American residential neighborhood on the northern side of Gulfport. We had a community meeting in the front yard of a family's home. Despite being well inland, much of the area had flooded. While people certainly weren't happy about the backwater flooding, their attitudes mirrored others we visited—they were all committed to the Coast, and they would all rebuild. In fact, some had already finished. I am convinced it was talking to these dedicated Mississippians and thousands of others like them that convinced dignitaries like Bill Clinton and corporate leaders that Mississippi was worth an investment.

Marsha Barbour

Throughout the early days and into the next weeks and months, if I needed a firsthand report on what was really happening on the ground, all I had to do was talk to my wife, Marsha. She had gone down to the Coast with the initial convoy on Monday and did so for nearly every day that followed until almost Thanksgiving. She and three Department of Public Safety officers—Sam Owens, Mike Cooper, and Wade Parham—would gather supplies in the morning and, as they liked to say, "head out" to areas that Owens had identified from his conversations with local officials to find people who needed help and assistance.

It was on one of their earliest trips to Hancock County that Marsha realized FEMA was not bringing in any diapers or formula for babies; so for weeks every state or National Guard plane or helicopter flying to the Coast from Jackson had "baby stuff" crammed into every open spot. Marsha told me at one point she and her team were told about a place where they could definitely find supplies of this kind: The Gulfport WIC (Women, Infants, and Children) Center, is a local distribution center for the federal program. When Marsha and company found the center, it was closed because the storm surge had blown out the front windows. The building, however, still contained stores of supplies of "baby stuff"—just what Marsha was looking for. They loaded up and resumed their rounds with plenty of supplies for young mothers and their babies.

Wherever Marsha could find supplies in those early days—from a frozen food locker in a local Coast high school to the food pantry in the Governor's Mansion—she would deliver them to needy families throughout the Coast.

When the FEMA trailers started arriving and people needed electrical hookups, she would call Anthony Topazi at Mississippi Power. As noted earlier, because of the destruction of our utility infrastructure by the storm, virtually every FEMA trailer brought to a site had to be set up for occupancy. But no pole or meter, and the FEMA trailer couldn't be occupied. So when Marsha would learn of a family ready to move into a FEMA trailer that was not hooked up for electricity, she'd call Anthony on his cell phone. After a couple of months of Marsha's repeated calls, I saw Anthony at a meeting. He said Marsha called him almost every day to give him addresses and directions for FEMA trailers that were ready to be set up. He laughed and said once Marsha called to ask for a FEMA trailer hook up but gave him a rural address in the service area of Singing River Electric Power, a local electric cooperative. Anthony said he told her, "Marsha, that is not in our service area." She replied, "Anthony, don't start making excuses!" Anthony told me he suspected that Mississippi Power hooked up dozens, maybe even a hundred FEMA trailers that weren't in the company's service area because Marsha made it plain there were people who needed help and we all needed to do whatever it took to make sure they got help!

And Marsha reminded me that FEMA trailers didn't come stocked with bed linens, housewares, or cooking utensils either, so she set out to find as much of that as she could. If FEMA paperwork was getting in the way of what a family might need, Marsha and her officers would head straight to the FEMA office on the Coast to work on the problem. Marsha and the three officers had plenty of interesting episodes with all sorts of volunteers, including several celebrities, one of whom was Whoopi Goldberg.

I'll never forget Nick Russo (who later succeeded Bill Carwile as our FEMA coordinator) telling me about the time he was at his desk in his office on the Coast when he looked up and walking toward him were Marsha and Whoopi Goldberg. Marsha, along with Sam Owens and Wade Parham, had run into Whoopi in East Biloxi, while Marsha was checking on Eddie Mae Smith, a widow in her seventies whose home had been terribly damaged. Because Eddie Mae wouldn't leave her house, Marsha checked in on her every couple of days. On this occasion Whoopi was there as part of her Mississippi Rising commitment, visiting Mississippi to give tents to those who were homeless. It happened that Whoopi and Marsha, neither of whom knew the other was in the area, bumped into each other near Eddie Mae's house.

Whoopi asked Marsha some questions and said she had some suggestions; so Marsha put her in the truck with her, Parham, and Owens and took Whoopi to the FEMA office. That's when Russo looked up and saw them approaching him. Russo's office was a cubicle, so Marsha gave Whoopi the only other chair and waited while Russo and Whoopi talked. Russo answered her questions and heard her suggestions. Then Marsha took Whoopi back to her group in East Biloxi. Whoopi Goldberg, an international celebrity and renowned movie star, came to the Coast to help people. She didn't want or ask for special treatment. She was extremely generous, giving large numbers of families tents they could use for shelter. Later she sent a large number of bicycles to the area because she had seen Eddie Mae's niece riding a bike through East Biloxi to run errands. She gave one of the local charities all these bikes so people could get around since so many cars had been lost to the storm surge.

Eddie Mae Smith was an elderly African American widow who lived alone in a house in East Biloxi. She was one of several people Marsha "adopted" because she wouldn't leave her home. Eddie Mae was full of personality and wisdom, and Marsha became especially fond of her. Ultimately volunteers completely stripped her home down to the studs, cleaned off the mold and rebuilt the walls, floors, and ceilings. Eddie Mae was in her totally restored house within a year.

Another character who won Marsha's loyal attention was Billy Boy Arceneaux. Billy Boy was a displaced, one-legged fisherman in his fifties who had a German girlfriend who tried rather unsuccessfully to make him behave. Billy Boy liked to drink. Yet he was also very artistic, which led to his method of making something of a living (thankfully, his girlfriend worked.) Billy Boy made fishing nets by hand, but the stores and fisherman to which he had sold them before Katrina were gone. Marsha brought his problem to me, and I put her and Billy Boy in touch with Wal-Mart. Before you know it, Wal-Mart gave Billy Boy a contract for all the fishing nets he could make for months. It was a small but very meaningful act by the world's biggest retailer, Wal-Mart.

At Thanksgiving we were still in full recovery mode on the Coast, and philanthropy was pouring in. One donor volunteered thousands of turkeys for the holiday meal, and FEMA set up a distribution center at the Coast Coliseum. While I was really impressed by the generosity, Marsha instinctively realized hundreds of families living in FEMA trailers still had no transportation. Marsha and her team spent the days before Thanksgiving delivering turkeys to hundreds of families in need who couldn't get to the distribution center. That was typical of not only her affection for the folks worst affected but also her practical insight into their needs. She was my eyes and ears on the ground, and her commitment to the people of Mississippi had no equal.

State Workers

Sam Owens, Mike Cooper, and Wade Parham were just three of the thousands of state workers who gave a lifetime of service in the months following Katrina's landfall. Not only did these state employees have their own families to see through the recovery but they also had responsibilities that took many of them from home for weeks or months at a time. For the employees we interviewed for this book, it was hard to remember specific dates because, as more than one of them remarked, "It was just a big blur; we were working all the time, from sun up to sun down, that time ran together."

The Department of Public Safety made huge demands on its patrolmen, investigators, and agents. The more than one hundred officers who moved to the Coast the night of the storm were there for several days, and when they were relieved, it meant a different hundred or so officers had left central and northern districts shorthanded. So across Mississippi for several weeks, all state law enforcement personnel were working sixty- or seventy-hour weeks, as were local police and deputies in the bottom half or two-thirds of the state. Indeed, many local officers in north Mississippi were deployed to the south over the following weeks.

More than a dozen local teams of emergency medical and firefighting personnel from the upper half of the state came in to South Mississippi and the Coast right after the storm cleared to help with search and rescue. Along with the local first responders from the Coast and the other hardest-hit areas, they joined with search-and-rescue teams from the state and our sister states, which played a large role in limiting the number of fatalities in Mississippi to only 238.

And don't let me leave out the military: not only the National Guard from our state and so many others but also those valiant young Coast Guardsmen in helicopters during the first few hours and days. Of special note is the Mississippi guardsman who lost his life while responding to a wreck, in Pearl River County.

Health Department and Human Services personnel also stood out. The provision of health care took a huge hit, with damage and sometimes destruction of medical facilities on the Coast and well beyond. Health department workers helped manage the location and relocation of patients requiring hospitalization all across the state. The University of Mississippi Medical Center managed a large warehouse of pharmaceutical and medical supplies donated by the pharmaceutical companies soon after the storm. Human Services workers met the needs of many who weren't able to take care of themselves before the storm.

A group of Human Services workers moved into a motel in Columbia, some ninety miles from the Coast, and drove back and forth every day to make food stamps and assistance payments available to beneficiaries, often out of the trunks of their cars in the parking lot or on folding tables in the street next to where a destroyed welfare office used to be. They did this for two weeks or more.

You can imagine my pride in Mississippi's state employees. They rose far above the call of duty.

Help from Other States

Not only did our own state workers go far beyond the call of duty, the same could be said for the outpouring of assistance we received from our sister states for weeks and even months after the storm. A wonderful example were the Kansas and Georgia Bureaus of Investigation. For weeks after the storm there remained a significant number of people who were unaccounted for. Obviously the families and friends of these missing persons were concerned and often distraught. The Mississippi Bureau of Investigation worked with local sheriffs and police, but into the fall there remained hundreds of people unaccounted for. On September 26 the Katrina Missing Persons Task Force was created by the Mississippi Department of Public Safety. It included the Georgia and Kansas Bureaus of Investigation as well as Mississippi's Bureau of Investigation. On that date, 1,876 people from Mississippi were unaccounted for.

With help from several other state and federal agencies, the Task Force accounted for all but eleven, or more than 99 percent, of the missing. It was another example of the effective support we got from the employees of our sister states and the federal government, which just added to the stamina and determination of our own state employees, who really were heroes.

Later in the spring and into the summer of 2006, as I went into areas where there were many volunteers, which I did every day I was on the Coast and in any of the affected areas, people would stop me to talk. They would say, "Governor, last year I was sent here by my state's Department of [pick a department, whether law enforcement, wildlife conservation, National Guard] to work with your folks on the search and rescue or the recovery. It was such an experience, I wanted my family to see it and be part of it. Can I introduce you to my family?" This happened to me dozens of times, and it thrilled me.

What a wonderful perspective from these loving, giving, caring Americans! They had been sent to Mississippi to help others they didn't know, yet these helpers felt like they got so much out of the service that they wanted their spouses and children to have a chance to experience this uplifting opportunity to help people who needed it. And the sentiment displayed by these special people was a common, almost universal refrain among the nearly six hundred thousand volunteers who came to Mississippi in the first twelve months after Katrina's deluge.

Not only states but towns and cities joined in the recovery efforts. One program in particular—the "adopt-a-city" initiative—sprung up from interest the call center received from communities all across the county. Travis Schmitz volunteered at the call center when he was not working at the University of Mississippi Medical Center and helped to coordinate at least thirty "adopt-a-city" programs. Some places were interested in supporting similarly sized communities (i.e., we are a city of 5,000 people and we would like to support a town like ours). Others wanted to adopt cities with similar names (i.e., Long Beach, New York, wanted to help out Long Beach, Mississippi). The end result was just one more way Americans came to our rescue.

Corporate Citizens

A few days after the storm, I received a phone call from Pete Correll, the chairman and CEO of Georgia-Pacific, one of the largest employers in Mississippi. While the company no longer had timber holdings in the state in 2005, it operated two paper mills, six sawmills, and two or three plywood plants as well as other facilities throughout the Piney Woods. Pete was in the state meeting with his employees and checking on damage to his sites when he told me he wanted to come by for a visit. He walked into my office, and I'll never forget what he said: "Haley, what do you need?" His gesture was genuine and heartfelt, and I told him we needed hope for our working people and small business people—we needed jobs to generate income to help kick-start the recovery. After telling me he would "get back with me," Pete recalled that on the plane ride home he was shocked at the huge amount of timber that was blown down throughout South Mississippi— "thousands of trees scattered like matchsticks." He knew that unless that timber was hauled to a central site where it could either be processed or watered down, the bugs would soon destroy it. He also knew that timber represented the annual income or the life savings for many families who woke up the day after landfall only to find timber on the ground with no place to take it.

And the idea was hatched. Georgia-Pacific would reopen a sawmill in Roxie and a plywood plant in Gloster to generate an additional five hundred jobs and create more market for all that downed timber. There was so much timber on the ground that Georgia-Pacific established ten wet wood yards, satellite receiving sites throughout the southern two-thirds of state where the downed timber could be stored and treated until the mills could process the wood. And that took three years. That's how many trees Katrina blew down, and that's how many trees would have been ruined, along with no telling how many incomes and savings accounts, had Georgia-Pacific not stepped up to my challenge. As Pete once told me, "I don't know that it was the best thing for our shareholders at the time. The plants were higher cost than the plants we were already running, but it provided jobs in Mississippi when the state needed those jobs, and it was the right thing to do."

Northrop Grumman was another great corporate citizen. Before Katrina hit, its Ingalls Shipyard in Pascagoula, builder of Navy destroyers and assault ships as well as large cutters for the Coast Guard, had nearly 13,500 employees. Katrina destroyed 80 percent of the cranes and 90 percent of the equipment, and left every building on the eight-hundred-acre site damaged. The entire electrical grid and thirty miles of cable were destroyed by the saltwater flooding. But even while workers were waiting for the yard to be repaired, the company not only kept current with the payroll but employees from the other Northrop Grumman sites all over the world raised more than $1 million for their fellow employees in Mississippi. Ingalls was back in business two weeks after landfall, and by the middle of October more than 8,700 workers were back on the job. This was a huge boost to our struggling economy on the Coast that fall. Much like Ingalls, many of the closed coast casinos and their hotels announced they were paying their employees their full salaries for at least ninety days.

One reason Ingalls could get back on line so quickly was its location. Not far down the road was the Chevron refinery and Roland Kell. When Ingalls needed fuel for all the construction equipment and the generators, Roland told them where to bring the fuel trucks. And when FEMA needed a lot on which to set up a number of FEMA trailers for some of the employees, Jim McIngvale, the communications director for Ingalls, gave them written permission on the back of an envelope to use an abandoned company lot near the shipyard. It was that kind of corporate commitment and out-of-the-box initiative on the part of their officials that made all the difference in the world to Mississippi's ability to recover as quickly as we did.

Many companies that made significant contributions had no facilities here, but they wanted to help. GlaxoSmithKline is an international pharmaceutical company based in the United Kingdom. Within a few days of Katrina's landfall the company's U.S. president, Bob Ingram, called from North Carolina. An old client and friend, Ingram told me Glaxo and several other major pharmaceutical companies wanted to contribute millions of dollars' worth of product to Mississippi, knowing that large amounts of drugs had been lost to the storm. These companies couldn't just give us their products because a secure warehousing and delivery system needed to be in place first. For example, many of the painkillers Ingram wanted to contribute were at the top of the list of drugs that criminals liked to steal.

It didn't take long for us to locate a small warehouse in Simpson County, make sure it was guarded round the clock by state law enforcement and National Guard, and create a secure distribution network that was managed by the University Medical Center. Over the course of the fall, Mississippi was the beneficiary of truckloads of pharmaceuticals worth tens of millions of dollars. GlaxoSmithKline, Eli Lilly, Pfizer, and others were very generous, and the security system worked perfectly.

Within a week of the storm I got a call from David Oreck, whose family made vacuum cleaners in Long Beach. Although their facility was damaged and much of the equipment was inoperable, Oreck, a great salesman, had an idea. He wanted to have a big news event and announce that the Oreck plant had reopened and would be making vacuum cleaners there the following week. And that is exactly what he did. Marsha and I went down for the event, and the media coverage was fabulous. Many of their employees were at the plant, where the announcement was made and lunch was served. As you can imagine, the Oreck announcement was a major event and a very positive element of our effort to give people regular doses of good news, news to give hope and confidence that their communities would come back and that they ought to stay and be a part of it. Interestingly, Oreck moved its production to Tennessee in 2007 because wages on the Coast became so high, and the labor supply so short. But even though Oreck eventually moved its operations to Tennessee, that early announcement and the early jobs were a much-needed boost during the days following landfall.

Corporate philanthropy, too, was a big boost for those trying to recover in the early days after Katrina. Burlington Northern Santa Fe, a major railway company that serves the northern part of the state, made a $1 million donation to the Red Cross for the benefit of Mississippi.

And the Biloxi *Sun Herald* and its parent company, Knight Ridder, were a beacon of hope on the Mississippi Gulf Coast. For one thing the paper endured, which a lot of survivors were trying to do. It was published every day, and not just online. A newspaper—made out of paper—was available in the readership area every single day. And because of the *Sun Herald*'s grit and determination, it was the source of information about Katrina and the damage caused, and for places to seek help and the types of help available—to whom and from whom. Ricky Mathews and his team deserved the Pulitzer Prize they won for their Katrina coverage. I know thousands of Coast residents who returned to their communities to rebuild their lives were infected by the spirit of the *Sun Herald* and are grateful to this day that newspaper played the role it did so powerfully.

Indeed, the *Sun Herald*'s role after Katrina was beyond any I have ever seen or heard of for a newspaper. The *Sun Herald* led the community, providing news at a time when information was hard to get and driving opinion on the Coast—and it did so in the most positive way imaginable. The voice of the *Sun Herald* was a call for recovery, rebuilding, and renewal; it was a voice that spoke to but also for the strong, resilient, self-reliant people of South Mississippi who had the character to overcome the worst natural disaster in American history and build their communities back bigger and better than before. Ricky Mathews and his team were indispensable.

Volunteers and the Spirit of Giving

Many a motor home, trailer, and pickup truck was driven to the Coast and South Mississippi in the first few days, though, quite honestly, law enforcement and the National Guard in the most damaged areas joined me in discouraging this. Despite the big hearts and good intentions, I urged the public not to go to the Coast until full security was restored and more cleanup had been accomplished. Before long, though, it was futile. Mississippians, just like other Americans from coast to coast, wanted to help their family and friends and, frankly, people they didn't even know.

The number of volunteers from out of state would only grow. This was made clear to me in personal encounters I had during President Bush's third trip to the state on September 9. We toured around in a motorcade, making a couple of stops to allow him to see damage, observe progress in debris removal, and meet people. Soon we went to a major feeding station in Gulfport run by the Salvation Army with support from some church groups. It was pretty large, and there were a hundred or more people there, even though it was well into the afternoon. Before working the crowd the president and I met with the news media for a quick question-and-answer session.

After walking into the tented area with the president, I broke off from him, not wanting to interfere with folks trying to shake his hand. I went over to the edge of the tent fifty or more feet away, where there were a half dozen men standing in front of a line of eighteen wheelers. I walked down the line of men, shaking hands and noting most were not from Mississippi.

The last man was a small, older man who had an accent very different from mine. After introducing myself to the man, who said his name was George, I asked where he was from. George told me he was from Vermont. I smiled and asked how he had made it down to the Mississippi Gulf Coast. George grinned and pointed, saying, "I got down here in that truck. A bunch of people in my community gathered up a trailer full of supplies, and I drove them down in that truck." Just as I was about to thank him, George raised his hand and said, "This is my third trip!"

It took my breath away. Here was this man, a truck driver, who in the eleven days after Katrina, had made three trips from Vermont.

As more and more of these hundreds of thousands of volunteers arrived, the logistics of providing for them so they could help us became increasingly difficult. As you might expect, based on what I said previously about the government policy of not allowing FEMA to pay for temporary housing to be used by labor or nonresident volunteers, finding places for these volunteers became a huge challenge, especially in the first couple of months, and it never was satisfactorily resolved. That being said, the good work done by these volunteers and their organizations far outweighed the logistical challenges we faced.

Most volunteers came from churches and other faith-based organizations and in a lot of cases were housed by local congregations in their existing or renovated facilities. There were also large contingents from charities like Habitat for Humanity, the Salvation Army, and the Red Cross as well as hundreds of smaller groups. The young people from AmeriCorps, federally funded through the Corporation for National and Community Service, were critically important to many communities; they arrived early and stayed late. College-aged or barely older, these young people were hard-working, dedicated, and they made a contribution that far exceeded their members. Most of the volunteers stayed about a week. In a day or so they'd be trained and then spend several days cleaning, feeding people, rebuilding, or virtually any other task that needed doing. Then they would leave and another group of volunteers would start the cycle again. The AmeriCorps members stayed for months at a time. They soon were training each new wave of volunteers and helping supervise things. They were tremendously valuable!

Before the first couple of weeks were over, I could sense the influx of volunteers quickening. Many in the first few days were Mississippians, often family members of those who had suffered damage or worse. But there were also groups like the physicians organized by Dr. Jim Sones, today the chairman of the Department of Gastroenterology at the University of Mississippi Medical Center. Dr. Sones and his colleagues in Jackson filled up trucks with medical supplies and medicines and drove to the Coast to deliver them to physicians in the area whose offices and supplies had been destroyed.

One great gift to housing volunteers and workers was made by the Morrell Foundation of Salt Lake City, Utah. The Morrell Foundation is affiliated with Morrell Corporation, a large construction company in Utah, which is Mormon-owned. The Morrell team reached out to me a few days after the storm and told me they'd like to build a large temporary housing complex for labor and volunteers, and that they didn't find Louisiana to be interested. Morrell, as it turned out, had built a lot of the temporary housing for athletes for the Winter Olympics in Salt Lake City in 2002. They wanted to use that model and experience to meet this needs gap for the Gulf Coast.

We were just getting access to electricity, but we had to find a large site, as Morrell intended to build a facility that would sleep some six hundred to seven hundred people as well as have sanitary and cooking and eating accommodations. It took us much longer than I liked to find a location and get electricity, water, and waste water disposal hooked up. We couldn't find a private site that worked, so the actual site was a state park in Hancock County. Buccaneer State Park sits just across Beach Boulevard from the Gulf of Mexico, slightly west of Waveland. Within a matter of weeks the giant tent was constructed with hundreds of small rooms throughout. The Morrell Foundation bore the total cost, with help from The Church of Jesus Christ of Latter-day Saints' (LDS) charitable arm. Marsha and I flew down in October for the grand opening. We flew into Stennis International Airport in Hancock County, several miles north of the Coast. Stennis continued at the time to be a major warehouse and staging area for both government and charitably donated supplies, so it was bustling.

As we drove down to the beach, we could see that some county and city buildings had been replaced by portable facilities that were the equivalent of mobile homes. (These would be used for years before the rebuilt office buildings were constructed.) Other than these trailers, the landscape revealed no pre-Katrina structure was fully intact, and the vast majority were simply gone: wiped away. The trees still had no leaves, and much debris was piled up along the roads on private property.

When we got to Buccaneer State Park, we saw the huge tent with a large covered area near the road with support structures holding up the roof but no walls. The luncheon was to be held in this open area. We got out of the patrol car, and, as we approached the site, there were a couple of hundred people standing among tables and chairs in the dining area. Looking beyond the crowd I saw a large vehicle that appeared to be a motor home, on the side of which was written in three-foot-tall letters: Adventists in Action. Here was this enormous contribution made by Mormon groups with a Seventh-day Adventists group doing the cooking!

Marsha and I worked the crowd, trying to meet everybody. A number were from the Coast area but either had participated in the construction, were staying in the Morrell facility, or were helping put on and serve the lunch.

After lunch, I spoke to thank the Morrells and the LDS Church. I asked how many in the crowd were Mormons, and there were twenty or so, about one-tenth of the crowd. I asked for a show of hands of Seventh-day Adventists, and there were eight or ten who had helped with the meal. The vast majority were Catholics or mainstream Protestants, consistent with our local population. Most weren't from the Coast or even from Mississippi, but they had come to help as part of church groups from their hometowns and were being directed by the local churches affiliated with their denomination. This was typical of hundreds of thousands of volunteers for years to come. Baptists, Methodists, Episcopalians, Lutherans, Presbyterians, and Catholics were organizing missions of service from all over the country, and when they arrived, they became part of a stupendous religious charitable outpouring where they worked side by side with Pentecostals, Mormons, Adventists, Mennonites, Church of Christ, Church of God in Christ, Jews, and Muslims.

In fact, after the Morrell event, as Marsha and I walked back to the car, an older man approached us. He introduced himself as Harold and said his son was a rabbi in New York City, where Harold lived. He said, "Governor, I asked my son if I should come home to New York for the High Holy Days. My son said, 'No, Dad, you are likely closer to God down there than if you returned home.'"

This old Jewish gentleman made a powerful point: many, many of the wonderful volunteers who came to the Coast to help their fellow Americans did it out of service to God. It was a mission of religious conviction that made the volunteers feel better about themselves and feel closer to their God. Regardless of their own theological beliefs, their religious hearts bound them together in a rewarding way.

At this stage of recovery most volunteers in the hard-hit areas were primarily engaged in cleanup at homes and small commercial buildings that had a chance of being repaired. The work was dirty as these structures had been flooded from the storm surge, sometimes a foot or two deep but more often several feet deep or even over the top. After all the contents had been removed and usually disposed of, because little could be cleaned and used again, the house was typically stripped of sheetrock down to the studs. The studs then would require rescrubbing with Lysol or some similar product to remove the mold that started accumulating soon after the water receded. Some floors could be saved; others had to be ripped out and replaced.

Many of these wonderful volunteers in the early months—and sometimes far into 2006—spent their time doing strenuous cleanup work of this type. Later, and for years afterward, volunteers built everything from parks and playgrounds to homes. Ka-Boom and other children's charities built a number of playgrounds, where dozens of volunteers in one day would help one or two professional engineers or construction workers erect the playground's swing sets and other equipment as well as create sandy areas. Habitat for Humanity ultimately engaged large numbers of volunteers over a several-year period in actually building homes, typically working with the family that would own the home once it was completed.

Typical of the hundreds of volunteer stories I could share was the way in which Ellen Ratner and Cholene Espinoza ended up making a huge contribution to our recovery. Coming back from a business trip in Texas a week or so after the storm, Ellen's flight stopped in Jackson on its way to Washington. As fate would have it, onto the plane walked Shantrell Nicks and her two children, who were leaving Pass Christian to stay with relatives for a few weeks while her husband, a local school principal, was working day and night to get the school cleaned out. Ellen was so moved by Shantrell's description of the damage that she called Cholene and proposed the two of them head to Mississippi. Cholene described her response in a book she later wrote about her Gulf Coast adventure: "I was skeptical when Ellen first suggested that we—two gay women—should drive down to the heart of the Bible Belt, to one of the reddest of the red states, and camp out with two churches." But they did and ended up leading an effort to build a new community center for Pass Christian in Delisle, which was graciously named the Marsha Barbour Center.

The volunteers, no matter what kind of work they did, seemed glad for the opportunity to help. Over and over someone would say to me, "Governor, I feel like I have gotten more out of this myself than the good I've done for the people I came here to help." Perhaps that is the essence of the volunteer spirit; the heart of the Good Samaritan.

As the first month after landfall was drawing to a close, more had been accomplished than was generally recognized nationally; we who were living through the recovery could see the progress but could also see the enormity of all that remained to be done, and we were beginning to realize how long it would take and how difficult the conditions would be as we rebuilt the Coast.

CHAPTER 5

Special Legislative Session and Gaming

D URING THE FIFTEEN YEARS LEADING UP to the summer of 2005, since the state had legalized gaming along the Gulf Coast and the Mississippi River, we had become the third-largest gaming destination in the country, trailing only Nevada and New Jersey. By the time Katrina hit the Gulf Coast, there were twelve casinos operating in Hancock and Harrison Counties employing some fourteen thousand people directly and another seventeen thousand indirectly. Many people will argue it was the advent of gaming that had rescued tourism for a coast that had never fully recovered from Hurricane Camille in 1969. In August the Coast casinos had generated more than $105 million in gross gaming revenues. For September, October, and November, that figure was zero.

In a surprising turn of events during the 1990 session, the Legislature had authorized what came to be known as "dockside" gambling: casinos were required to build on water and actually float on "movable" piers or barges, though the law allowed permanent construction of hotels, restaurants, and parking garages on land adjacent to the casinos. Prior to 1990 casinos were housed on ships that had to travel into the Gulf and back. That arrangement proved economically untenable, so the 1990 legislation served as a compromise between ship-based gambling and permanent on-land casinos.

This compromise turned out to have devastating ramifications when Katrina and its storm surge hit the Gulf Coast. Nearly all of the casino barges were torn from their moorings and several of them were firmly deposited onto land, including two that ended up on Highway 90. In addition to losing the casino barges, all of the hotels and restaurants sustained heavy water and wind damage.

The most expensive casino-hotel on the Coast at the time was the Beau Rivage. It was built by industry innovator Steve Wynn in the late 1990s, before he sold his company, Mirage, to MGM. The Beau, as it is commonly called, cost some $700 million to build with its twenty-nine floors, more than 1,740 rooms and suites, Las Vegas–class entertainment areas, and restaurants. The large casino area floated on barges, as state law required, but it would take an expert eye to find where the on-land construction left off and barge area began.

To protect its barges Wynn's team had designed and built suspension and mooring systems far more complicated than any other. When Katrina hit with a storm surge well above twenty feet at the Beau's location, no barge broke loose and none damaged the hotel itself. Yet storm surge waters got as high as the third floor reception areas and ballrooms. Remarkably, above the third floor level through which Gulf waters had flowed, there was not a broken window in the building—but ironically, the lack of any airflow in the building effectively sealed it airtight and hastened the growth of mold throughout the structure. The hotel ultimately stripped rooms to the concrete structure and rebuilt from there. The cost exceeded $600 million, almost as much as the original cost, which had included the steel and concrete support structure.

Next door to the Beau the brand new, just finished Hard Rock Hotel and Casino was actually preparing to open on Friday, September 2. With fewer guest rooms than the Beau, the Hard Rock was to be a classy entertainment as well as gaming venue. Of course, the

Hard Rock couldn't open. Indeed, it was smacked with storm surge waters through its first three floors and wind and water damage above that. Instead, it would not open for more than a year. Every casino on the Coast suffered severe damage, as did all of the adjoining properties.

Getting Casinos on Land

A few days after landfall, Jerry St. Pé, the chairman of the Mississippi Gaming Commission, flew to Las Vegas with the commission's executive director, Larry Gregory, to meet with the executives of all the companies that had businesses on the Coast. St. Pé had worked for Ingalls Shipyard in Pascagoula for forty years, the last sixteen of which he had served as president until he retired in 2001. He had lived through Camille and like all of us never thought he'd witness anything worse than that 1969 storm. I got lucky when he agreed to serve on the gaming commission; there's nothing like having one of the top businessmen from the Coast chair a commission that regulates the largest industry on the Coast when a hurricane hits. In a whirlwind nine hours, St. Pé and Gregory met with every CEO of every company that had a presence on the Gulf Coast.

St. Pé's message to them was simple: we've got to have you back; what do you need to come back? Late that night I received a handwritten three-page fax from Jerry, giving me some good news. Every CEO wanted to return to Mississippi, and they had all the intention in the world of coming back, but they needed two things: first, assurance that the state and local taxes imposed on casinos would not be increased, and, second, the flexibility to rebuild on land so as to protect their investments during the next hurricane.

Not raising taxes on casino gaming had in fact been a pledge I had made in my campaign for governor two years before. My view was simple: If you want less of something, tax and regulate it. If you want more of it, keep taxes low and regulation rational. Casinos and their hotels, restaurants, bars, and other properties employed more than

29,000 Mississippians along the Coast and the Mississippi River, including those employed at Choctaw Indian casinos. The private casinos had invested billions of dollars in land-side facilities such as health clubs, tennis and golf courses, theaters, and parking garages as well as hotels, restaurants, and bars. We needed to keep the casinos in Mississippi.

The state collected an 8 percent tax, and municipal or county governments received another 4 percent, for a total tax of 12 percent on gaming. Annually that brought in about $190 million to the state, plus sales taxes, hotel taxes, and income taxes on the companies and the 29,000 employees. All combined, it was 6 to 8 percent of the state's revenue. Even more important, gaming brought millions of people a year to Mississippi: a substantial percentage of Mississippi's tourists wouldn't visit our state if not for the casinos and their amenities. I often told legislators, "If we could get another $50 million in taxes from the casinos, I'd decline it, if they would put that money into more hotel rooms, golf courses, theaters, and parking garages. Increasing those amenities will help our state more."

The second request—moving casinos onshore—was going to be more challenging. The only way to allow casinos to build onshore was to amend the 1990 law. I already knew we needed a special legislative session in the fall to deal with a variety of laws that had to be changed, and I also knew that putting forward a bill to change the 1990 law would force the issue front and center. That meant a debate over whether we should do what it would take to continue gaming on the Mississippi Gulf Coast, which meant a debate all over again about whether we should have gaming in the state at all. Again, my position was simple: we had gaming; businesses had invested billions of dollars in our state to engage in a lawful activity; the casinos had kept their end of the bargain; and we needed those 31,000 jobs to rebuild the Coast. So I was prepared to support their request.

What was remarkable, though, is that the casinos started the planning and cleanup necessary to rebuild before the Legislature's special session. I'll never forget that corporate show of support.

At the same time, we knew there were a number of other laws that needed to be redone—some temporarily, others permanently—in order to facilitate a rebuilding of the Coast. In the days following landfall, our staff solicited local officials for their thoughts about laws that needed changing, and other suggestions came our way unsolicited. For example, a number of laws affecting school testing and budgeting had to be waived for schools that no longer existed or were severely damaged; municipalities and counties needed similar exemptions to purchasing, personnel, and budgeting laws. The hurricane was so destructive that one request was to allow one of our counties to change its seat of government because of the natural disaster.

Yet another proposal would have created extensions on tax returns that were due in the fall and at the end of the year. To help college students coming from Louisiana, the Legislature was asked to provide for a one-year waiver of out-of-state tuition for state universities and community colleges. Finally, because our state revenue estimates were so uncertain at the time of the special session, the Legislature authorized the State Bond Commission to borrow up to $500 million to create a line of credit for the operations of state government. To put that number in perspective, at the time it represented about 13 percent of the state's entire general fund budget!

We settled on Tuesday, September 27, as the date for a special session, hoping the Legislature could get its work done before the weekend. At the time, the State Tax Commission was estimating that the state could sustain revenue losses of $213 million to $272 million.

The Special Session

At 11:30 on the morning of September 27, four weeks to the day after I had taken my first helicopter ride over a devastated Gulf Coast, I was escorted to the House chamber to address the Joint Session of the Legislature. The sight of what I had seen then led me to open with ". . . and the miles upon miles of utter destruction is unimaginable, except to those who have witnessed it with their own eyes, on the ground."

Beyond describing the changes to laws I was hoping the Legislature would pass, I wanted to use my speech to single out and thank the people who had shown an extraordinary amount of courage and resilience in helping South Mississippi and the Coast start the process of recovery during that previous four weeks. These included the first responders, hundreds of local officials and those from other states, and many of our own citizens. As I said at the time, "The stories of ordinary people displaying extraordinary courage and uncommon selflessness are, well, extremely common."

But it was the end of the speech that I used to articulate what had become so clear to me in the days following Katrina's landfall: "In thirty years, when I'm dead and gone, people will look at what the Coast and South Mississippi have become. If it is simply a newer version of today, we will have failed those people, our children, and grandchildren. If, on the other hand, it has become what it can be, bigger and better than ever . . . then those people in thirty years will say these folks after Katrina, they got it right and we're grateful to them."

The highlight of the session was the move to give more flexibility to casinos. One key decision was how far onshore casinos would be allowed to build. Would they have to be next to the water? Would they have to locate between Highway 90 and the water? Could they go inland within a certain number of feet or yards from the water? And, of course, the water's edge varied from day to day and from high tide to low tide, so how would that edge be defined in the law? Through many discussions with lots of people, a consensus began to emerge that the law would use a distance measure from the water as a boundary within which gaming companies could build permanent casinos.

We had been told early on that the Republican leadership in the Senate wanted the House to send them the gaming bill, so it would have to originate in the House and have a House bill number. It always amazed me how legislators could get wrapped around the axle by that kind of petty stuff. But the Senate leadership was dug in. That meant the Speaker of the House would have to allow the House to take the lead. So I walked over to the Capitol office of Speaker Billy McCoy to convince him that the future of the Mississippi Gulf Coast depended on this legislation, and the only person who could make it happen was McCoy himself.

The previous year, my first as governor, Speaker McCoy, a Democrat from Northeast Mississippi, had served as my nemesis. Aside from disagreements over various spending issues, our biggest battle had been over tort reform, or ending lawsuit abuse in Mississippi, as I expressed it. It was a battle royale. The state Senate passed comprehensive tort reform legislation three times during the regular session, but McCoy, a very canny legislative leader who had mastered the powers of the Speaker's office and the rules, kept any tort reform bill from getting to the House floor. Tensions were high and were about to get higher because after the Legislature adjourned to end the regular session on Sunday, I announced Monday that I was calling a special session on tort reform to start Wednesday.

It was brutal, but tort reform had been a major part of my campaign the year before, and the public strongly supported my position. Our grassroots supporters had been pushing tort reform in their home counties throughout the regular session, and they ramped it up for the special session. The Speaker didn't relent at first, but his supporters in the House were being worn out by their constituents at home. Still, by way of effective use of parliamentary procedure and strong loyalty from many Democratic House members, Billy successfully stopped two more Senate-passed bills from getting to the House floor in the special session.

Only after the Senate passed a third bill in the special session (the sixth such bill that the Senate had sent over to the House), and after several of Billy's loyal Democrats told him they couldn't afford politically to stand in the way of passage any longer, did the Speaker relent. He gave us a procedural vote, and the pro–tort reform side won by twenty votes. The Speaker then let the bill come to the floor, where it passed by a vote of 78–39.

A few months later, Billy and I were at it again, this time over state spending priorities and Medicaid spending. The standoff was so tense that we were able to adopt a state budget only days before the start of the new fiscal year. Now, little more than eight weeks later, I was walking that hundred or so feet to Billy McCoy's office to ask for his help. I found Billy exasperated with the Senate and sharply critical of the lieutenant governor's unwillingness to bring the onshore gaming bill to the Senate floor first.

And, of course, I was in his office to ask him to do what the Republican leadership of the Senate refused to do. Although Democrats had a majority in the Senate, the Republican lieutenant governor was president of the Senate, appointed committee chairs, and controlled the flow of bills as McCoy did in the House. And Lt. Gov. Amy Tuck ran a tight ship.

My point to the Speaker was simple: while I knew he opposed casino gaming in the state and his constituents in the Northeast Mississippi counties of Prentiss and Alcorn would probably vote to abolish it if they could, if he didn't permit the onshore casino bill to come to the House floor, the Mississippi Gulf Coast's prospects for a real recovery would be enormously reduced. He was the only one who could let the Legislature do its will; whether the Coast would come back bigger and better was in his hands.

I will always admire Billy McCoy for his decision. He was personally opposed to gaming; support for the bill was not in his political best interest, and he was helping me, the guy with whom he had been battling for a year and a half. Yet he agreed to do what I thought was right and what he ultimately believed was in the best interest of Mississippi.

The proposal I made to the Legislature at the beginning of the session limited casinos to coming onshore no more than 1,500 feet. It became clear early on that most in Jackson thought that was too far inland. Over the first few days of the session, we were able to agree on an eight-hundred-foot limitation, and that was the bill Rep. Bobby Moak, chairman of the House Gaming Committee, brought to the floor two days after the special session had opened.

In spite of a Gulf Coast that lay in ruins, and in spite of a recognition that gaming provided a level of jobs that was virtually required to sustain any recovery, allowing casinos onshore was far from certain in the Mississippi Legislature. Not everybody was as strong as Billy McCoy.

The power of religious leaders and their opposition to gambling along with a personal feeling among some legislators that gambling should not be a part of the state's economy meant passage of this legislation was not a given. At the same time, there were some legislators, like the Speaker, who knew the Coast needed this legislation and were willing to support the bill even though they knew the majority of their constituents back home were opposed to expanding gambling in any form, even by eight hundred feet. It was for all these reasons we had agreed with legislative leaders to pass the bill on Friday—get it done before the weekend church services when legislators would be at home.

So on Friday morning, Chairman Moak called the bill up for discussion on the House floor, explained the provisions, and, after the adoption of several amendments, offered a motion to limit debate so we could pass the bill and get it over to the Senate. That motion prevailed 76–38, though the bill was adopted by the much smaller margin of 61–53. The difference is the number of representatives who wanted to help the Coast but who knew what their constituents wanted.

As I've organized my memories and experiences about Katrina for this book and had time to examine all of our work, I am amazed at all of the coincidences that occurred that helped facilitate the recovery. Anyone in Mississippi could have been chairman of the state gaming commission, but at that time we had a seasoned business executive from Jackson County. And any of the fifty-two senators could have been chairman of the Senate committee that had jurisdiction over gaming, but in 2005 it was Tommy Robertson, a veteran legislator, also from Jackson County. And a little before ten o'clock Friday night, his committee received the bill from the House, discussed it, and in about an hour had reported it favorably to the full Senate.

At 11:02 that night the full Senate reconvened to, I had hoped, debate and pass the bill. They had fifty-eight minutes since at midnight their rules required them to adjourn for the day. And the single most important point all of us were making to the senators was to avoid any amendments. Passing the bill in the same form as the House meant it came straight to me for approval. Passing the bill with amendments meant it had to return to the House for concurrence—or worse, conference—and none of us wanted to risk another vote on the House floor. Delay would be a friend to our opponents.

But as the debate began and amendments were offered, it became clear our opponents were working to drag out the debate until the midnight deadline. But then came the surprise. A group of senators led by Gulf Coast Senator Billy Hewes (now mayor of Gulfport) offered an amendment that apparently sought to ensure that the "onshore" provisions did not apply to the various bays that were fed by the Gulf Coast waters but that were well inland. To my dismay and disappointment, the amendment was adopted about the time midnight arrived. Lt. Gov. Amy Tuck, the presiding officer in the Senate, ordered the Senate to reconvene at two o'clock Monday afternoon. We had work ahead of us over the weekend.

Saturday's *Sun Herald* led with the headline "Casino Plan Stalls in Senate" and put the blame squarely on Billy Hewes while rightly praising the decision by McCoy to "oppose gaming but support the Coast."

At the same time that I was asking the Legislature to make a tough decision to bring casinos onshore, I was asking them to vote against their own housing plan. The House had passed a $100 million proposal to spur housing, and the Senate had increased it to $500 million. With uninsured loses approaching $5 billion, I thought this amount of money was more symbolic than substantive—an effort to get political credit "for doing something." Moreover, my first priority was to obtain the billions we needed from the federal government, and I worried this legislative initiative would be used as an excuse by many in Congress and the administration to undermine our request for unprecedented assistance from Washington, D.C. As a result, the tough vote I was requesting was to do nothing, which is ultimately how it ended. Asking legislators to take a politically risky vote in favor of gaming yet decline to make a politically helpful vote on housing meant asking them to have faith in the direction we wanted the recovery to take. Enough of them joined with me, but others just couldn't.

I woke up Monday morning hoping that our work over the weekend had not only convinced Billy Hewes to withdraw his amendment and that the support I knew we had on Friday among the senators would hold. Billy had met with a number of his supporters and business leaders on Sunday, and with Larry Gregory, and he became convinced the bill as passed by the House would not allow for casinos to be located on any of the back bays in Harrison County.

The Senate convened at two o'clock that afternoon, and I knew right away our side was intact when they defeated a move by the opponents to once again amend the bill. Then Billy offered his motion to reconsider the adoption of his Friday amendment and pull it from the bill. This was approved, and the language was removed. After another attempt by a north Mississippi senator to weaken the bill failed, the senators finally voted and approved the legislation by a margin of 29–21.

The Tuesday newspapers all carried headlines about the passage of the gaming bill—"The Coast casino industry is back in business"—but that morning when the Senate convened, Jack Gordon, a wily senior Democratic senator from north Mississippi, offered a motion to hold the gaming bill in the Senate, where it would not move until a separate bill, known as the Tidelands Bill, was written to his satisfaction. As the *Sun Herald* put it, "Moments before an onshore casino bill would have headed to the Governor's Office to become law, some in the Senate took it hostage over another bill—this one about state tidelands leases. Gordon held the bill on a motion to reconsider, claiming it should not become law until the House and Senate agree on a separate bill on casino tidelands leases. Tuck backed what Gordon did."

Gordon was chairman of the Senate Appropriations Committee at the time and was generally recognized as the Legislature's expert on the state budget. He had become convinced that moving the casinos onshore could potentially impact the money the state made from leasing the land it owns along certain parts of the coastline (known as tidelands). Working through changes to that law took another five days, so the Legislature didn't leave town until Friday of that week, when they adjourned and sent me the casino bill and the Tidelands Bill at the same time.

I figured the session had been a success when I read a *Sun Herald* article by reporter Geoff Pender, who wrote that "House leaders left claiming they had saved the Coast's tourism industry, Senate leaders claiming they had saved the tidelands fund." Lobbying and politics will teach you to find a way to give everyone involved in a fight a way to claim victory. Sometimes compromise is about finding a way to give somebody something rather than making someone else look like a loser.

Soon after the session ended, Emily Pettus, an Associated Press reporter, wrote a column describing how my active support for the gaming legislation had cost me some "political capital." While many people in the state, including religious conservatives who had strongly supported me for election as governor two years earlier, opposed letting casinos on the Coast come onshore, I chose to follow Ronald Reagan's advice: At the end of the day, good policy is good politics. Pettus even mentioned that vote in the context of rumors that I may jump in the 2008 presidential campaign.

All in all, the special session lasted for two weeks and resulted in the passage of twenty-four bills, including, among others:

- an exemption for schools affected by the disaster from certain testing requirements;
- an authorization for state government to borrow money for expenses in case revenues dipped below budgeted forecasts;

- an authorization for counties and municipalities to donate supplies and labor in the stricken counties;
- an extension of the time within which money borrowed by a school district in anticipation of tax payments could be repaid; and
- something as unforeseen as an allowance for a county to temporarily change its county seat because the buildings associated with the one stipulated in state law had been obliterated.

Clearly, state law had never anticipated a disaster on the scale of Hurricane Katrina. What I had learned since landfall is that recovery from a disaster of this magnitude operates on many different fronts, and that recovery doesn't stop for a legislative session. All of us in the Governor's Office were used to devoting the bulk of our time and attention to the Legislature whenever it was in town. But the fall of 2005 was different, and we had to adjust. We were all focusing on two or three initiatives at any one time, and there was no time to enjoy the accomplishments of the session and take some time off. There was no demarcation from passing the bills to coordinating new recovery operations on the Coast to engaging the federal government. This gave "multitasking" a magnified dimension in the lives of all of us involved in our efforts for recovery, rebuilding, and renewal. And the Legislature surely did its job with the Katrina special session.

President Bush visited Mississippi for the eighth time in the days following the special session, but for many of us the end of the session opened a window for us to devote more time and energy to working with a group of men and women who were serving the Coast and the entire state on the Governor's Commission on Recovery, Rebuilding, and Renewal, or the Barksdale Commission.

CHAPTER 6

The Barksdale Commission

T HE CALL CAME FROM RICKY MATHEWS on Wednesday afternoon, two days after landfall, from his satellite phone to my cell phone. As I learned later, Ricky was standing in the parking lot of the *Sun Herald*'s damaged offices because that was the only place from which the newspaper's satellite phone could reliably make a connection. An unusual location to be sure, but when he got through, I clearly understood and appreciated his message: He and other business, government, and civic leaders from the Coast wanted to actively participate in making the recovery successful.

The question we both raised: What should the recovery process look like? Mathews suggested a meeting at the newspaper's offices at three o'clock Sunday afternoon. I agreed, and he said he would invite others from the Coast to join us. Just forty-eight hours after Katrina had left South Mississippi, we had set a date to start designing the process of recovery.

Mathews and I didn't talk again until I walked into his conference room at the *Sun Herald* that Sunday afternoon, and I'll never forget the scene—individuals from all parts of the Coast had somehow found a way to get to Ricky's office to not only talk about the future but to start planning the rebuilding. Seeing people I knew and others I didn't all crowded in that small room, surrounded by near-total devastation, looking to be part of a team that would help rebuild their communities—this was a constant source of motivation to me for the remainder of my time as governor.

Everyone there knew work had to continue on the rescue and cleanup, but everyone also wanted to start a separate track that would focus on rebuilding their communities and the Mississippi Gulf Coast as a whole. They had saved a space for me at the head of the conference table and wasted no time in getting to the point of the meeting—where do we go from here? Thinking back on the conversations all of us had in that room, several themes emerged that guided much of our work that followed. First, the planning effort needed to be focused on South Mississippi, not just the Coast, and not just individual communities and individual counties. Our planning and programs had to be done with the entire geographical area in mind.

Second, the more people who could be involved, the better. People throughout the affected areas needed to know that their part of Mississippi was going to get help to be rebuilt, and they were going to have a say in that process.

Third, the leader of this planning process did not have to be from the Coast.

While people from the central and northern parts of our state think of folks from the coastal counties as one group of "coast residents," those who live in these coastal communities think of themselves as citizens of their towns and counties rather than of the region. The post-Katrina landscape offered a real opportunity to get leaders and citizens of the Coast and South Mississippi to think and act regionally, and some of the people in the room were clearly pushing for that.

An unrelated fourth point from the meeting was that there was no question that the success of the recovery was linked to the willingness of the gaming companies to rebuild their casinos, which meant allowing them to come onshore.

The more we talked, the more the idea of a broad-scale commission emerged as the vehicle to continue these discussions. When I left,

I made a commitment to consider creating such a commission, appointing a chairman and staff and establishing a process. My instinct was to appoint as chairman someone who was not from the Coast. My own experience, confirmed by the meeting, was that the three counties and eleven incorporated municipal governments didn't have a history of working together well. Not only was there a lot of competition among the communities and the various elected leaders, there was a lot of jealousy. For example, there had never been a coastwide business organization to work for the benefit of the entire Coast. The more I thought about it, the more I thought of only one person as chairman.

Jim Barksdale is one of the most successful business leaders in Mississippi history. He had recently retired as CEO of Netscape, a hugely successful information technology company headquartered in Silicon Valley. His spectacular business career included early success at IBM and FedEx, he still served on the board of FedEx at the time of Katrina, and he had a stint as the CEO of McCaw Cellular in Seattle.

Jim lived in Jackson and was from a prestigious, highly respected Mississippi family. His ancestor was a Confederate general who had been killed at Gettysburg on the second day while attacking Union lines. Many a town in our state has a Barksdale Street. Jim was a little older than I, but I had gone to Ole Miss with his brother Bryan, now a physician; to law school with his brother Rhesa, now a federal judge; served on the board of Skytel, a publicly traded telecommunications company, with his older brother Tom; and worked on Thad Cochran's first Senate campaign in 1978 with Jim's youngest brother, Claiborne. The little brother of Jim's first wife, Sally, Dr. Fred McDonald, an Ole Miss classmate, had been one of my campaign leaders in Copiah County when I was elected governor in 2003. Mississippi is not a big state!

But the icing on the cake was that Jim Barksdale had been the largest personal contributor to the campaign of my 2003 Democratic opponent, Gov. Ronnie Musgrove. Not that Jim was a Democrat. He was a Republican, and he had been active nationally in GOP campaigns, including a leading role in supporting President Bush's election. No, Jim's problem with me was I had been a lobbyist for Microsoft during my career. Indeed, I was the first outside lobbyist hired by Bill Gates and Microsoft in the late 1990s.

Jim was CEO of Netscape, and the companies were bitter competitors. He had never forgotten or forgiven my representation of Microsoft, and although I asked him and Sally for their support, he politely declined and contributed more money to Musgrove's reelection campaign than any other Mississippian.

This made him an even better choice for chairman.

I wanted people to understand I was serious, and that the commission chairmanship wasn't some political reward for a supporter. This appointment needed to be seen as the result of my effort to pick the "best person available," a serious and capable leader for a hugely important assignment.

Governor John Bell Williams had appointed a commission after Camille, and the next year they were building gas stations on the beaches. That result was unacceptable to me. It wasn't for me to decide how the Coast and South Mississippi would be rebuilt, but it was my responsibility to lead the process.

In addition to getting the commission off the ground, I found myself engaged in work on a number of fronts: managing state government's response to the disaster; leading the acquisition and management of unprecedented support from the federal government and our sister states; attracting and guiding the expected outpouring of philanthropic giving and volunteer efforts; and, most of all, giving the residents and businesses that had resided in South Mississippi before the storm hope and, subsequently, confidence that their communities and the Gulf Coast area would not only recover but would be even better places to live, learn, work, and worship than they were before Katrina's devastation. An active, participatory, far-sighted commission led by an outstanding chairman like Jim Barksdale would be a powerful force in giving folks that hope and confidence as well as setting a high bar for what people could expect for the recovery operations going forward.

For my own confidence, I asked Henry Barbour, my nephew and the campaign manager of my successful election campaign two years before, to serve as volunteer executive director of the commission. Henry knew how I thought and knew my senior staff in the Governor's Office, plus a lot of others in the administration. Further, I trusted him and knew Jim Barksdale would grow to trust him too.

Henry helped us find really strong volunteer staff for the commission, starting with Brian Sanderson, an outstanding young lawyer on the Coast, to be deputy executive director and general counsel. One other very important commission appointment I made that week was to ask former governor William Winter, a Democrat, to serve as outside counsel.

William Winter is the most popular and respected living former governor of Mississippi. In his eighties at the time, he was still very active, practicing law daily (as he does to this day as well!). For me, Governor Winter had a lot to contribute in terms of perspective and process, but he also gave the commission a bipartisanship that helped achieve its critical goal of giving "hope and confidence" because he helped give us credibility and trustworthiness. It was for the same reason Derrick Johnson, the state NAACP president, was asked to serve as one of the five commission vice-chairmen.

A week after landfall, it had become clear to me that recovery would take many months, even years, and that rebuilding would take even longer. Not only did we need to create a process for people to participate in the recovery and rebuilding, but that process needed to help people stay strong and hopeful as they began to realize that the time frame for recovery was long, not short. The more we could create a vehicle for people to ask questions, offer solutions, and participate in a concrete way in the rebuilding, the more we could channel their energy into something constructive while helping them stay optimistic through what would be many dark hours ahead.

Two other reasons to get the commission up and running were obvious. We were beginning to gather suggestions for the special legislative session, and our congressional delegation in Washington was asking us what we needed. Commission deliberations would generate suggestions for both purposes. For all these reasons, the commission needed to be named sooner rather than later. I set Friday, September 9, less than two weeks after landfall, as the deadline to get it done and to make the public announcement.

After meeting with me at the Governor's Mansion on Monday, Barksdale quickly agreed to serve as chairman, though at one point in the conversation, he looked at me and said something like, "Since I didn't support you in the election, is this offer because you are acting like a statesman, or is it retribution?"

We decided to break up the work into specific issue areas. As Barksdale liked to say, the only way to tackle a big problem was to divide it up into a lot of little problems. So we created public policy committees focused on such issues as infrastructure, transportation, housing, education, agriculture and forestry, tourism, and health and human services as well as geographic committees that could focus on specific regions of the southern half of our state. We then asked business and community leaders, such as Ricky Mathews, Mississippi Power CEO Anthony Topazi, Hancock Bank CEO George Schloegel, Viking Range CEO Fred Carl, Sanderson Farms CEO Joe Sanderson, and former Ingalls Shipyards CEO Jerry St. Pé to chair those committees.

In creating the commission I wanted to be able to say that no public funds would be used to staff and cover its expenses. Since no one had any time to raise private money, the money was raised in two calls—Ricky Mathews arranged for the John S. and James L. Knight Foundation, which was affiliated with the parent company of his newspaper, to give $1 million, and Jim Barksdale contributed $1 million out of his pocket.

In the meantime Jim, Henry, and I met with the committee chairs, began to identify others to serve on the commission, and began making the calls. In the end, nearly fifty men and women from all over

South Mississippi joined the commission. Every single person we called agreed to serve, and every person served for free. The list of commission members is provided in the sources. Beyond the members, more than five hundred other individuals volunteered their time on more than twenty committees and task forces. We estimate the work of the commission represented an investment of more than fifty thousand man hours dedicated to planning for the future of South Mississippi.

In making the announcement on September 9, I summarized my vision for the commission: "I am utterly confident that we'll come back; that in six months we will see that single great surge; in two or three years the Coast will be better than we've ever known it; that thirty years from now people will look back and say, 'That terrible, dreadful storm that was so bad in many ways actually was an opportunity for us to make Mississippi what it could have been but had never been before.' I am committed to going beyond recovering and rebuilding. I am committed to our having a renaissance on the Gulf Coast that makes it bigger and better, and everything that it can be."

While this was my vision, I considered it absolutely essential that neither I nor anyone else in Jackson or Washington, D.C., would decide or dictate how the Coast and South Mississippi would be rebuilt. That was up to the leaders and citizens of the local areas themselves, and the commission was intended to give everyone interested a way for his or her voice to be heard and ideas to be considered. It was the commission's job to create a process that brought local decision makers the best and brightest ideas for renewal, so then they could decide which made sense for their areas.

A lot of people from outside came to Mississippi and made a lot of suggestions, some of which were very helpful. The key, however, was that these smart people from elsewhere were never allowed to impose their ideas on the locals. I strongly believe in the doctrine of subsidiarity: the government that is closest to the people governs best. I'm proud that in Mississippi we followed this principle; I may not have agreed with every decision, but the right people got to decide.

As it happened, on the Monday after the *Sun Herald* meeting, President Bush made a visit to Poplarville to meet primarily with elected officials from the affected communities across South Mississippi. An auditorium at Pearl River Community College in Poplarville, some forty miles inland, was the nearest intact hall that could hold a couple of hundred people, and it served as the meeting site. Through the heroic efforts of electric utility crews working for Mississippi Power and perhaps rural electric co-ops, too, the lights and— importantly in Mississippi during the first week in September—the air conditioning were on for us that day. A week after the storm, the local officials had more questions than we had answers. They were polite to the president, but it had to have been frustrating for community and city leaders who were trying to dig out from millions of tons of debris, not to mention trying to account for what were then still several hundred missing persons, after having buried more than two hundred of their fellow citizens.

While there were some questions and comments about long-term plans, the vast majority dealt with the task at hand: the never-before-confronted federal rules for removing and disposing of more than twice as much debris as previously left behind by a hurricane (the previous record was Andrew in Florida in 1992, with 23 million cubic yards, and the 47 million cubic yards we ultimately removed was only the debris in Mississippi!). It seemed the paperwork required to permit and get reimbursed for the removal and disposal was as mountainous as the debris itself.

The president was well received, for he was clearly not only sympathetic but was also committed to eliminating as much bureaucracy as he legally could and committed to the federal government's paying the maximum share of the costs it could under law.

On the way back to Air Force One, which was at Stennis Airport in Hancock County, the president and I discussed my staff's following up with FEMA, the Office of Management and Budget, and other federal departments about the large number of questions generated at the Poplarville meeting. My staff spent several days running down answers and getting them over to local officials. Our team, plus FEMA and MEMA officials on the ground, continued to follow up on these issues for months since they were shared by others throughout the affected areas.

Before we got to the plane, the president and Marsha talked about what she was seeing in her almost daily visits to the hardest-hit areas. Like me, the president seemed to learn a lot from her reports. She was very straightforward and made plain that for many, particularly those who had little before the storm, recovery had hardly begun. Sleeping in shelters, eating at feeding stations, homes destroyed—they were down and dizzied but not defeated. And they really needed help.

I took a moment to mention the commission to him. He and I agreed it would be good to have him appear and speak to the commission at its first meeting. My office reached out to the White House scheduling office the next day while I was in Washington and settled on September 20 for what would be the president's third trip to the Coast and the first meeting of the commission. I thought, "What better way to impress upon everyone the seriousness of this commission and its work than to kick it off with the President of the United States." So, we had eleven days to get everything organized and up and running. As Barksdale said in an interview for this book, "It's amazing how much can get done quickly if everyone says 'I just want to help,' and you have no bickering or politicking and everyone trying to one up someone else. And that's how we got started and that's how we were able to produce a report before the end of the year."

That week I also got Jeb Bush's ideas about a commission. For months Jeb served as a mentor and sounding board for me. He was a great resource because he shared not only Florida's hurricane experience, he also sent us hundreds of state and local law enforcement officers and thousands of other Florida employees and officials. From my standpoint, I wanted the commission's recommendations in my hands by the end of the year, which would give us a chance to consider them during the regularly scheduled legislative session that began in January 2006. For Barksdale, that date gave him a deadline and ensured that the commission's work would not drag on; still, we all knew we were compressing a lot of work into less than four short months.

We also agreed the work of the commission would be accomplished through the committees, and the report would consist of committee reports and recommendations. We didn't have time for long meetings of the full commission to debate what we anticipated would be several hundred findings and recommendations from the committees. As it turned out, Jim would be the final arbiter of what recommendations got published in the final report, and in an interview for this book, he indicated that he signed off on virtually any recommendation approved by a committee. As Barksdale said, "If they worked on it and they submitted it, we were going to put it in the final report, whether I agreed with it or not."

The Tent Meeting—September 20, 2005

While we wanted to have the first commission meeting on the Coast, the question became where to have it, especially now that the meeting would involve President Bush. We soon realized there was no suitable building left undamaged that could host such a meeting, so the inaugural meeting of the Governor's Commission on Recovery, Rebuilding, and Renewal, with President Bush as our special guest, was held in a tent in the parking lot of an outlet mall in Gulfport. The opening paragraph from the *Sun Herald* article captured the spirit of the meeting:

> President Bush sat quietly for nearly half an hour, listening as Governor Haley Barbour and local business and government leaders kicked off their first meeting on how best to rebuild Katrina-ravaged South Mississippi. Bush told the local leaders he didn't want to interrupt business because he believes it's important that Mississippi people lay out the vision for what this important part of the world was to look like

when it's rebuilt, not the federal government . . . what you need to do is develop a blueprint for your own future.

For me, the president's remarks set the right tone. South Mississippi's citizens had a choice: They could control their own future, or someone would do it for them. And the commission offered them the vehicle to do just that. Ricky Mathews remembered that meeting when he said in an interview that the "tent meeting" was a "rare moment for South Mississippi to come together and find our common issues and rebuild."

At the same time, with the president and the national press that came with him, the commission sent a different but critical message to the rest of the country: "Mississippi has its act together. We've got plans we are working on, and we will put them into action. We are coming back stronger and better." That tent meeting also confirmed for me that I had made the right choice for chairman. When President Bush saw Jim Barksdale, he called him "Jimmy." Previously the president had appointed Barksdale to the President's Foreign Intelligence Board, and they had become friends. There's nothing better than having your commission chairman on a first-name basis with the President of the United States!

Throughout the meeting people brought up not only planning but also specific ideas that should be considered. It was more than conceptual; one could tell that only three weeks after Katrina had left utter obliteration in its wake, local leaders—in a tent on a shopping center parking lot—had already conceived of specific projects, identified keys to rebuilding in ways better protected from future hurricanes, and committed themselves to making their communities better and more livable than before. At some point during this process, Leland Speed, who was then chief of the Mississippi Development Authority, asked me if I had ever heard of Andrés Duany, an architect and urban planner from Miami. Leland told me Duany was at the forefront of a group called The New Urbanists, who were designing new and exciting city centers and neighborhoods, and that I should contact him about getting involved.

I asked Leland to call Duany instead, and out of the conversations with him came the idea of hosting on the Coast a week-long session of architects, planners, and engineers from around the country, for all-day and all-night sessions of dreaming about how the Coast might look. This kind of brainstorming session is called a charrette, which is a French word that means "cart." French architects use "charrettes" or carts to move plans, drawings, and their other papers around the office or building. The word morphed to describe a meeting of architects and other professionals involved in designing a building project. As time went on, these charrettes had become much bigger and more elaborate. The charrette following Katrina began on October 13 and involved more than one hundred professionals from outside of Mississippi and several hundred from within the state.

This period, from the middle of September forward, may have been the busiest time during the twelve months I cover in this book. We were getting the commission up and running while planning for the charrette, getting ready for the special legislative session, and beginning to put together our request to Congress for the special disaster appropriation. We were creating plans on multiple fronts in addition to managing the recovery. But we were also benefiting from the fact that everyone on my senior staff was working with each other on these multiple fronts and thus sharing information, learning about new problems or solutions, and gaining new insights by virtue of their work with the commission.

The *Clarion-Ledger*'s Sid Salter caught me on a plane ride about that time and captured what I was feeling, that planning was one thing but delivering on those plans was the hard part: "There will be billions of dollars available to Mississippi with which to rebuild. How we manage this will determine how much help the federal government can and will be to us, and that's the message I'm trying to get to my colleagues in state and local government. Each day I try to remember that the kind of job we do in managing this disaster will in great measure determine the quality of life for many Mississippians for decades to come. People are depending on us to help them get back on their feet as best and as soon as possible. There are some good plans to do that on the table, but now the job is getting the toothpaste out of the tube."

The special legislative session ended on October 7, and the next day I signed the bill giving casinos the ability to build onshore. A month after my Sunday meeting at the *Sun Herald*'s office, we had accomplished one of the crucial goals. In another three weeks we would present to Congress our comprehensive request for federal rebuilding funds. But in between, Mississippi hosted one of the most extraordinary meetings in which I have ever participated.

The Charrette—October 12–17, 2005

The official title was the Mississippi Renewal Forum, but it quickly became known as "the Charrette." It took place in the badly damaged Isle of Capri casino-hotel. To get to the upper floors where all the activity took place, participants had to walk through the first floor area, which Katrina had destroyed with its storm surge. This served as an apt juxtaposition for bringing some of the country's smartest architects, planners, landscape designers, transportation specialists, building code experts, and engineers to Biloxi to help us consider the possibilities of what a rebuilt Gulf Coast could look like.

The proposal was to put one hundred of the country's best thinkers in the same room with more than five hundred of our local officials, business leaders, and developers to see, over a period of seven intense days, what kind of innovative and imaginative ideas they could generate. We also emphasized that we were using this process to create planning and architectural tools that local officials could use in the rebuilding of their own communities. As Barksdale wrote in his letter of invitation, "It is important to emphasize that these tools and designs will be made available to local stakeholders, but not forced upon them. We realize that the community leaders of the Coast will make the decisions—we only want to provide a mechanism that will hopefully lead to a bigger and better Mississippi Gulf Coast that we all love so dearly." I want to make the point that many of those experts came to Mississippi free of charge, and for nearly all of the rest, we only covered their travel expenses. I am forever grateful for the willingness of these professionals to donate their time and energy to our recovery, and I also appreciate the Knight Foundation for paying all the costs we did have to absorb. When this happened on the Gulf Coast ten years ago, it was the first time that a charrette on this scale had been accomplished in this country.

The charrette focused on the Gulf Coast communities because that is where the geographical slate had been wiped clean, often literally. I had never heard of the word "charrette" until Andrés Duany proposed one. As I said in my speech opening the convocation, I knew only two French words before that week—bourbon and bonbon—and now I knew a third–"charrette." After I admitted how little French I knew, I shared with everyone there—the experts, the local officials, the business leaders, the neighborhood activists—my commitment to allow local citizens to decide how their communities would be rebuilt. The role of all the experts and visionaries who had come to the Coast was to show the locals what other communities had done; how other communities were designed and organized; and what others viewed as attractive, livable, and efficient plans. That is, the charrette would lay out various versions of what could be if the citizens of the community wanted it. As I laid out this oft-repeated theme, I noticed the energy in the room, for the participants in this large exercise were excited about what they were about to try to do. And every time I returned to the charrette at various hours and met with different groups, I noticed that excitement, the thrill of being part of something important and unique.

Essentially, the week-long charrette consisted of small teams of experts combined with larger groups of local officials and business leaders developing plans for ways communities could be rebuilt. The work included tours of the affected areas, access to incredible amounts of demographic and geographic data, and work areas that encouraged different groups to interact with each other.

A week later, on October 18, we opened the workspace at the Isle of Capri for the media and everyone else to see the results, including a number of proposals to rebuild the downtown areas, relocate the CSX rail line north of the interstate and replace it with a light rail transit system, and construct mixed-use areas that included residential and commercial areas together as well as new ways of building hurricane-proof housing. Several of the depictions of how rebuilt downtowns and other destroyed areas could look were stunning and drew much attention.

Another important development from the charrette came to be called the "Mississippi Cottage," which was initially proposed by a couple of architects, one of whom was from New York. She recognized the gross inadequacy of the so-called FEMA trailers, the standard temporary housing provided to families whose homes were destroyed or uninhabitable in a disaster. While we were just learning the sad reality that nearly all FEMA trailers were campers, she displayed at the charrette a sturdier, larger, portable cottage that was far superior to what FEMA offered. These cottages would have made an enormous difference for the tens of thousands of Mississippians who lived in campers for one, two, or even three years. Talk about durable people, and determined!

As the recovery and rebuilding stretched out, the architect's observation about FEMA trailers became more and more obvious. In 2006 House Speaker Denny Hastert of Illinois led a congressional delegation to check progress on the Coast. Marsha met them and, while traveling with them, she showed the Speaker a FEMA trailer. It was eye-opening to the group, but particularly to Denny. She had him go into the bathroom so he could see for himself that a full-sized, grown man couldn't turn around in the tiny bathroom with the door closed. No doubt this helped convince Congress to encourage FEMA to allow us to build about three thousand Katrina or "Mississippi Cottages," as they were variously known.

These cottages were the length and width of full-sized mobile homes, and they had to be and were transportable like trailers. But they were built to withstand 150-mph winds, and they could be taken off their wheels and set up on a hurricane-proof foundation. The cottages were about eight hundred square feet plus a small covered front porch. Some had two bedrooms and others three bedrooms, with two baths. There was a small kitchen that opened over a counter into the living area. While they were incomparably superior to a camper, the cost over time was not that much more. We considered it the right solution for housing after a megadisaster, when families would require emergency housing for several months or years. The cottages could be removed from the storm foundation and retransported. In fact, that was a requirement to meet FEMA rules, which was an appropriate requirement.

Several years after the commission's report was published and after we had received funding and clearance to build the cottages, I attended a ribbon cutting for one of the first ones to open, in the devastated neighborhood of East Biloxi. A woman in her seventies with a French last name like many of the old families on the Coast was moving into the cottage that day. She and I met, and she was very excited, having lived in a FEMA trailer since a few weeks after the storm, her modest home having been destroyed.

There was a lot of media, and I stood on the porch, explained the cottage program, and told how superior it was to the FEMA trailer standard. Then I introduced the home's new occupant, and she stole the show. She said she had lived in East Biloxi all her life, always within a few blocks of this spot. "This is the nicest house I've ever lived in," she told the crowd. And that was undoubtedly true. That idea from the charrette, a seeming afterthought from a young architect from New York, had proved far-sighted and achievable. For the three thousand or so families for whom we were able to obtain approval to build a cottage, their quality of life was greatly improved while allowing them to stay in their communities on the Coast and in South Mississippi.

Following the charrette, the staff and commissioners held a series of public forums in the eleven coastal towns—"mini charrettes"—presenting the ideas that had been developed specifically for each of those communities. From there the local officials could decide which ideas they wanted to implement. It was at the Renewal Forum that Jim Barksdale met Gavin Smith, a former emergency management official in North Carolina who had been retained by FEMA to provide consulting advice to Mississippi. Smith was debating some of the New Urbanists, and Barksdale, who was in the audience, afterward asked him to join the team. The two hit it off so well that Smith left FEMA and joined the commission staff.

Gavin Smith was the closest we had to what you might call an out-of-state expert on responding to natural disasters. We had many people offering a lot of advice in the days and weeks following Katrina's landfall, but surprisingly, except for FEMA officials, there was not a core of people who had been through a major disaster before and who were available to move to Mississippi to help guide our efforts. A number of engineering and contracting firms visited with us, for example, but none of them offered the kind of advice we ended up developing on our own during the course of the commission's work. In short, there was no "disaster response" consultant we could retain. There are such people now.

Smith finished helping us close out the commission and then became director of a new office I created in early 2006—the Governor's Office of Recovery and Renewal. After leaving that job toward the middle of 2006, he returned to his home in North Carolina and has since further developed an academic and professional specialty for rebuilding in the wake of major disasters. There are now national meetings dealing with the very things we more or less pioneered in Mississippi.

We reached out to Smith in writing this book to discuss what he had learned since 2005–6 and what he remembered about Mississippi. In our conversation, he talked about how important resilience is in the success of recovery:

There are a lot of different dimensions of resilience. It's not just physical resilience, the ability to rebuild a community after disaster in that thoughtful way that makes them less vulnerable physically, but there's also an economic resilience, the idea, the degree to which small businesses and corporations come back and reemploy people in the area. There's a social resilience, some would say social capital, the strengths and bonds of people that exist at the local level. And I will tell you that's something that really struck me in Mississippi. I think about this often, and it's really pretty humbling in many ways, the social resilience of the people of Mississippi. I've been in a lot of disasters and seen a lot of different events and people react differently. It was amazing to see, for example, the Governor's Commission come together and the number of people who were engaged to go to the public meetings and see people in a meaningful way engaged. I remember people coming to the meetings, but stopping at places along the road where others had dropped off clothes, because people had lost everything they owned. People would pick up clothes and put them on. They might have been ill fitting, but they were going to public meetings in those clothes they had picked up on the side of the road. It was very humbling for me to see that.

The Ocean Springs–Biloxi Bridge

One of the most fascinating byproducts of the commission was the way it served as a venue for substantive decisions to get made, decisions that usually are made behind closed doors by governmental officials as part of their normal course of work. In the months after Katrina, with so much of the normal routine of conducting business upended, and with so many decisions having to be made in such a compressed time frame, the commission, and especially the various committees, became informal venues for government officials and involved private citizens to come together to resolve issues and make decisions.

The broad scope of the commission's membership helped, and certainly the great stature of Jim Barksdale and many other commission leaders such as Anthony Topazi, William Winter, Joe Sanderson, Ricky Mathews, and Jerry St. Pé gave it enormous credibility. Yet I think the key to its successful functions may have been the work done by the individual committees. Each committee was tasked to focus on one specific issue area, and most came to involve many more people than just the members—important stakeholders who knew the public policies and had "skin in the game"—through hearings, neighborhood forums, and informal discussions. The committees provided opportunities for people to collaborate on ideas and proposals and, while that process was designed to result in recommendations of the commission, it also provided solutions to problems that were pressing day to day, including the development and timing of FEMA flood maps, the ways in which those maps influenced local building codes, and what kinds of temporary housing should be used. Hundreds of people were getting information and ideas from the committees' activities.

One of my favorite examples of how this informal process worked involved rebuilding the bridge connecting Ocean Springs and Biloxi. The communities along the Coast are connected by U.S. Highway 90, which runs from the Louisiana line to the Alabama line and connects the major cities in the three coastal counties. Those three counties are separated from each other by two bays that enter the Gulf at the east and west ends of Harrison County, respectively. Before the storm, the bridge across the Bay of St. Louis, from Pass Christian to the town of Bay St. Louis on the west, and the bridge across Biloxi Bay, from Biloxi to Ocean Springs on the east, connected everyone. Katrina's surge was so strong that it lifted the concrete roadbeds off the support structures of both bridges and left nothing but the pilings. Getting those bridges rebuilt was critical to transporting workers and tourists as well as construction crews and commercial delivery vehicles.

Rebuilding the Ocean Springs–Biloxi bridge proved most conten-
tious, and it was a great example of the balance we were constantly
faced with in the days and months after August 29: getting something
rebuilt—a downtown, a park, a major road, a school, this bridge—as
quickly as possible versus taking the time to agree on an improved
design to better serve generations for long periods to come. Both sides
of that equation have valid and important considerations, and having a varied group of people associated with the commission made
achieving that balance easier but not always easy!

As for the bridge, on one side was Biloxi's mayor, A. J. Holloway,
who rightfully argued the bridge needed to be rebuilt as quickly as
possible to allow workers to get to construction sites and tourists to
find the casinos. Quite frankly, he didn't care much what it looked like
so long as it could get built and opened quickly. Mayor Connie Moran
of Ocean Springs was pushing for a design that included a walking/
bicycle lane. She also wanted decorative designs and lighting on the
concrete railings, along with substantial landscaping on the landing
pads on either side of the bridge. There were public and private argu-
ments about the extra time and cost needed for Connie's design versus the need to get it rebuilt quickly.

This disagreement was exacerbated by an earlier delay over the
question of how high to build the bridge. Not only were aesthetics and
recreational utility pitted against the practical need to reestablish the
ground transportation link as quickly as possible, there was also a critical maritime transportation issue. Biloxi Bay is a busy channel of
ingress and egress to a number of large and extremely significant industrial sites located on the "seaway" on the inland side of the bridge.
Significant seagoing and barge traffic must pass through the Biloxi
Bay Bridge. This had been achieved for decades via a drawbridge that
was opened and closed as needed, often daily. The drawbridge was no
longer accessible because the bridge of which it had been part was
no more, and it was impractical to rebuild the collapsed bridge.

As Governor I learned things every day, and the Biloxi Bay drawbridge taught me that all drawbridges are built to spec, and there is

no inventory of parts to put together a drawbridge when one is needed. Every piece of metal has to be manufactured from scratch. So if you want to replace a drawbridge, it will take years. Thus, having a new drawbridge was out. That meant a critical early decision for the Ocean Springs–Biloxi bridge was how high the span clearance would have to be at the point the ship channel passed under the bridge. Industries on the seaway above the bridge from the Gulf included a major electric power generation facility—Plant Watson—that was coal-fired. Its owner, Mississippi Power, brought nothing taller than barges loaded with coal through the bridge. But there were other industries that would have vessels go under the bridge less often, and they would move or go out of business if their vessels couldn't go under the bridge. These included one company that built yachts and service vessels for offshore oilrigs, while another was connected to the shipbuilding operations at Ingalls in Pascagoula. Since a drawbridge was not an option, we agreed after some time that the clearance under the bridge should be ninety-five feet and we designed what a bridge constructed to those height dimensions should look like.

No sooner had the federal government approved the clearance height solution than the argument about the walking and bicycle lane on the bridge got even hotter. The issue would surface any time the transportation committee met, and no decision was being reached. As the federal deadline to use the money approached, I began pushing commission members to work with the Mississippi Department of Transportation to reach an agreement, though even my own skepticism led to a brief argument with Ricky Mathews, where I told him the grade of the bridge would be too steep for anyone to walk or bicycle anyway. Mathews said, "Haley, if we don't do this, we will all regret it." I groused and then told him to get it resolved.

George Schloegel was chair of the transportation committee, so he convened a meeting of all the stakeholders, about fifty people, which filled up the city council chambers at the Biloxi City Hall—mayors, supervisors, interested citizens, business leaders. All morning they tried to resolve the issue and couldn't. At one point, Schloegel, thinking this was going nowhere, called "time out" and decided to break for lunch but asked the five or six key players to stay behind for a smaller meeting—Jim Barksdale, Biloxi mayor A. J. Holloway, Ocean Springs mayor Connie Moran, MDOT executive director Butch Brown, Anthony Topazi, and maybe one or two others.

As the story is told by people we interviewed for this book, Brown said, "I've only got a certain amount of money for this bridge." Moran argued again for the walk/bicycle lane, at which point Brown said, "I don't have enough money for that because of the way we've designed the bridge." Moran and Holloway continued to disagree, and at some point Barksdale looked over at Brown and said, "Butch, how much would it cost to include the features that Connie wants?" Caught a little off guard, Butch estimated about $9 million, at which point Barksdale asked, "Can a private individual just pay for this $9 million difference?" When Brown said, "Well, yeah, I suppose they could," Barksdale's response was as direct as it was unprecedented: "Fine, I will either give $9 million or I'll get others to help me raise it. I'm good for it if y'all will just build this bridge. Now, what other issues do we have to discuss?"

As George Schloegel said in an interview for this book, "Everyone looked at each other and that was that." Moran, Holloway, and Brown agreed, so the larger meeting was reconvened. Schloegel reported on the compromise, which everyone accepted. As it turned out, the next day Brown called Barksdale to say MDOT had found the money to cover the cost of the bridge and not only would a walking trail be included in the Biloxi–Ocean Springs bridge, but the same design would be incorporated in the Pass Christian–Bay St. Louis bridge on the other side of the county.

So far as I can tell, everyone is extremely proud of the iconic new Ocean Springs–Biloxi bridge, and the number of people who walk and bicycle over it on a daily basis is incredible. There's no question that people were inconvenienced by the delays, and the recovery in the Biloxi area may have been slowed some by the additional time needed to redesign and rebuild the bridge, but I'm glad we took our time to get it right.

Andrés Duany contributed mightily to the rebirth of the Gulf Coast, but perhaps his most important contribution was articulating the standard against which we should evaluate how well we had done. He once said the measure should not be us or our children but our grandchildren: What will they say thirty years from now—would South Mississippi and the Gulf Coast be a better place for them had Katrina never shown up? The Ocean Springs–Biloxi bridge is proof that we were on the right track.

The Commission's Report

Early on I had concluded that the commission's report should contain recommendations to the governor and should be advisory in nature. It was the commission's job to involve the government, private sector, and nonprofit organization decision makers in the process; to create a team to present the best possible ideas for renewal; and to empower them to take action. As I wrote in a September 23, 2005, letter to the commissioners, "While I am sure the report will have many good ideas, the final vote on implementation of almost all the issues that the Commission will consider and recommend will be by mayors, supervisors, aldermen and private investors. That's why this process must be driven from the local community and not Jackson or Washington."

As I gathered up advice about the commission in early September, the choice was either a "top-down" commission with legal authority to supersede local governing authorities or a "bottom-up" group that sought to involve and persuade local officials. Do you "run over" local officials to impose a new vision for the Gulf Coast, or do you risk not adopting all the recommendations by giving those officials and other stakeholders the chance to say no? Once Jim Barksdale decided he would include virtually any recommendation generated by any of the committees, the report became a menu of suggestions, some more important than others, some more doable than others, some pie-in-the-sky, and some we should have done years ago. Katrina gave us a chance to consider them all.

Another decision we made was to divide the commission staff into two groups—those working with the committees and those who would be writing the report. In this way the report was an ever-changing document that improved over time as committee deliberations evolved, as more data and information were gathered, and as consensus developed over which proposals would be recommended. Henry Barbour made this decision for another very good reason. He and Barksdale were bound and determined to deliver the report to me by December 31, and because the committees were operating on such a short timeframe, there was no time for committee work to end and report writing to begin. It all had to be done simultaneously. Incorporating all of the committee recommendations into a single report and drafting a narrative that tied everything together fell to Brian Sanderson, a young lawyer loaned to the commission by the Butler Snow law firm in Jackson. To say he worked long hours to meet the deadline would be an understatement.

As it turned out, I was in Las Vegas at the end of the year and, sure enough, FedEx delivered a draft of the report to my hotel on New Year's Eve. It was the first time I had seen it, mostly because I had been in Washington for virtually all of December working to pass the congressional appropriation. The final report contained 238 recommendations from the eleven different issue committees. In formulating these recommendations, the commission had solicited input from thousands who attended more than fifty public forums and town hall meetings throughout the thirty-three-county region of South Mississippi. In addition, the commission staff received more than eight hundred written comments via email, fax, and letter.

Over the years, people have tallied up all of the ideas that were generated by the charrette and all the recommendations of the commis-

Image of Hurricane Katrina from NASA's Terra satellite at 1:00 p.m. Eastern Daylight Saving Time, Sunday, August 28, 2005. Credit: Jeff Schmaltz, MODIS Rapid Response Team, NASA/GSFC

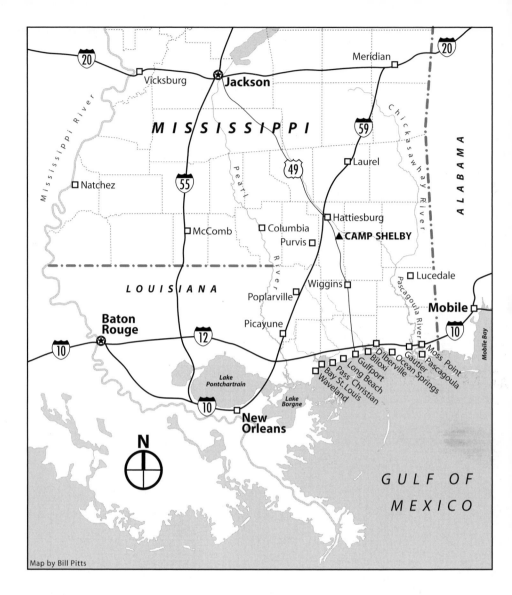

Map by Bill Pitts

MEMA Emergency Operations Center in Jackson on the day of landfall. Governor Barbour is speaking to the group, with MEMA Director Robert Latham standing to the governor's left. Credit: Mississippi Emergency Management Agency

The casino barge from the former Grand Casino in Gulfport sits astride U.S. Highway 90, locally known as Beach Boulevard, on Tuesday, August 30. Credit: Mississippi National Guard

Alison Dean saves a photograph of her parents as she explores her home in Waveland after it was destroyed by Hurricane Katrina. Credit: AP Photo/John Bazemore

Gulfport neighborhoods, taken from a National Guard helicopter, on Tuesday, August 30, the morning after landfall. Credit: Mississippi National Guard

Governor Haley Barbour, Colonel Don Taylor (Executive Director of the Department of Human Services), and team receive their first briefing from Mississippi National Guard Adjutant General Harold Cross on the morning of Tuesday, August 30, the day after the storm. Credit: Mississippi National Guard

Members of the New York City Urban Search and Rescue Task Force search through homes destroyed by Hurricane Katrina in Bay St. Louis, on Friday, September 2, 2005. Credit: AP Photo/M. Spencer Green

A coast resident on the beach the day after landfall. Credit: Marianne Todd

The remains of a residential street, cleared of debris. Credit: Marianne Todd

Marsha Barbour talks with volunteer John Boyle of Orange County, NY, outside an emergency operations center in Biloxi. Credit: *Sun Herald*, 9/29/2005. © 2005 McClatchy

Governor Barbour greets a survivor at a Hancock County distribution center in a shopping center parking lot a week after landfall. Credit: Marianne Todd

Senator Thad Cochran briefs the media on his tour of the Coast on Wednesday, August 31. Governor Barbour is in the background. Credit: Mississippi Emergency Management Agency

Ricky Mathews was publisher of the Biloxi *Sun Herald*, which won a Pulitzer Prize for its coverage of Katrina and served as a powerful force in the Coast's recovery, rebuilding, and renewal. The wreckage of the Treasure Bay Casino rests on the beach in Biloxi. Credit: Danny Rawls

Governor Barbour announces the creation of the Governor's Commission on Recovery, Rebuilding, and Renewal in early September 2005. Jim Barksdale, pictured on the right, served as the commission's chairman. Credit: Author's collection

President George W. Bush walks through an East Biloxi neighborhood on his first visit to the Coast on September 2, 2005. With him, from the left, are Biloxi Mayor A. J. Holloway, U.S. Senator Thad Cochran, and Governor Barbour. Credit: Eric Draper, Courtesy of the George W. Bush Presidential Library & Museum

Governor Barbour thanks conservation officers from Indiana who searched for survivors and bodies in Jackson County for several days after the storm. Credit: Mississippi Emergency Management Agency

Governor Barbour and First Lady Marsha Barbour tour the portable hospital North Carolina One, sent by the state of North Carolina and erected in a shopping center parking lot in Hancock County during the first days after the storm. Its doctors and nurses treated hundreds of Mississippians. Credit: Marianne Todd

In the first days after the storm, FEMA, MEMA, and private groups set up distribution and information centers in tents on parking lots across the Coast. Credit: Marianne Todd

Anthony Topazi, president of Mississippi Power Company during Katrina and a sensational leader after the storm, addresses the first meeting of the Governor's Commission on Recovery, Rebuilding, and Renewal in Gulfport with President Bush listening attentively. Credit: Mississippi Power

The cast of the Mississippi Rising concert, held at the University of Mississippi a few weeks after the storm, which raised more than $15 million for the relief fund. Credit: University of Mississippi

Actress Whoopi Goldberg with First Lady Marsha Barbour and Mississippi Bureau of Narcotics Officers Sam Owens and Wade Parham during Ms. Goldberg's visit to East Biloxi during the first month after the storm. Credit: Sam Owens

A meeting during the Mississippi Renewal Forum, also known as the Charrette. This gathering brought architects, planners, landscape designers, transportation specialists, building code experts, and engineers to Biloxi to consider what a rebuilt Gulf Coast could look like. Credit: John S. and James L. Knight Foundation

Governor Barbour holding a news conference at the U.S. Capitol with Iowa Senator Charles Grassley (left) and Senate Majority Leader Bill Frist of Tennessee (right) in October 2005. Credit: Author's collection

Speaker of the House Billy McCoy, who provided the leadership necessary during the special legislative session to pass measures allowing casinos to recover and rebuild on the Gulf Coast. Credit: AP Photo/ Rogelio V. Solis

Wayne Newton at a special fundraising event for Mississippi's First Responder families in Tunica in December 2005. Adjutant General Harold Cross is to Newton's left. Credit: Mississippi National Guard

Governor Barbour speaks to a reporter in August 2006 at the Governor's Recovery Expo in Biloxi. Accompanying him are Gavin Smith, director of the Governor's Office of Recovery and Renewal, and Ashley Edwards, a staff member of that office. Credit: Author's collection

First Lady Marsha Barbour at a post-Katrina event to restock the Pascagoula River with bass. Also pictured here is Melvin Tingle from the MPB show *Mississippi Outdoors*. Credit: Mississippi Department of Wildlife, Fisheries, & Parks

Governor Haley Barbour and Florida Governor Jeb Bush pose for pictures during a news conference Wednesday, October 11, 2006, in Tallahassee. Barbour was in Tallahassee to thank the first responders from Florida who assisted in the aftermath of Hurricane Katrina. Credit: AP Photo/Phil Coale

Governor Barbour and First Lady Marsha Barbour pose after thanking a group of AmeriCorps workers. The young AmeriCorps members played an indispensable role in the recovery, creating an impact far beyond their numbers. Credit: Carmen K. Sisson/Cloudybright

sion and wondered why more were never implemented. Some have even criticized both the charrette and the commission because more was not put in place. My answer is that I never wanted any of these to be viewed as top-down, with folks in Jackson telling folks in South Mississippi and along the Coast how to rebuild their communities. Ultimately, I agree with something Ricky Mathews said early on: South Mississippi has to be in charge of its own recovery.

I believe the commission succeeded enormously in illuminating for people what could be—showing community leaders their options, their alternatives, what other cities have done and why—and most especially in creating venues for hundreds of people from all over South Mississippi to voice their concerns and their hopes for the future during a time of incredible pressure and need.

We released the report on Wednesday, January 11. A local mayor summed up what many thought about the actual recommendations when he said it "was a mixed bag of reasonable guidance and unrealistic dreams." Jim Barksdale, on the other hand, echoed my position about the role of the commission vis-à-vis the role of local authorities: "The difference between something happening and something not is local officials." And a number of mayors and county supervisors and development officials did in fact use the planning recommendations to move forward with exciting projects, including those in D'Iberville, Gulfport, and Bay St. Louis.

I don't see the need to repeat the findings and recommendations from the commission's report, which is still available online. My aim here is to explain why we established a commission in the first place and why it was useful on a number of fronts. Nevertheless, many of the discussions, forums, and recommendations have led to improvements in a number of areas. These include improving local building and development codes; integrating the FEMA flood maps with community decisions about housing and business development; adopting new landscaping, public recreation, and lighting initiatives; promoting new and different tourism activities; rebuilding historic downtown

areas; creating venues for parent and community input in the rebuilding of schools; creating electronic records for health care facilities,
businesses, and government agencies; establishing regional water and
wastewater facilities and authorities; and improving our local emergency telecommunication systems.

Biloxi mayor A. J. Holloway offered a wise observation that greatly
affected the adoption of thoughtful recommendations. While many of
us at the time considered this the once-in-a-lifetime opportunity for
South Mississippi and especially the Gulf Coast to make revolution-
ary changes because Katrina had "wiped the slate clean," AJ reminded
us that in reality the slate was not as clean as it looked because virtually
all of the property that had been wiped clean was privately held—in
many cases by families with title to land that went back generations.
Getting thousands of individuals to make certain preconceived uses
of thousands of acres of private land was unrealistic even if it did
illuminate some very positive ways to improve their homes and
communities. And, of course, many of the building proposals required lots of money. While a substantial amount of money came to
the Coast, we were hit hard by the 2008 recession, which put a number of building projects on hold.

Two of the most far-reaching recommendations, both of which had
been discussed before Katrina but had gained new life through the
commission, were relocating the CSX railroad and expanding the size
and scope of the port at Gulfport.

The CSX railroad runs parallel to Highway 90 and through virtually every community on the Coast. In Harrison County, it crosses Biloxi Bay just north of Point Cadet (the easternmost point in the City
of Biloxi) and runs generally due west through residential neighborhoods in Biloxi and Gulfport until it crosses U.S. Highway 49 above
downtown Gulfport. From there it continues on its generally westerly
path through west Gulfport, Long Beach, and Pass Christian, where
it comes to the Bay of St. Louis. George Schloegel and others strongly
urged the purchase of the right-of-way of the CSX railroad and the
railroad's relocating its tracks to north of Interstate 10.

The railroad right-of-way in Biloxi and Gulfport would be stripped of the rail tracks and converted to a four-lane (or more) bypass to move traffic quickly through the heavily populated areas. That would greatly reduce traffic on Beach Boulevard (U.S. Highway 90) and allow it to become specifically a tourist route, with only short trips by them and locals. The through traffic and even traffic traveling from one part of the community to another part would take the new expressway, which would be limited access. All this, especially in Biloxi and Gulfport, would speed up regular traffic and make Beach Boulevard a far less crowded and perfectly paced beachside road.

More important from my perspective were the evacuation needs of a very crowded part of the Coast. Between U.S. 90 and Interstate 10 there was only one four-lane street, Pass Road. It had very few turn lanes, was totally open access to driveways and parking lots, and stayed extremely congested. While local leaders wanted to improve the tourist and pedestrian quality of Beach Boulevard, and the New Urbanists saw the CSX right-of-way as a virtual park with a light rail system, the real goal was to protect people against the next big hurricane.

When a major evacuation starts on the Coast, such as when big hurricanes approach, the first and worst traffic congestion is not on northbound roads, though that occurs. The worst is the traffic jam on east–west two-lane streets as families and businesses drive to get to the northbound roads. These east–west streets quickly resemble parking lots, and many people are put at risk. My main reason for supporting the CSX right-of-way purchase and the construction of an expressway at least through to Highway 49 was to facilitate evacuation and save lives.

Ultimately, we failed to make that case effectively to Congress when we returned in 2006 for a second round of special appropriation requests, so we were never able to secure the kind of money needed to cover the relocation and rebuilding costs.

Perhaps the best summary of why I think the commission's work was so important can be found in something Ricky Mathews wrote soon after the charrette. He focused on two aspects. First, he used the word "catalyst" to describe the commission:

> The word catalyst comes from chemistry. It refers to a substance that increases the rate of chemical reaction. In the case of South Missis-sippi's challenge, it refers to an event, a person or something that brings about an acceleration of our recovery and renewal. The Governor's Commission has created a framework for the conversations to take place. And within that framework, we are all learning the rebuilding language together. We are learning to appreciate the unique challenges that each of our wonderful communities is facing. We are finding our common issues. We are developing a compelling vision together.

Then he wrote of something I had not thought about in terms of creating the environment needed for the private sector to reinvest in South Mississippi: "FUD, which stands for Fear, Uncertainty, and Doubt. It refers to the perceived risks of making an investment. If the FUD is high, there will not be a renaissance. If the FUD is low, the money will flow as long as the opportunity to invest is there." The work of the commission over the four months following Katrina's landfall contributed enormously to reducing the FUD factor.

To find the money to put the commission's recommendations into effect required one of the most comprehensive and strenuous lobby-ing efforts ever carried out in Washington. So we return to October 25, the date we began to make public our special request to Congress for funds to rebuild the southern half of Mississippi. For much of the time the commission was developing its report, I was in Washington lobby-ing for funds to help turn many of those recommendations into concrete projects. That story is taken up in the next chapter.

CHAPTER 7

Congress and Recovery

HE FOUND ME AT THE GOVERNOR'S MANSION on Wednesday, two days after landfall, and said he had just finished his own helicopter tour of the devastated Gulf Coast. Thad Cochran, Mississippi's senior U.S. Senator, looked at me and said, "Tell me what you need, and I'll do my best to deliver."

This became a constant refrain: "You are on the ground and will know better than I do what Mississippi needs to rebuild." "Once you and your team decide, I'll try to get it for you."

My friendship with Thad Cochran went back many years. When he ran for and was elected to Congress the first time, in 1972, I had served as the Mississippi Republican Party's campaign director, trying to coordinate the efforts of three congressional campaigns (including Thad's) with an active U.S. Senate race and, more important, the campaign to reelect President Richard Nixon in Mississippi. Since we knew Nixon would do well in the state (Nixon ended up getting 78 percent of our vote), a key to the ultimate victories of Thad Cochran in the third district and Trent Lott in the fifth was to generate as much support as possible from those who voted Republican at the top of the ticket. The same year, my bride of six months, Marsha, was the first paid employee of Thad's campaign. So the senator and I go back a long way.

Cochran and Lott were thirty-four and thirty-one years old, respectively, when they won two congressional seats previously held by Democrats. Mississippi Republicans largely built their party around them for the next two or more decades.

I've been on the other side from Thad Cochran only once in my career, and that was in 1978, in the campaign to succeed retiring Senator Jim Eastland. I worked for Charles Pickering, who opposed Cochran in the GOP primary. Pickering asked me first, before Cochran had even decided to run. Pickering was a state senator, and Cochran was a U.S. Congressman. Both were good candidates, but Cochran's district covered more geography and population than did Pickering's and thus he had a higher name recognition and more contacts. The day after Cochran won the primary, I got a call from his campaign manager, Al Smith, saying Cochran wanted me to serve as the chairman of his general election campaign. We've been together ever since.

Twenty-seven years later, Thad Cochran was Mississippi's senior U.S. Senator, and at the time Katrina made landfall, he had earned enough seniority to have assumed the chairmanship of the Senate Appropriations Committee eight months earlier.

Cochran returned to Washington Wednesday night after Katrina, knowing he had to get an early infusion of money to FEMA. The agency had the spending authority to cover a limited disaster, like a tornado, but nothing on the scale of what he had seen on our Gulf Coast. Moreover, the federal government was one month away from the end of its fiscal year, which meant there was little if any surplus remaining in FEMA's disaster relief fund. As Mark Keenum, Cochran's chief of staff, told me at the time, "We all were in a state of shell shock, but Senator Cochran and the entire congressional leadership wanted to send a signal to everyone on the Coast that Congress would be there for them." So, after Senator Cochran and the congressional leadership conferred with the White House, the president submitted a request for an initial appropriation of $10.5 billion, with $10 billion going to FEMA and $500 million going to the Pentagon. Congress had to do this so FEMA could begin to draw down the money it needed.

There was only one problem. Congress was not in session; it was out for its August recess. So Bill Frist, Senate majority leader; Dennis Hastert, House Speaker; and Harry Reid, the Senate minority leader all got together with Cochran and other appropriation leaders and made use of House and Senate rules that allowed them to convene when Congress was out of session. On Thursday morning, September 1, Senators Cochran, Frist, and Reid gathered on the Senate floor and passed the special FEMA appropriation bill. Similarly, in the House, a few members convened the next day under special rules and approved the bill that the president signed later that day. Eight days later, with the full Congress back in session, another $51.8 billion was approved for FEMA and the Defense Department.

With its emergency account filled, FEMA had the money to respond to the needs for recovery. We could begin to focus our attention to planning, funding, and executing the rebuilding effort, though it was here that we came face to face with what is known as the Stafford Act. The federal government's legal authority to respond to natural disasters, through FEMA and other agencies, is governed by the Federal Disaster Assistance Act, otherwise known as the Stafford Act, after the senator who authored the original legislation.

Confronting damage on the scale left by Hurricane Katrina revealed the weaknesses of the Stafford Act. First, the law was designed for much smaller events. There was no organizational infrastructure in place to respond to the dislocation of nearly a million people and the obliteration of all associated infrastructure.

Second, the law required public facilities that are destroyed to be rebuilt on the same footprint and just as they were before the disaster occurred. The law doesn't provide for updates or improvements, nor, for example, would it pay to move a water line or sewage plant to a more secure location for the next hurricane.

Third, the law contained no provision to help people rebuild their homes. In the aftermath of a limited disaster, FEMA was designed to help provide short-term individual assistance, coordinate debris removal, supply temporary housing, and replace and restore essential public services. In Mississippi alone, we had more than sixty-one thousand homes that were uninhabitable and private insurance was not likely to cover the cost of damage for many of these homes since the damage was done by water, not wind, and thus was not covered by private homeowners' policies. This was a crisis the Stafford Act never contemplated.

To recover, Mississippi would need to do three things—get schools back up and running for all our children, provide the environment necessary to help businesses bring jobs back, and restore private and public housing. Given the statutory limitations imposed on FEMA by the Stafford Act, and given that very little was available under the Stafford Act to help restore jobs, relocate schools, and rebuild houses, we knew out-of-the-box thinking was required to help the southern half of our state recover and rebuild.

In 1987, after I left the Reagan White House, I began lobbying in Washington while still practicing law and living in Yazoo City. By 1989, while Marsha, the boys, and I continued to live in Yazoo City, I gave up my Mississippi law practice and began lobbying full time. When I ran for governor in 2003, my opponent was the incumbent Democratic governor, and his main attack against me was my career as a lobbyist. Ultimately I won by seven points, 53–46, and our polling showed that most people thought having an experienced lobbyist as governor would be more helpful to the state than harmful. Of course, nobody during the 2003 campaign foresaw Katrina and the requirements of recovering from the worst natural disaster in American history, but in the wake of the megadisaster, it turned out to be the optimum time to have as governor a former Washington lobbyist and national party leader.

For Mississippi to have been visited by such a horrendous and epic disaster, we were as well prepared to seek help from the federal government as we had been at any time in our state's recent history. President Bush was a close personal friend. I had worked with him during his dad's election campaign in 1988. Six years later he ran for and was elected governor of Texas while I was chairman of the Republican National Committee. He had been to Mississippi a number of times during my campaign and would end up coming to Mississippi almost a dozen times following Katrina's landfall.

For the first time in forty years, Republicans won control of both Houses of Congress in the 1994 election, while I chaired the Republican National Committee. Consequently, the leaders in both houses were allies and friends. Our other Mississippi senator, Trent Lott, had served as majority leader for six years and in 2005 was a senior ranking member on the Senate Finance Committee. Moreover, he had served in leadership positions in the House before coming to the Senate.

Rep. Chip Pickering was a vice chair of the Energy and Commerce Committee while Rep. Roger Wicker was a member of House Appropriations and a senior member of the House Budget Committee. Both Pickering and Wicker had worked on Senate staffs before getting elected in their own right. Rep. Bennie Thompson was the ranking Democrat on the Homeland Security Committee, which had jurisdiction over FEMA, while Rep. Gene Taylor was a senior Democrat on House Armed Services and a Coast resident.

The staffs of these members all knew each other and had years of experience working together and creating relationships throughout Congress and with the executive branch. I knew them all and counted them as friends, and I shared connections with many of them long before I became a lobbyist and they became congressional staffers. A typical example is Les Spivey, who was the number two staff member on the Senate Appropriations Committee. His dad was my dentist in Canton. Jim Perry, my senior policy director, and Les had known each other from the days when Perry worked in Roger Wicker's House office and Spivey worked for Senator Cochran. As Spivey described the network in an interview for this book, "All of us connected with

Mississippi had this working relationship thing down pat long before Katrina."

There's an old expression that lobbyists use—don't ever let your opponents see any daylight between you and your allies. In other words, so long as everyone sticks together and works as a team, your opponents will be unable to drive a wedge between you. It is the modern-day equivalent of preventing "divide and conquer." From the day Katrina made landfall, the six members of the Mississippi congressional delegation worked together for their state and constituents. In fact, the delegation did something it had never done before. Cochran convened all the members in his office in early September, the first time anyone remembers all six members coming together in one place to talk about one issue. But they did, and they received a briefing from my staff and me. They never looked back.

Lobbying and the Plan

I had learned over the years that getting a major piece of legislation adopted by Congress required at least three things—a plan, educating the members, and using your network of friends, contacts, and natural allies of the plan. Cochran knew this when he asked me for a long-term plan of what we needed, how we would spend the money, and how it would contribute to our recovery. He wanted a road map with details.

I asked Jim Perry, policy director of my staff, to take charge of writing the plan. It made sense that this was his assignment since Perry was not only my policy director but also a former Hill staffer in D.C. and the point man with the Barksdale Commission. In that way, he could take the ideas being generated from the commission and translate them into the requests we would be making to the federal government.

After talking with a number of people inside and outside of government, we settled on three major components. First, we knew we would need funding beyond what the Stafford Act would allow in order to rebuild schools, highways and bridges, and our public service and utility infrastructure and to help families rebuild the tens of thousands of units of housing destroyed by the storm.

Second, we knew our state budget would take a huge hit because of the loss of so much of our tax base in the southern half of the state. The easiest and most direct way to plug that hole would be to ask the federal government to cover the state's matching share requirement for Medicaid, which at the time was approaching $400 million annually.

Third, in addition to rebuilding the destroyed infrastructure, we needed new tax incentives for businesses to return to the damaged areas. It was not enough to restore our infrastructure, to get our schools up and running, and to rebuild houses. We had to bring businesses back with their jobs. And recruit new ones. So creating a series of tax incentives made sense to me. As I always said, "The private sector must rebuild Mississippi communities."

Approaching Congress with this kind of comprehensive package was unprecedented. Making this happen fell to our Mississippi congressional delegation, and in the months and years after Katrina, they came together like never before and used all of their connections, influence, and years of seniority and contacts to persuade Congress to pass this kind of once-in-a-lifetime legislation.

An early call went to Chip Pickering about Medicaid. Since the House Energy and Commerce Committee, of which he was vice-chairman, had jurisdiction over Medicaid-related legislation, we asked him to take the lead on this and to host a meeting with everyone involved to try to get the most he could for us. At the time, Mississippi's match rate was about 25 percent—that is, the state had to pay approximately one-fourth of total Medicaid spending in Mississippi while the federal government paid the remaining 75 percent. I was hoping he could get that down to 10 or 15 percent. Pickering decided that if we were asking him to "get all he could," he would go for a zero percent match rate.

As it turned out, the chairman of Energy and Commerce was Joe Barton, a longtime representative from Texas whose state had also been affected by hurricanes and who held Chip in high regard. Barton had named him as one of his vice-chairmen earlier in the year. To our great relief, Barton gave Pickering the authority to negotiate this issue on behalf of the entire committee—thus, effectively, for the entire House of Representatives. Medicaid also is handled through Senate Finance, one of Trent Lott's committees; whatever Pickering could get through the House, Lott would be in a great position to have the Senate concur. The challenge would be getting the White House to buy into our proposal.

A similar call went to Trent to help with the tax legislation, of which the Senate Finance Committee also has jurisdiction. Over on the House side, the corresponding committee was Ways and Means, whose chairman was Bill Thomas from California, a good friend of Lott's from his days in the House. It just so happened that one of Chairman Thomas's key members was Congressman Jim McCrery from Louisiana, while the number two ranking member was Clay Shaw from Florida, both of whom knew something about hurricane damage. Both men were generous with their help throughout this process. All of these key House members had been friends and allies of mine during my days in Washington, both at the RNC and during my lobbying years.

Congressman McCrery had in September quickly moved through Congress legislation that provided tax breaks for hurricane victims, including the elimination of withdrawal penalties on retirement accounts and flexibility in using these funds to rebuild houses; created temporary tax credits for employers in the stricken areas for hiring employees; and increased a variety of incentives for charitable tax deductions for contributions given in the four months following landfall.

As Senate Appropriations chairman, Cochran had to handle the additional funding we needed, with Roger Wicker helping in the House. Cochran's counterpart at the House Appropriations Committee was Chairman Jerry Lewis from California, a friend who wanted to help Mississippi but who had his own priorities as well. The number two Republican on Lewis's committee was Bill Young from Florida, who had been through plenty of hurricanes himself. The layout was looking good for us.

Looking back on it ten years later, I remain extraordinarily impressed by the way our delegation and staff worked the legislation through Congress. They were in constant motion, always talking to anyone and everyone, thinking through ideas and possible partners and giving us feedback. There was a never-ending loop of conversation between the team in Washington and those of us in Jackson developing the request. House members teamed up with senators, staff members teamed up with each other, and they all teamed up with their colleagues from other states, including Bill Frist, the Senate majority leader from our northern neighbor, Tennessee, and the Republican senators from Alabama, Richard Shelby and Jeff Sessions.

As for the White House, we came to realize that, while the president would try his best to help us, there would be resistance on other executive branch fronts. Likewise, on the House side of the Capitol, Speaker Dennis Hastert from Illinois and Majority Leader Roy Blunt from Missouri were old friends who wanted to help, but—like the White House—they were worried about setting precedents that could be not be sustained in future natural disasters. For them, it could be difficult politically to differentiate or to tell one region of the country or one group of states what Congress had done for Mississippi and Louisiana they were not going to do for someone else.

This was the legislative context in which we operated in the fall of 2005. None of the Republican leadership wanted our request to set a precedent for all the storms that followed; our response, of course, was that this storm was unprecedented. Nothing like it had ever happened before. When a natural disaster wipes out much of the infrastructure, institutional capacity, and economies of an entire region, Congress should be prepared to take unprecedented action. The worst natural disaster in American history required a similarly massive response.

In the end, there was only one way to overcome these objections, and that was by talking to members individually and in small groups, telling them about the destruction, giving them tours of the Coast, and explaining the weaknesses of the Stafford Act. At the time there was plenty of consternation in Mississippi and, I'm sure, Louisiana over the length of time it took to get the special funding and tax packages approved. I tend to agree with an assessment Chip Pickering once offered: "Partly because the earlier appropriation had taken care of short-term needs, this was like a pause in the debate over what to do over the long term and this was precedent setting. You first get what you can through traditional means, then move on. The special appropriation was an unprecedented response to an unprecedented disaster for a long-term recovery plan that should have and did take longer to get through."

The Plan

After initial discussions with the White House and leaders in the Congress, we learned the president would be submitting a request for supplemental funding to cover needs beyond the Stafford Act, mostly for the Department of Defense bases affected by the storm. Our first priority, then, was getting as much as possible of what we needed included in the Bush proposal to Congress.

First and foremost was housing. The Stafford Act was (and is) gravely insufficient because it provides no funding to rebuild houses. There was simply no way for us to recover without replacing housing. And this was not a case of making renovations to damaged houses; in tens of thousands of cases, there was no house to repair, only a concrete foundation. Mississippi's problem was that while many of these houses were outside the flood zone—and thus not required to have flood insurance—they had been totally destroyed by flood waters. And it was for that unique circumstance that I sought assistance from Congress.

My rationale for federal involvement in replacing or repairing the homes located outside the flood zone was simple: the federal government delineates the flood zone and only the federal government offers flood insurance. For those who live in flood zones, you buy flood insurance. For those who live outside the flood zones, you don't. That is factually irrefutable. Our point was, "I am a good citizen. I went in to close my loan to buy my house, to get my mortgage. And the government's agent tells me my new house is in a flood zone, and I can't get a loan unless I buy flood insurance. Or the agent says I don't have to buy flood insurance since I am not in the flood zone." So that good citizen has relied to his or her detriment on the federal government, which has told him or her, "You don't need flood insurance, and by the way, we are the only ones who sell it." If the government tells you something and you rely on it to your detriment, who ought to pay? The citizen? I didn't think so. I thought the federal government should reimburse people whose houses were destroyed or damaged by flood waters outside the flood zone. Otherwise, these homeowners would most likely never rebuild and our chances of recovery would be compromised.

Electric utilities were another issue of confrontation. Our investor-owned public utilities—Entergy and Mississippi Power—had spent hundreds of millions of dollars to restore power in record time. The magnitude of the damage was unprecedented, and if we were to create an environment that allowed our state and citizens to recover and begin rebuilding, we couldn't allow the massive 35 percent rate increases that would be necessary for the utilities to recoup those costs, as required by the law. The Bush Administration was initially opposed to our request to provide funding for these utilities, arguing that it amounted to nothing less than a "federal bailout" and was inappropriate. We maintained otherwise, especially since the government's policy is to allow federal funds to reimburse municipally owned and cooperative utilities for their restoration and rebuilding costs. We also knew the federal government had provided money to New York utilities following the 9/11 crisis. While not a natural disaster, I saw no distinction between the needs of the citizens.

At one point, Entergy's executive vice president of external affairs, Curt Hebert, told me about a meeting he had three or four weeks after landfall with Al Hubbard, assistant to the president for economic policy and director of the National Economic Council. In addition to its subsidary in Mississippi, Entergy owned the utility in New Orleans, which had been completely wiped out, and was a few days away from declaring bankruptcy. Hebert was there asking the White House for help in avoiding bankruptcy but ultimately was forced to file. Hubbard was frank and to the point: "No, the White House would be offering no help." I remember Hebert telling me the meeting became very emotional when Hubbard refused all help, leading Hebert to ask him, "If this were in Los Angeles or New York City, would you be acting in the same way?" which provoked Hubbard to "storm out of the room, only to return later and apologize." This was obviously an issue I would have to take up directly with the president.

Finally, we had massive rebuilding needs for the Gulf Coast's public infrastructure, including roads, bridges, water and sewer facilities, and public buildings—all of which we wanted to build back better, and many of which we wanted to relocate and make changes in anticipation of future hurricanes. Much of that was not allowed under the Stafford Act.

It was for all these reasons that we knew we would have to seek a special appropriations package from Congress, so we began to put pencil to paper to develop a plan and a lobbying strategy. Then, it almost fell apart.

Friday, September 23, 2005, started out as a good day for us. We were in the middle of what would be a productive special session of our Legislature; we had encouraging conversations with folks in Washington; President Bush had just signed Congressman McCrery's individual tax legislation; and agency personnel were coming together in Mississippi to help develop the components of our plan. Then the *New York Times* broke a story about the amount of money Louisiana would be requesting from Congress, a whopping $250 billion for that one state alone. All of a sudden our attempts to move Congress in the direction of considering additional spending ran headlong into the buzz saw of, "Haley, if Louisiana's Plan is your idea of a reasonable request, you can forget about getting anything from Congress."

It would be another month before we were ready to submit a plan to Congress, but Louisiana's outrageous request caused the kind of negative reaction and pushback in Congress we had not anticipated. Ironically, over the long term, I believe it actually helped. Their proposal was so inflated and contained so little Katrina-related justification that over time we would gain support for our proposal by coming in with a significantly smaller amount that was full of details and documented rationale. And that's exactly what Jim Perry and his team set out to provide.

In between a special session and general recovery efforts, Jim Perry and I made trips to Washington almost once a week to talk with whomever we could schedule meetings—testing ideas, testing legislation, testing budgets. Often members of our delegation would host meetings with congressional staffers and executive branch officials; other times, we would meet individually with members. Our constant refrain was simple—we know what we are asking for is unprecedented, but this disaster is unprecedented.

In addition to identifying the amount of money we needed and how we would spend it, we needed to decide the way in which we would ask Congress to get the money to Mississippi. Because what we were requesting had never been done before, there was no existing federal program specifically established to handle such spending. We went back and forth about different ways to obtain the funding: should we start a new program or tap onto an existing program, something like FEMA's Hazard Mitigation Grant Program? We ultimately decided to ask Congress to appropriate the bulk of the money through two existing block grant programs—the Community Development Block Grant Program (CDBG) and the Social Services Block Grant Program (SSBG). CDBG was much bigger than SSBG in terms of money. Cochran and his staff liked it because we were not asking Congress to create a new agency or a new program. We'd be using an existing programmatic framework that would save time because there would be little need for new regulations, much less a totally new regulatory regime, and it would give Mississippi maximum flexibility.

In this early stage, then, we had two political imperatives—wait to release our plan until after the president's plan was released (so he was not upstaged) and make sure the president's plan contained a block grant component (even if it was modest and even if it didn't contain housing). Our friends in Congress had let us know it was much easier legislatively to expand a provision that was already in the president's plan, such as a block grant program.

After learning that the president's plan would be released toward the end of October, we created a goal of getting ours out by November 1. Though we had numerous meetings with White House and administration staffers, we asked for one official meeting with the president to make our case and ask for his help. The meeting took place in mid-October in the Oval Office, and I was pleased the key staff was there since I knew how much influence staff has on White House decision making. The president was friendly, and he made plain he knew what our requests were but expressed concerns about the precedents he might be setting if he signed on to them. Still, he was clearly sympathetic; yet I understood it isn't the president's job to say "No." That is what staff does.

During this White House meeting, Al Hubbard continued to adamantly oppose my plan for the state to use federal disaster funds to reimburse investor-owned utilities. Hubbard and I had been friends for years; he had been Indiana Republican chairman in the 1990s, when I was chairman of the national GOP. Nevertheless, Hubbard was dug in against my proposal, and he spoke vigorously against it during the Oval Office meeting. Even though I had previously mentioned to the president how critical it was in getting the electricity back on to get a recovery going, he didn't comment. In fact, soon after my exchange with Hubbard, the president left the meeting, leaving me with the staff.

While I knew Hubbard was doing his job, objecting to what many feared would set a bad precedent that would be hard to distinguish against in the future, I didn't like it. In fact, by the end of the meeting, I had been told a lot of reasons "why not" and had no commitment that the president or his staff would support my plan. Frankly, I couldn't believe it. Some of these guys had been my friends for many years. I had not only chaired the Republican National Committee when President Bush was elected governor of Texas in 1994, but we'd been friends when his dad was vice president. I'd been one of his ten-member national steering committee that launched his 2000 presidential campaign. And they were not committing to support my state in its darkest hour of need.

I was disappointed and angry when I bumped into Andy Card, the president's chief of staff, as I was leaving the White House after the meeting. He could tell I was agitated, and he said for me not to do anything rash, that they had to be careful, but we'd get it worked out. I wasn't convinced.

I had phone conversations with two of my closest D.C. friends, whose experience in politics and federal affairs I trust and value most. I told them both I was really upset by the lack of support from the White House. When my state was in its greatest hour of need, the president wasn't going to help me. Not only that, but I was the governor who had refrained from publicly attacking FEMA and instead had praised them for the things they'd done right. If the president opposed our package, as I feared, I said to each of them, I would have to put my state first and publicly break with the president. That was terrible to contemplate, as close as I'd been to George W. Bush and so many in his administration. I was pretty miserable and called Marsha to tell her about it. She agreed with my assessment, even if it ruptured our friendship with the president, who had always been extremely gracious to her.

My gut-wrenching subsided a little when, later that day, I met Jim Perry at the JW Marriott hotel to review our plans, and he soon received a call from Steve McMillan, a senior director at the Office of Management and Budget, home to the accounting and financial staff for the White House. McMillan had been in our meeting, and he told

Perry that we were going to get line items for both CDBG and SSBG block grants. That made me feel a little better, and Jim and I had a celebratory drink.

Later Andy Card called me. Andy was a great old friend. He and I had served together in the Reagan White House, he as the director of the Office of Intergovernmental Affairs and I as director of the Office of Political Affairs. Andy is a straight shooter.

He had called to say that the president "is fine on your utilities deal." That was also great news. More importantly, Andy asked me not to fall out with them over the meeting. He said they wanted to work with us. Without saying it, however, he left me with the impression the White House staff wanted the president to be careful about endorsing provisions that could turn into bad precedents after future disasters. "We're going to work through all this, we just have to do it our way." Of course I could accept that. Their job was to protect the president.

In the end the White House never came out for our package, but they never opposed it either. I couldn't say it publicly, but my take was the president would not oppose anything Congress would give us. His staff didn't want him to put his endorsement on anything, but they figured we could get Congress to pass anything we wanted within reason. We were on our own, but they weren't going to make it harder for us.

In the meantime, Chip Pickering was making progress with Medicaid, and Trent Lott was moving forward with the tax-incentive package for businesses, which came to be known as the Gulf Opportunity Zone Act of 2005, more commonly known as the GO Zone Act. Getting the federal government to pick up part or all of our match on Medicaid funds could mean several hundred million dollars a year.

It helped when Pickering would show up for meetings with staff from all the relevant committees, my staff, and staff from Cochran's office; the executive branch officials knew they were facing a united front and ultimately a losing battle. To our great relief, and my surprise, they ultimately agreed to a plan that provided Mississippi with nearly $600 million in Medicaid funding for two years. This was a huge help to our state budget and would give us enormous flexibility in responding to other budget requests.

The Plan Goes Public

In late October, President Bush formally asked Congress for $17.1 billion for Katrina relief. One newspaper report included this detail: "In the reallocation of FEMA money request was a White House proposal that $1.5 billion be redirected to the CDBG program operated through [the Department of Housing and Urban Development] HUD." The president had also included a line item for SSBG spending. Cochran now had his vehicle.

Still there were some disturbing omissions, especially the $4 billion we estimated would be needed to cover thirty-five thousand homeowners outside the flood zone who had lost their properties from flood waters. As I told the Biloxi *Sun Herald*, still smarting from our White House meeting, "I am disappointed in the President's recommendation to Congress. I'm not just a little disappointed. It's undeniable that the federal government played a major role in thousands of Mississippi residents relying to their detriment on the federal government's advice that they were outside the flood plain and didn't need it."

On Thursday, November 1, I presented our plan for Mississippi to the president and Congress. It came to $33 billion over ten years, with $24 billion needed for the next two years. The major components of our plan included nearly $4 billion for homeowner assistance; $600 million for regional water and wastewater improvements; $325 million for utility ratepayer mitigation; $500 million for Port of Gulfport reconstruction and enhancements; $600 million for community revitalization; $1 billion for highways; $700 million for Medicaid, and more than $550 million for K–12 and postsecondary education.

Les Spivey arranged for me to describe the plan to the full staff of the Senate Appropriations Committee, more than one hundred people in all. We had been blessed in that ten days before Katrina hit, many of the key committee staffers had spent several days in Mississippi, including the Coast, visiting places where Cochran had received requests for funding. Throughout the entire fall, the committee staff were our allies and proved to be a huge help in getting our legislation adopted.

A few weeks later I made our case in front of the entire House Republican Conference, though I couldn't tell them what my friends at the White House had implied to me, "You can get this done, but we can't help you, we can't set the precedent." During my presentation there were a number of questions, all of which I answered, but there was no open opposition or incredulity. Congressman Tom Cole of Oklahoma told the group, "Haley's plan seems comprehensive and conservative."

From then on, except for a trip I took to Iraq and Afghanistan during Thanksgiving to visit our National Guard troops and express our appreciation to them, I was talking to House members about our plan, either in groups or in front of an official committee meeting or with countless individuals. I thought Cochran and Lott had the Senate, and while I knew the House leadership was sympathetic, we had to get the votes. There was only one way to get this done, and that was through individual and small group meetings with members in the House. There was no other way. In order to overcome the resistance to doing something that had never been done before and to overcome the resistance to spending billions of dollars of federal money in the Katrina states, I had to explain what was at stake and why it was the right thing for the federal government to do this.

One day, as I entered the House side of the Capitol building, I bumped into Congressman Barney Frank of Massachusetts. He and I hardly knew each other; we had both been on a television panel show one time. Frank called me aside and told me he had heard Mississippi had developed a plan for Katrina recovery. When I confirmed that, Frank told me, "I want to help. Get me your plan, and I'll write a letter to every Democratic Member of the House and ask them to support it." Here I was—a conservative, Southern Republican, and former RNC chairman—and a liberal Democrat from New England offered not only to write his colleagues but in doing so, to put his reputation and credibility on the line, which he did.

I have since thought Barney Frank personified the attitude of not only most in Congress but also of most citizens. Americans wanted to help us the best way they could. His support also reminded me of an important but often ignored adage, "In politics there is no such thing as a permanent enemy. You never know whom you will need to help you or who will be willing, if asked." Not a bad lesson for life, either.

On the Senate side, Thad Cochran was in charge, and few if any senators were of a mind to question what he wanted to do for the states hit by Katrina. Senate Republican Leader Bill Frist of Tennessee was supportive. We had made the decision how to provide the money to the states—through the block grant programs—and now was the time to determine what legislative vehicle we could use to pass the bill. Because of concern about opposition from some Republicans in the House, we worried about passing the bill as a stand-alone measure. We needed what we lobbyists call "must-pass" legislation to which we could attach our appropriation as an amendment.

We got yet another break when it became clear in the closing months of 2005 that the president had to have a new appropriations bill to continue funding the wars in Afghanistan and Iraq. And he needed that bill to pass by the end of the year, or funding for the Pentagon would expire. The man responsible for managing that supplemental defense spending bill, for determining whether or not it would pass, was the chairman of the Senate Appropriations Committee: Thad Cochran.

We had our "must-pass" legislation, especially after the chairman of the Defense Appropriations Subcommittee, Senator Ted Stevens from Alaska, told Cochran he would not oppose our amendment. Stevens had himself served as chairman of Senate Appropriations, and he wanted to support Cochran and his leadership. Ranking committee

Democrat Senator Dan Inouye also supported Cochran's bill. Using the Defense bill also gave us grounds for a great argument for those who wanted to oppose our plan: you are willing to spend hundreds of billions of dollars in a foreign country but unwilling to spend far less to rebuild your own country?

We had our plan. We had our proposal to spend the money. We had our legislative vehicle to enact the spending. We had our deadline, since the end of the year is the Christmas season. We all knew no member of Congress wanted to spend the holidays in Washington. So we had a deadline with some punch. And what became clear to everyone as the days brought us closer to the end of the year was that Thad Cochran was not going to back down but was going to support Mississippi's request all the way, even if that meant scuttling the Defense appropriations bill.

House members knew Cochran had the support of the Senate, and they knew he wasn't going to back down. They knew when I made my pitch I was speaking for the senator. There was no daylight between Cochran and me. And as he told the influential *Roll Call* newspaper, "I am prepared to use all the power I have. These needs can't be postponed." In an interview for this book, Cochran's then chief of staff, Mark Keenum, explained why Cochran's position was so important: "As chairman of the Appropriations Committee, Senator Cochran had a lot of power . . . He held the pen that wrote the numbers; and Senator Cochran wrote the numbers that the governor needed."

In passing something like our proposal, it helps to take advantage of every opportunity. One was the work of the various congressional committees investigating the response of the federal government to the hurricane and the breakdown of FEMA's logistics. The work of these committees kept Washington's attention on the issue and helped sell our argument that the government should do something to make amends for what it had failed to do in the aftermath of Katrina's landfall. I was joined at one hearing by a delegation from Mississippi, including Gulfport mayor Brent Warr, Waveland mayor

Tommy Longo, Harrison County emergency director Joe Spraggins, Hancock County emergency director Bobby Strahan, and our own MEMA director, Robert Latham. It was difficult for House members to hear those testimonies and not be moved to ultimately honor our request.

By the end of November, I was telling the press that delay was our enemy. The winter was almost upon us, and thousands of Mississippians did not have adequate housing. The feelings in Mississippi were summed up by a *Sun Herald* editorial that argued that Congress should not take a holiday until it passed the relief legislation for Katrina victims. During one of President Bush's trips to the Coast, the *Sun Herald* committed its front page to an editorial entitled, "An Appeal to the President of the United States: It Is Time to Renew the Commitment and Rekindle the Compassion."

That being said, folks opposing our request would plant stories in Capitol Hill newspapers, like the one that appeared in *Roll Call*:

"The needs of the Gulf Coast are real and deserve to be addressed, [while] balancing the proposed spending against other needs and the goal of being fiscally prudent," said a Senate GOP leadership aide. "I think there's going to be some push-back," said one aide to a House GOP conservative, given that the House conservatives called on leaders to offset the costs of rebuilding the Gulf Coast. The aide also questioned whether the House and Senate leadership's current strategy of using the must-pass Department of Defense appropriations bill to carry the Katrina reallocation, along with emergency spending for bird flu preparedness and home heating assistance, will fly with conservatives who are increasingly concerned about what they see as out-of-control Congressional spending.

The *Sun Herald* even quoted a congressional staffer as saying that Mississippi's congressional delegation was in "panic mode." Meanwhile, the White House's budget office was telling anyone who would listen that their $17 billion proposal was sufficient.

The December 2005 Offensive

As we left the Thanksgiving holidays behind, the proposal became more complicated because the appropriations bill had to factor in not only all of the states hit by Katrina but also new damage inflicted on Texas and western Louisiana by the late-September Hurricane Rita, and it would only provide funding for the upcoming fiscal year, while our Mississippi proposal of $33 billion was a multiyear proposal. In the end, the key fight became twofold—how much money would be appropriated for the first year of the recovery and would we be able to use some of the money coming to Mississippi to provide grants to homeowners outside of the flood zone to rebuild their homes.

So our goal for the month of December was to convince the Republicans in the House to join Cochran in approving our request. And in that quest we had many friends and allies. Congressional delegations from Texas, Louisiana, and Alabama joined with ours to uniformly support Cochran's proposal. Lobbyists with companies and organizations in these states testified to the enormity of the problem. Congressional staff worked with us every step of the way, asking us to help them think through tough drafting issues. As for our constant meetings with House members, Roger Wicker summed up our strategy: "The relief we were asking for was unprecedented. A lot of members of Congress didn't understand the justification until we repeated it over and over."

In early December I told the press, "We are at a point where our recovery and renewal efforts are stalled because of inaction in Washington, D.C. The delay has created uncertainty that is having very negative effects on our recovery and rebuilding. It is taking the starch out of people who've worked so hard to help themselves and their neighbors." At the same time we were pushing for the appropriations legislation, other committees were working on the Medicaid appropriation and the tax-incentive or GO Zone legislation, which passed a first test in the House in early December by gaining approval by a margin of 415–4.

Trent Lott and Gene Taylor did a great job during the fall of carry-ing our message to the press, that what the president was proposing was insufficient. They were so vocal and so articulate that it let me play the proverbial "good cop" role. Typical of Lott's comments came in early December: "Mr. President, the recovery is not going exactly right. We've dusted ourselves off and are working to restore our in-frastructure and residential and business tax base, but . . . we need your leadership to ensure that the federal government fulfills its com-mitment to help Mississippians get back on their feet."

Roger Wicker and Chip Pickering chose to focus on the delegations that had a stake in the federal government's appropriately respond-ing to the megadisaster, and they did so very effectively. We had com-bined the needs of Texas, Louisiana, Mississippi, and Alabama for the ensuing fiscal year into one proposal; had come up with a figure of $35 billion for one year only; had secured the support of those con-gressional delegations; had refined our message; and now we had to spend as much time as it would take educating key members of the House. That fell to me as well as to all of the delegation members. While I made clear publicly that we thought we needed more money, I also made clear that was our final position.

Pickering and Wicker decided to up the ante in December with a private meeting with Speaker Hastert. They had polled their fellow Republican members in adjoining Southern states and took a mes-sage to the Speaker: "Until Katrina funding gets done, we will block any rule that would authorize debate on the House floor on any other measure. We have the votes to do it, and we are going to die in this ditch." Pickering's point was there were enough GOP votes from Mississippi, Louisiana, Alabama, and Texas to shut down the House. He was clear, and Cochran was holding the defense bill and would settle for nothing less than the $35 billion. There was no daylight.

On December 14, the White House tried to undercut Cochran by increasing their funding proposal to $24 billion. They were begin-ning to see the need to resolve this fight, knowing that Cochran was holding tight. And by this time, all of the southern delegations were working in tandem. The question now became: Who was going to blink first? Cochran made clear it would not be him. Ever.

And we now knew the Speaker wanted to help the White House, but he also had a House to run; he wanted to be fiscally responsible, but he also knew about the bad press on the Coast and elsewhere; and he needed to move beyond Katrina because the midterm elections were coming up and the focus needed to change. Midterm elections are when majorities are lost, and the House leadership was beginning to realize they needed to be responsive to Katrina and put this fight behind them. Our deadline was working.

By the middle of December, we were making progress. Leaders in the House had allowed me to meet privately with the Republican Whip Organization, the group of members who count votes among their peers. The House Appropriations chairman agreed to attach the Katrina funding to the Defense bill and agreed to several of our key programs, including funding for the housing program. Then things started happening pretty quickly. The deadline was fast approaching. As Mark Keenum put it, "Deadlines make things happen." Leaders in the House approached Cochran with a possible compromise level of $29 billion, and I got a phone call from the Speaker's office. Hastert and I had met early on so I could brief him on our request. I was transparent with him then: the law didn't provide anything like what we needed, and more members were agreeing with us as they learned about our situation.

We were a week away from Christmas when I got the call on Friday from Mike Stokke, Hastert's political aide, who told me that later that evening the Speaker would want to talk with me. After making my rounds of talking with House members that day, I made my way to Cochran's office and waited for the call. As it turned out, it was near midnight by the time we got the call, and it took about ten minutes for Jim Perry and me to walk from Cochran's office in the Dirksen Senate Office Building to the Speaker's office in the Capitol. We assumed the meeting would be all about resolving issues and developing a plan to come to closure.

Republican majority leader Roy Blunt, who was also in this meeting, had earlier raised a concern brought to him from private insurers about our housing proposal. A sticking point among these companies was that if the government paid for people's houses when they were destroyed by a disaster, people would quit buying homeowner's insurance. If it got out that sixty thousand people on the Mississippi Gulf Coast got the equivalent of an insurance check, others might say, "Well, man, I'm going to quit buying homeowner's insurance." And Blunt told me early on, "This is a problem."

At our midnight meeting, I told Blunt that under our program, in order for someone to get a federal grant, he or she had to meet three requirements: you had to be outside the flood zone, you had to have had homeowner's insurance, and you had to agree to carry flood insurance for the future or elevate out of the flood zone. That made Blunt comfortable with supporting us.

Denny Hastert and I had a very friendly, warm relationship, and he was a great ally. He was a former high school wrestling coach. Levelheaded, calm. Tried to do what he thought was right. He had a lot of authority because people trusted him. And I had known Roy Blunt more than ten years.

Although we were friends, in the Speaker's office at midnight a week before Christmas, they wanted to know more details in the bill: why CDBG, what about insurance, how would the programs work. They were interested in how the provisions would be implemented. It was all public policy. They were getting comfortable with the amount of money and how we could defend that amount. In the end, the Speaker became convinced and called House Appropriations Committee chairman, Jerry Lewis, before we left and said, "This is over. We need to get this done." I walked back to Cochran's office early on Saturday morning, where Mark Keenum and a few other staffers were waiting with a celebratory drink.

While this was a huge breakthrough, the devil is always in the details. Cochran asked if we could live with the $29 billion compromise offered by the House, and I said yes, so long as we could work through the many small decisions to make sure the language of the bill would give us the flexibility we needed to move forward with the programs we had outlined, in particular the allocation of CDBG dollars. We could make $29 billion work if Louisiana didn't get all the block grant money. The legislation did not specify how much each state would get, and if we were not careful, I could envision a scenario in which the overwhelming share would get funneled to Louisiana. Based on their September plan, they certainly thought they were entitled to get the lion's share of the money. We knew how much we needed for the first year (about $5 billion), and we knew how much CDBG would be allocated in the final bill ($11.5 billion). So Cochran's staff made sure there was language in the bill that limited the amount of CDBG funding that any state could receive to 54 percent of the total. As Les Spivey said in an interview for this book, "That is the strongest language that we've ever written. Those few words. Probably over 90 percent would have gone to Louisiana without that provision. Mississippi would get a few scraps and Alabama and Texas a few things here and there. But putting that language in there is how we got our money. The devil is always in the details." While we wanted $5.4 billion, the compromise gave us $5.2 billion. That was enough to get the job done for a year; then we were confident there would be future, smaller appropriation bills for Katrina relief.

Saturday, then, was a good day all around. Even though the newspapers were writing articles about the differences between the two Houses, they were twenty-four hours behind the story. We knew $29 billion was the figure, as was the $11.5 billion CDBG amount. Cochran and Lewis agreed on the figure during a meeting on Saturday and then spent the day working through all the details. Members and staff from both appropriations committees started drafting the language while Lott finalized the tax-incentive legislation.

As for the GO Zone legislation, the House prevailed on its insistence that casinos be cut out of the tax-incentive package, although Lott was able to secure a compromise that would allow the casino companies to take tax breaks to rebuild their hotels and restaurants but not their gaming halls. The bill, approved by voice vote in the House and Senate, would allow states hit by Katrina and Rita to offer tax-exempt bonds to rebuild infrastructure through "opportunity zones" or the geographical areas most damaged by the storms. In Mississippi alone, close to $5 billion of GO Zone bonds were issued for more than eighty construction or financing projects. The legislation contained a variety of other federal tax breaks that provided the kind of economic incentives businesses needed to rebuild and expand and create jobs that could fuel our recovery. While I have given more attention to passing the appropriation bill, chiefly because it was by far the most controversial part of our package, I don't want to minimize the significance of the GO Zone legislation and how much it contributed to our eventual recovery. Although it never garnered the public attention that a multi-billion-dollar housing grant program could generate, the bill's many tax provisions fueled thousands of individual decisions by Mississippi businesses that led to the kind of rebuilding effort we had to have.

Sunday morning's *Sun Herald* had the story from Cochran's office we all remember: "We have a deal, Sen. Cochran told his weary staff. They'd endured an all-night marathon of negotiations Friday and a week of intense haggling to overcome concerns about the spending by House GOP leadership and a lack of support from the White House. It was less than the $35 billion Cochran wanted but far more than Bush's $17 billion." The article quoted me as saying, "It's not everything we asked for, nor is it all we need, but it's an amount that we can use to do the most important things facing us."

Then on Monday, with less than a week before Christmas, we caught one final break. The compromise had been reduced to legislation on Sunday by staffers on both sides of the Capitol. The House went first, took the bill up early, passed it, and moved it over to the Senate, though it came with a very controversial provision attached to it that had nothing to do with Katrina relief. Representatives in the House had added language to allow for oil and gas drilling in Alaska's Arctic National Wildlife Refuge, a cause that state's senior senator, Ted

Stevens, had pushed for as long as I had known him. Stevens decided to go all out and try to force the Senate to keep the drilling provision—described by the *Washington Post* as "the mother of all pet projects"—in the bill. This was easily the most hotly debated environmental issue in Congress at the time, and by raising it front and center in the closing days of 2005, Stevens and his allies did us a favor by diverting attention away from the hurricane-relief funding. All of a sudden the media's attention and congressional debate was focused on Ted Stevens, the Alaska wilderness, and drilling. Our package was, mercifully, off the radar screen.

Even though we had less than a week before Christmas, Stevens forced the Senate to debate the issue for two days while Democrats and some moderate Republicans were threatening to derail the whole enterprise—war funding and all—if drilling stayed in the bill. Stevens, though, knew what he was doing. As chairman of the Armed Services Committee, he was the lead author of the Defense appropriations legislation on which we had hung our Katrina funding. He was also Thad Cochran's predecessor as chairman of the Appropriations Committee and, as such, knew how to use Senate rules governing funding bills to help his state. While he had a lot of favors he could call in, he also had to get sixty votes on a key procedural move to keep drilling alive.

I knew we'd have to let Stevens play this thing out, but I also suspected he wouldn't have the votes. In the end, we would get the bill. In the meantime, on the other side of the issue, environmental groups launched a full frontal attack on the amendment and, while many Democrats joined with the environmentalists, others, such as West Virginia's Robert Byrd, opposed Stevens because they didn't support using an appropriations bill as the vehicle for an issue that had nothing to do with funding the government.

On Wednesday time had run out on debate, and the full Senate had to make a decision. Either Stevens had the votes or he didn't, and when the roll call began I still thought he would lose. Sure enough, he got fifty-six votes, but he needed sixty on the procedural motion to move forward. We were done. Immediately after the vote, Cochran and the GOP leaders huddled on the floor; Stevens agreed to take the language out of the bill, but not before he was allowed a separate up or down vote on the drilling issue, which he lost 45–48. The Senate unanimously passed the final bill containing our unprecedented special disaster assistance package!

The House quickly accepted the Senate changes and sent the bill to the White House. Whether he intended to or not, Stevens had done us a favor. By raising a controversial issue and stringing out the debate well into the week leading up to Christmas, when members of Congress were tired, ready to go home, and willing to vote for almost anything in the bill—except for drilling in Alaska—Stevens helped us. Our Katrina package was not the focus of debate; our package remained intact and became law when President Bush formally signed it on December 30.

The lead story in *Congressional Quarterly Today* on Wednesday gave Cochran and the team the credit:

> After months of lobbying, negotiating and sometimes pleading, Gulf Coast lawmakers are on the brink of winning a much-needed boost for their constituents—at least $29 billion from federal taxpayers for rebuilding levees, schools and highways and aiding state and local governments. That state's lawmakers were helped in recent weeks by influential and frustrated Mississippi officials, who pushed Republican Congressional leaders to provide additional aid before year's end. After months when it appeared that Congress and the Bush Administration had lost interest in rebuilding areas devastated by Hurricane Katrina, appropriators at the last minute came up with legislation that would address many of the infrastructure problems faced by business and community leaders in the region. That happened in part as a result of increased pressure from Mississippi lawmakers, particularly Senate Appropriations Chairman Thad Cochran, who has been dissatisfied with the Bush Administration's funding strategy for the rebuilding effort.

Senator Stevens had helped us, but we had helped ourselves. I have no doubt Cochran would have held out for our $35 billion number. He is a quiet, polite gentleman; but he is tough as nails. And he may have prevailed at $35 billion. We didn't ask him to do that because of something I learned from my old boss, Ronald Reagan, a former union president: In a negotiation, do not require perfection to accept a good deal; if you get 75–80 percent of what you want, take it, and come back for the rest later. Reagan also taught me you must not bid against yourself. Reagan would set up his position, and then he would refuse counteroffers until he got what he considered the best deal he could get, if it gave real progress and most of what he needed.

That is how we tried to negotiate our special disaster appropriation: We set up what we needed in an honest way, in this case $35 billion for a year; then we didn't give any ground when the White House raised their offer to $24 billion from $17 billion. We didn't budge; in fact, we loudly said we'd take nothing less than $35 billion. We took the House offer of $29 billion, more than 80 percent of what we had requested, but we were only able to do so because of the limitation that no state could get more than 54 percent of the first-round of money. That gave Mississippi about 97 percent of what we had fought for. Accepting that compromise was not a hard decision, especially since we knew there would be more rounds of disaster appropriations in the coming years.

The whole week was a good one for Mississippi: Congress completed work on the tax-incentive legislation—the Gulf Opportunity Zone Act of 2005—which the president signed on Tuesday. On Monday the conferees crafting the legislation that would permit the federal government to cover a portion of our Medicaid match agreed on a conference report, which the House approved that day. The Senate took it up but postponed a final vote until the New Year, which they then approved and which the president signed in February. That single piece of legislation alone freed up nearly $600 million in our state budget for other recovery priorities.

As the year ended, Congress had come through for Mississippi and the many victims of Hurricane Katrina. The delegations from the stricken states had worked together as one.

I missed the final Senate vote because I had returned home to pick up Marsha and drive to Birmingham where Celeste, the wife of our older son, Sterling, was scheduled to give birth to our first grandchild. He was born Thursday afternoon, December 22, at St. Vincent Hospital, part of the large UAB Medical Center downtown. They named the healthy little boy Adyn Sterling Barbour. I was a grateful man that Christmas of 2005.

CHAPTER 8

Christmas 2005

A BILOXI *SUN HERALD* PHOTOGRAPHER captured the scene that appears on the back cover of this book and that Marsha and I used as the cover of our 2005 Christmas card. While we wanted to remember the damage and heartache, we also wanted to recognize the progress we had made and the hopeful and enduring spirit of the Mississippi people. We thought there was no better verse from the Bible to use on the card than Jeremiah 31:7: "There is hope for your future, says the Lord. Your children will come again to their own land."

Christmas came to the Gulf Coast three days early in 2005: the Imperial Palace, or IP, as it is known in Biloxi, became the first casino to reopen its doors after Katrina's landfall. As the Biloxi *Sun Herald* put it, "The racket of slot machines never sounded so beautiful." Larry Gregory was executive director of the Mississippi Gaming Commission at the time, and early on the morning of December 22, he had signed the papers indicating IP had met all the regulatory requirements to reopen. He remembered looking out of his hotel window later that day, wondering if anyone would show up, and instead seeing cars backed up on the interstate, waiting to park and enter the casino. The surge of people was so great that special crowd control measures had to be quickly adopted and put into place.

Four days later, the Isle of Capri's general manager, Bill Kilduff, cut the ribbon on his newly renovated and rebuilt casino and resort. As a result of the law passed by the Legislature back in early October, he welcomed "thousands" of guests to the first casino built on land in Mississippi with "let the good times roll!" Other casinos would open throughout the spring and summer, bringing jobs and tourists back to the Coast and the kind of economic stimulus the region desperately needed. In addition to the psychological boost these large businesses had on the Gulf Coast, getting them open provided hundreds of jobs at the facilities and hundreds of other indirect jobs. Not only were jobs coming back as a result of the casinos, but all the repair and renovation and new construction projects that were underway by the end of the year were generating their own fair share of jobs.

The end of 2005 also meant the end of one of the most tumultuous school semesters in the history of education in our state.

Education and Schools

I have highlighted earlier in this book the many ways in which the timing of Hurricane Katrina coincided fortuitously with people in positions of leadership who would make a difference. Mississippi's senior U.S. senator, Thad Cochran, was chairman of the Appropriations Committee. Mississippi's other U.S. senator, Trent Lott, lost his Gulf Coast home and used his position as a ranking member of the Senate Finance Committee and former Senate majority leader to our state's advantage. The chairman of the Mississippi Gaming Commission, Jerry St. Pé, was a Gulf Coast business leader who had lived through earlier hurricanes.

Then there was Hank Bounds, who had been named state superintendent of education in June of 2005. Although in his thirties—young for a state superintendent—Bounds had come to the State Department from Jackson County, where he had been a principal and then Pasca-goula district superintendent for six years. He had been through ear-lier hurricane warnings and evacuations and knew virtually all of the region's school officials because of his involvement in the Gulf Coast Education Initiative Consortium, an organization of every superinten-dent from every district south of Hattiesburg.

Because Bounds had served on the Coast and had been active in the consortium, he knew all of the superintendents, and they knew him. So when Bounds took a leadership role in coordinating the re-covery, it was a natural fit. The superintendents were all friends and could cry and yell at each other and not take it personally. Bounds remembered one school superintendent who "got mad at me a dozen times and he called me back a dozen times and said, 'Hank, you know I'm not mad at you. I'm just upset for my kids.'"

Bounds had started his first official day on the job on August 1. Twenty-eight days later, he was leading a system of elementary and secondary education that had nearly 450,000 students out of school, or 90 percent of our state's children who attended public schools. Of the state's 152 school districts, only 14 did not experience "missed days" as a result of the storm. More than 260 schools in half of the districts were damaged to some extent. In the lower 6 counties, 16 schools were destroyed and another 24 severely damaged while the 80,000 children who attended these schools, and their parents, had no idea how, when, or where school would resume.

Bounds said in an interview for this book, "In previous hurricane years, we might lose a roof or get some windows blown out or a door blown out or get some water in a building, but did anyone ever antici-pate losing 16 schools? No."

Soon after landfall Bounds and I talked, and we agreed he would coordinate and be responsible for making sure school personnel and students were safe and accounted for, assessing the damage to school property, and, most important, finding a way to get students back in school as soon as possible in a reasonably "normal" educational envi-ronment. As I did with virtually every other department head with whom I worked, I told Bounds to call me if he needed anything; otherwise, I wouldn't bother him. As I came to learn, whenever I saw Bounds's number show up on my cell phone, he was calling with a specific problem that I needed to handle.

In the week after the storm, Marsha told me about the first conversation she had ever had with Bounds. She was somewhere on the Coast and reached Bounds, who was driving to Pascagoula, on his cell phone. She told him she had learned that the Harrison County School System office had a huge freezer full of food, that people had no food, but the freezer was locked. Her question to Bounds was, "Can you suggest how I might deal with that?" Marsha loved his response, "Find someone with bolt cutters. Cut the locks off. Use the food. If someone gets upset about it, blame me."

Bounds and I agreed about the three keys to recovery: people had to have a place to live, a job, and a school for their children. And as Bounds liked to tell me, he was not going to be the leg of the stool that delayed a community from turning back on.

A week or so later, I had a number of agency heads with me, including Bounds, for one of our daily press briefings in Jackson. As we are walking down the hall to the press conference, I looked over at him and said, "Well, Mr. Superintendent, what can I tell the state and the nation about when we can expect to get all the schools open?" He stopped me dead in my tracks when he said, "No later than mid-October." In fact, I remember stopping so quickly that people following me actually ran into me. "Surely you don't want me to tell people that!" And he said, "Governor, we'll get them open. Some of them won't be in the same buildings they were originally in, but schools will be open." I didn't think he could get it done, so I didn't mention what he had said at the press conference. Now I know I should have.

Two to three weeks after the storm, most Mississippi schools north of Interstate 10 were open. Six weeks after the storm, in mid-October, all districts in the state except one on the Gulf Coast—Bay–Waveland in Hancock County, the hardest-hit area of the storm—were back open. Bay–Waveland accepted students on November 7, and it would have been able to accept students in October if their temporary classrooms had arrived on time.

Not only was opening schools a challenge, but dealing with the way in which families had relocated because of temporary housing meant students were attending different schools. In fact, by the first of November, almost ten thousand students were attending different schools from the ones they attended before the storm including many from Louisiana. Mississippi reopened all of its public schools before New Orleans had reopened any of its schools. It was an incredible achievement, so I want to outline how Hank and his team did it.

First, everyone associated with the schools effort gave this the urgency it needed, in the same way as others in our recovery effort. They dropped everything else and focused exclusively on working with local officials to get schools back up and running.

Second, Hank and his staff literally moved their offices into the old Central High School in downtown Jackson and worked every day for the next month. They brought in cots, opened up a kitchen, and never let up.

Third, they created communication networks among the superintendents so everyone would know what was available from MEMA and FEMA and what everyone else was doing. Sharing information and challenges was critical to the recovery. The Gulf Coast Consortium had its first meeting a week after landfall and became a communications hub for the recovery in the south. Meetings with groups of superintendents and individual superintendents were held once or twice a week. Communication became essential because different FEMA case officers were assigned to different schools, so if one district was getting a particular kind of FEMA assistance through one case officer and another school district was not getting similar help through a different case officer, the differences could be resolved.

Hank remembered the first meeting of the superintendents along the Coast:

I recall very few dry eyes in the room. Everyone was very emotional. The Bay St. Louis and Pass Christian superintendents were saying they had lost everything, but their staff and teachers needed to be paid. And they were sitting there hand-writing paychecks to hundreds of employees and just sobbing because their school districts had been obliterated and some teachers and students were still missing. Hard to imagine it could even happen. And there's just every emotion in the room, from deep sorrow because they had lost children or lost faculty members or lost friends or relatives to wondering how were they going to run schools. I said to the group that we've got to find a way to get the schools open. If we are going to survive this, we've got to get schools open so parents can clean up and find jobs. And the turning point in the meeting was when Harrison County Superintendent Henry Arledge stood up and said, "Hank's right. Let's get the schools back open."

Fourth, they created specific teams to focus on specific issues—textbooks, portable classrooms, buses and transportation, insurance and FEMA issues, counselors for working with traumatized students, classroom equipment, and supplies. Individuals were given specific tasks and accepted specific responsibilities within the team, regardless of any job title they may have had prior to the storm. One team was organized to locate all of the students, teachers, and staff and make sure everyone was accounted for. Another team worked with local schools throughout the state to ensure that students who had left the Coast and were living temporarily in a different school district could attend school in that district.

Yet another team connected school districts outside of Mississippi that wanted to "adopt" schools in the state as well as volunteers who wanted to donate anything they could to help. Chevron stepped up and donated the funds necessary to build the website and software that helped make all this happen. Milton Kuykendall, the superintendent of suburban DeSoto County, which is adjacent to Memphis but in Mississippi, called Bounds one day and told him he could have seven buses and as many classroom chairs as he could handle. Bounds also met with Crockett DuBose, the chief of staff of the Galena Park School, which serves an area of Houston, Texas. Even though the school had low-income kids, they saved "their pennies and nickels" and delivered more than $10,000 to Pascagoula schools along with two trailer trucks of equipment and volunteers who spent more than a week helping to clean and get schools ready.

If you think about it, the issues were enormously complex. Opening up portable classrooms meant dealing with site preparation, getting electric service, finding water and wastewater hookups (most of which had been destroyed throughout the coastal area by the floodwaters), making sure the classrooms were handicap accessible, creating dining facilities, including kitchens from scratch, and supplying the classrooms with supplies and equipment (which we couldn't get on the Coast because all the stores had been destroyed). On top of that, we had to find buses that worked, and fuel for the buses, and— even more important, we had to identify routes where children were living in a geographical area that had no resemblance to the streets and neighborhoods prior to landfall. And since everyone knew these temporary classrooms would have to last at least a year until the new schools could be rebuilt, we all wanted to make sure they could stand the test of time.

Speaking of fuel for buses, I remember at one point, a week or so after the storm, getting complaints from metro-Jackson area schools that they were ready to accept students but couldn't get fuel for their local buses. A quick call to Bounds's office revealed he had directed the limited fuel we had in the state at the time to the Gulf Coast where search and rescue and recovery were still underway. Being able to prioritize and make choices is critical for a successful recovery program.

Because of the speed with which students returned to school, Hank was repeatedly asked for tours from officials all over the country. He told me of the time in December he gave the U.S. Treasurer a tour of schools in Jackson County. At the last school in St. Martin, Bounds walked into the school, introduced the treasurer, and then asked the kids some questions for the benefit of their guest. How many of you lost your home or were flooded by Katrina? Everyone raised their hand. How many of you are now living with a relative? A few students raised their hands. How many of you live in a FEMA trailer? A few others raised their hand. Before he could go on to other questions, "a little kid grabs my pants leg and says, 'Hey, mister, you didn't name where I live.' And the treasurer says to the boy, this is like a fourth grader, well where do you live? And he said, 'Oh, we're in a tent.'" Now, this is December, and it's cold outside, raining, and this boy and his family were still waiting on a FEMA trailer, as were many others through the winter.

Of all the times Bounds called my cell phone, and there were plenty, the one that meant the most in terms of dollars to Mississippi came after Congress had approved the special legislation appropriating money to our schools. We left Congress in December, thinking that Mississippi would get about $300 million.

But, as we all know, the devil is in the details. Under the legislation, Secretary of Education Margaret Spellings had the authority to draft the regulations detailing the way in which states would get reimbursed. Well, as Bounds told me after the first of the year, Margaret had developed regulations based on "dislocated" students, and under the regulations Mississippi would get closer to $30 million because our students were no longer "dislocated" as described in the regulation. Rather than provide funds to schools that were back online and accepting students, the department was proposing to give all of the money to schools that had accepted dislocated students. In other words, we would be punished for getting kids back in their own schools so soon, even though those school systems had lost virtually all of the property tax base they needed to financially support their schools. This was certainly not what we had intended in the appropriations bill Congress had passed back in December.

As Bounds explained, he had had several discussions with Spellings, and she wasn't budging. I was scheduled to be in Washington later in the week, so Hank and I met that morning in Rep. John Boehner's office. He wasn't the Speaker then but was chairman of the House Committee on Education and the Workforce, the committee that would have jurisdiction and oversight of these funds. He said he would take care of this, but first he asked that we visit with Spellings and get her side of the story.

I had known Spellings for a number of years, early on, when she was Gov. George W. Bush's policy director in Texas, and we were able to get an appointment with her later in the afternoon. After Bounds described our position, I argued emphatically that the special appropriations bill was not written to punish a school district that had overcome all kinds of hardships to reopen in record time. She started to see this was something her staff should have thought about and hadn't. While there was still some resistance, I left confident that she was going to tell her staff that the regulations should recognize schools that had reopened. She knew Boehner would support us on this, and I suspect she knew the White House would as well. A few weeks later I learned that the regulations had been rewritten. Mississippi ended up receiving $323 million for our K–12 schools.

Thanks to FEMA money and the funds received through the special appropriations, schools were repaired or rebuilt, teachers and staff were paid, and most districts were largely reimbursed for revenue they would have lost because their property tax bases had been all but obliterated. The Bay–Waveland lower and upper elementary schools were rebuilt and opened in the summer of 2010 while two new elementary schools were built in the Hancock County district and opened in September 2008. In Harrison County, new facilities in D'Iberville and West Harrison High School were finished in summer 2009. Both of these schools were hardened to serve as storm shelters, are able to hold up to 2,500 people, and can withstand 200-mph winds. Pass Christian finished the elementary and middle schools in August 2009 while Long Beach finished construction on its elementary school in November 2009. New schools were completed in Gulfport, Biloxi, and Jackson County, all opening between 2007 and 2009. These new schools, plus many renovated schools, offered at least some compensation for what our boys and girls had to endure in the fall of 2005. By the 2009–10 school year, K–12 enrollment in the lower six counties was just a little short of where it was pre-landfall.

Our postsecondary institutions enjoyed similar results. The University of Southern Mississippi's Gulf Park Campus in Long Beach sustained major damage to every building, but by the fall of 2010 the campus had surpassed previous enrollment records. Since Katrina, the campus has repaired almost 140,000 square feet of classroom and office space of the original 270,000 square feet lost. And by the fall of 2010, Mississippi Gulf Coast Community College had reached 95 percent of its pre-Katrina enrollment.

Sometime in the fall I received a call from a friend, George Argyros, a self-made billionaire who had made his fortune doing real estate development in Orange County. Argyros, a former U.S. ambassador to Spain, said he wanted to help. After several conversations about all of the needs we had, he landed on postsecondary education. He came to the Coast, toured the Gulf Park Campus and made a $1 million contribution toward its rebuilding effort.

In the years following Katrina, all the coastal districts had achieved high scores on the state's accountability assessments; in fact, for the 2005–6 year, the schools that showed the greatest academic progress were the ones that sustained the most damage on the Coast.

Bounds remembered a reporter from one of the national educational publications who called about a month after the storm, asking about the tests, "What were you going to do about state tests?" Bounds's response was nicer than mine might have been: "If you visited this place, you would never ask me that question. I don't give a hoot about a test, and if I have anything to do with it, we won't take a test in this state this year. We've got kids who we still can't find. We're still missing 400 students. I don't know if they are in harm's way, but we just can't find them. We've got kids living in tents, living in gyms, living with other people and no end in sight to this, and the worst possible conditions. No six year old should ever have to endure any-thing like this, and you're asking me about a test?"

I wholeheartedly agree with something Bounds said in his inter-view for this book: "Superintendents and principals, especially on the Coast, deserve a hero's welcome because of the work they did to lead their school districts and get them open and provide for the needs of the students, because they all lost their homes too."

Transportation

I thought about whether I should even try to describe the scene in this book: standing on Highway 90 in Gulfport two days after the storm, looking at the Grand Casino, a 2,000-ton barge that had three days earlier been moored in the Gulf's water—now resting on the highway. Neither words nor photographs can do justice to what everyone felt who was staring at it.

Butch Brown, the executive director of Mississippi's Department of Transportation and the man responsible for getting Highway 90 back in operation, looked over at Wayne Brown, the elected trans-portation commissioner for the Southern District, and said, "Wayne, we've got to get rid of that boat." As Butch told me later, he was thinking, "How do we move it?" Well, as it turned out, Wayne knew of a contractor on the Coast who wouldn't move it but would cut it up and haul off the pieces. After working out the details with the ca-sino's owners and the insurance companies, Wayne's friend had the Grand out of the way in less than a week.

North of Interstate 10, the Transportation Department faced the huge task of clearing debris from virtually every state and federal highway in the southern half of the state. Its crews essentially pushed the debris off the roads to make them passable, knowing they could come clear the right-of-way later. The greater challenges, however, were along the Coast: Part of the interstate had washed away in Jack-son County, creating huge traffic bottlenecks for people trying to get to Mississippi from Alabama and Florida; the Interstate 110 draw bridge, connecting Interstate 10 to Biloxi and Highway 90, was left inoperable by Katrina; Highway 90, the main artery from one end of the Coast to the other was impassable, with much of the actual road-bed washed away; and the two biggest bridges, as I described in an earlier chapter, no longer existed. Over the next thirty months the department spent close to $1.3 billion rebuilding our transportation infrastructure.

Twenty days after landfall Interstate 10 was fully open, and two weeks later Interstate 110 was back in operation. Another two weeks later much of Highway 90 had at least two open lanes for traffic (all four lanes were rebuilt by January 2006). With the full backing of his commission and the Federal Highway Administration officials—whom Butch Brown couldn't praise enough in an interview for this book—Brown executed contracts that gave substantial incentives to companies that finished ahead of schedule and imposed substantial penalties if they were late. T. L. Wallace Construction, of Columbia, Mississippi, completed the work on the two legs of the interstates well ahead of schedule.

Recognizing he had to run several major rebuilding projects at the same time, Brown and his staff brought in URS Corporation, a major national engineering firm, to serve as project manager for the two bridges, and they contracted the construction to two separate companies. In the spirit of other agency heads and officials who have been portrayed in this book and who understood that any delay could hinder the recovery, Brown's conversation with a friend at URS went like this:

BUTCH BROWN: Your firm has been recommended to help us in reconstruction and we need your firm to be project manager on two bridges. Can y'all handle that, and how soon can you have someone over here?
URS: Let me see what I can do.

BROWN: How long is it going to take for you to get back with me?

URS: I'll be back within two weeks. We'll have something.

BROWN: I need you at 8:00 in the morning.

According to Butch, URS spent the night pulling engineers from projects all over the country, and when they had a meeting the next day, URS was on the job.

Not long after Cotton Fore, a local contractor, had begun to tear out all the remaining piers of the Bay St. Louis bridge, Butch got a call from Congressman Gene Taylor: "I want all of that rubble. I want you to build me two fishing islands." As a result, virtually all of the demolished pieces from the bridges ended up being used to construct new fishing habitat near Bay St. Louis.

As I mentioned earlier, Mississippi is the only state in the country that vests all of its highway maintenance and construction with a three-member commission independently elected from individual districts. There is no department in state government that is more closely aligned with its counterpart in the federal government than a state highway agency, and there is probably no more complicated and complex set of federal regulations than those having to do with the connection between the Federal Highway Administration and a state transportation agency. And when you add to this mix a strong executive director, you have the possibility that infighting, turf wars, and bureaucratic imperatives could have easily overtaken our overwhelming need to rebuild our highway and bridge infrastructure. But all three elected commissioners—Bill Minor, Dick Hall, and Wayne Brown—our Federal Highway Administration state director, Andy Hughes, and Butch Brown set all of that aside and worked as a team to deliver results in record time. Spending more than a billion dollars in less than three years to essentially rebuild the major highway corridors for South Mississippi—and to do it in a way that clearly is better than what we had before—speaks volumes about what public officials can do when everyone is working together.

The Middle East

While thousands of men and women served their state with distinction and honor as members of our National Guard during the days and weeks following Katrina's landfall, Mississippi had more than three thousand of our soldiers stationed in the Middle East as part of the War on Terror in Iraq and Afghanistan. Thanks to a special effort by Gen. Harold Cross and many others at the Pentagon, I was able to join the governors of Georgia, Michigan, and Kansas on a trip to the war zones to spend Thanksgiving 2005 with the troops. Cross and I spent Thanksgiving Day on helicopters visiting Mississippi soldiers operating in four bases outside of Baghdad. That evening the other three governors and I had the privilege of serving Thanksgiving dinner to all of the troops in a huge commissary on the main American base in Baghdad.

Throughout that day, I was struck by the number of men and women who had families back in Mississippi who were recovering from the devastation of Katrina, all of whom wanted to know details about their particular hometowns but who also felt a sense of duty to serve their country. Hearing the individual stories and realizing the sacrifices these families were making at the time was about the most humbling experience I had as governor.

The New Year

The day after the Legislature convened in 2006, we did something a little different. The legislative leadership allowed me and several of the department heads involved in the recovery to stand in the well of the House of Representatives and answer questions from any legislator about what we had done the previous four months and what our prospects were going forward. I made opening remarks before we took questions.

We were about to receive unprecedented appropriations and other funding from the federal government to help our recovery. The

Barksdale Commission would be presenting its report in the next week, though its work was already being put to use throughout South Mississippi. Casinos had begun to reopen, jobs were returning, and kids were back in classrooms.

It seemed important to talk not only about all these and other accomplishments but also to state frankly that we were still in the middle of the recovery stage. Not only were tens of thousands of Mississippi citizens still in FEMA trailers, there were thousands more still awaiting a FEMA trailer. There were mountains of debris still to be cleared in certain areas, and lots of kids were attending school in portable classrooms. There were many unsatisfactory conditions across South Mississippi and especially on the Coast, so it was no surprise some questions from legislators were direct and even testy at times. But what had become apparent to us, and was slowly becoming apparent to others, was that recovery, especially on the Coast, would take years.

At the same time, I believe I got across to the legislators but also the media and the public that real progress had been made; that we were receiving incredibly generous support from the federal government, our sister states, corporations, and individuals were helping through record charitable giving and outpouring of volunteers; and all this was being put to good use and making a difference. I assured our legislators with no reservations that our state employees had performed magnificently and were a group they could be proud of.

The questions with the most emotion behind them focused on housing. There were tens of thousands of Mississippi families who had spent Christmas in FEMA trailers, hotel rooms, and other makeshift arrangements. Rebuilding much of the housing infrastructure on the Gulf Coast was going to take longer than any of us wanted. How we tried to address that problem is covered in the next chapter.

CHAPTER 9

The New Year

IN THE FOUR MONTHS SINCE LANDFALL, South Mississippi was beginning to recover. Children were in school; jobs were returning, especially now that some casinos were coming back online; much of the debris was cleared; roads had been rebuilt; and plans were in place to rebuild the two bay bridges on the Gulf Coast. At the same time, FEMA had paid out close to $1 billion toward the recovery and insurance companies had processed more than 200,000 claims totaling $6 billion.

Nevertheless, as Mississippi began 2006, more than 97,000 individuals were living in some 35,000 FEMA trailers. This is why we had devoted the bulk of our special request to Congress to housing. As I previously explained, many of these families had relied—to their detriment—on the federal government's determination that their houses were not in any flood zone and didn't need flood insurance. I believed Congress needed to compensate these individuals for the federal government's miscalculation, and Congress overwhelmingly agreed.

While the appropriation bill signed by President Bush on December 30 provided an unprecedented $2 billion to a special homeowner assistance program in Mississippi, it left the details to be worked out with HUD. It was our good fortune that the HUD secretary was Alphonso Jackson, a friend from my tenure with the Republican National Committee. He used to introduce me as his "brother by another mother." Scott Keller was his deputy with responsibility for the CDBG program, the HUD office that would fine-tune the regulations and provide the oversight for this critically important initiative in our state. Since CDBG funds normally are run through the Mississippi Development Authority (MDA), it became the point agency in state government for these new programs. And just like virtually every other state agency employee who was involved in the recovery, two MDA officials rose to the challenge of creating multi-billion-dollar programs where none has heretofore existed—Terri Hudson, MDA's chief financial officer, and Donna Sanford, MDA's comptroller. They worked with my office, particularly Policy Director Jim Perry and his small team, to create and execute a successful plan.

The key question was, of course, how to distribute $2 billion to homeowners on the Gulf Coast and that led to a huge meeting in Washington with HUD officials. Everyone was seated around a large conference table, thinking through the best ways to make whole (or partly whole) those homeowners who had relied on the federal government's telling them they didn't need flood insurance. The imperative was to get the money into the hands of homeowners as quickly as possible. If we were going to jumpstart the housing recovery and keep families on the Coast, we needed this funding available as soon as possible. But it was at that meeting that we came face to face with the usual HUD way of handling housing grant programs, a way that could delay for months—even years—getting the money into the building pipeline.

Because HUD wanted to ensure that the federal government's money was actually spent on rebuilding or repairing houses, its normal policies effectively would have required Mississippi to get into the construction business, to write checks directly to contractors and subcontractors doing the actual work on a homeowner's house. When you are talking about ten houses, that's one thing, but when you realize we were estimating this program could reach thirty thousand houses, then you can grasp the kind of state bureaucracy we would have had to create to administer a building program of that magnitude. But that's not the worst part. The worst part is that any building program like this would be subject to the provisions of the National Environmental Policy Act.

Which brings us back to the meeting in Washington, when all of my staff met with all of Scott Keller's staff. It became clear to the Mississippi contingent that subjecting thirty thousand individual construction projects to stringent environmental regulations would quickly amount to a bureaucratic nightmare, not to mention the enormous challenges we would face if required to keep track of thirty thousand construction projects. This was obviously not a scenario that was going to result in homeowners getting quick access to this funding.

At this point, the Mississippi group laid out the plan we had proposed to Congress. Our eligibility criteria was consistent with what we had told House Majority Leader Blunt and others in Congress and the Administration, plus we had "going forward" requirements for those who actually would receive a grant. Indeed we thought of it as a replacement for the flood insurance check homeowners would have received from the federal government had they been told they were in a flood zone!

Then something remarkable happened that day in January. The people in the room put the goal first and foremost and asked, "Is there another way we can get this done" that will live up to what I committed to Congress in asking for homeowner assistance? And, sure enough, there was. It was called a compensation program. So long as the State of Mississippi gave the money to the homeowner and did not formally require the homeowner to use it for home repair or construction, we could avoid the reach of the environmental regulations, and we could rely on the decentralized private market—individuals dealing directly with contractors—to handle the rebuilding.

Of course, one aspect of a compensation program meant we couldn't require homeowners who received the grants to spend some or all the money to repair or rebuild their homes, or to build new homes on the Coast, in Mississippi, or anywhere else, for that matter. The money would be akin to insurance proceeds.

Thus, the conundrum: it was important to the Coast and the state to get the population back permanently, and rebuilding was the best way to ensure that folks returned and stayed. So my strong interest was in requiring people to rebuild. But common sense told me using the standard HUD process would leave us in quicksand and bog down the rebuilding for God knows how long. Indeed, we subsequently were told Louisiana and Texas did their programs in a way that forced them to account for the environmental impact, slowing them down so much they were unable to begin general rebuilding for more than a year after us. HUD staff showed us how to fine tune our plan so it qualified as a "compensation" plan that avoided the long delays I feared would cause families to abandon rebuilding on the Coast.

There were further wrinkles. For example, in order to make sure we kept the support needed to get the special emergency disaster appropriations bill passed through Congress, I had to expressly agree we would not establish a program that directly or indirectly had the effect of discouraging people from buying homeowner's insurance. The property and casualty insurance industry had lobbied hard and effectively for the premise that the disaster assistance package not result in disincentives for people to purchase homeowner's insurance. Their argument was, if you didn't have homeowner's insurance, but the federal government paid for you to get a new house anyway, why would you buy homeowner's insurance in the future? The expectation would be that the government would bail you out.

That argument was logical and persuasive to many on the Hill and in the administration, so we had to solve it if we were to get our disaster assistance package enacted. It was at the midnight meeting in Speaker Hastert's office that we offered the stipulation that grant recipients must have owned a home that was outside the federally delineated flood plains in Hancock, Harrison, Jackson, or Pearl River Counties; must have lived in that home as of August 29, 2005, the day of the storm; must have maintained homeowner's insurance on the property; and must have received flood damage.

Those who met these eligibility qualifications also would be required to have "going forward" covenants if they received grants: to elevate new homes above the to-be-published revised federal flood elevations; to build in accordance with new stronger building codes; and to not only carry flood as well as homeowner's insurance but to also put in the covenants of any deed of sale that future purchasers would have to carry homeowner's and flood insurance. The maximum grant was $150,000. These requirements and covenants eliminated the opposition of the insurance industry, though mortgage banker groups fought us on another issue, as will be seen later.

As these regulations were being developed and discussed publicly, several people, both on and off the Coast, began to complain that the housing grant program was offering nothing for people who lived in the flood zone or for people who lived outside the flood zone but who had failed to maintain homeowner's insurance on their houses, especially low-income homeowners.

There were also complaints that the grants were limited to houses with flood damage; they wanted people who received wind damage but not any flood damage to also receive compensation.

Notwithstanding the merits of all those complaints—and the insurance requirement was not a part of our original plan—none of what these advocates and organizations wanted had even a one percent chance of passing Congress in the fall of 2005. Four hurricanes had destroyed or damaged thousands of homes in Florida the year before, and there had been no special federal disaster relief for those homeowners. They were expected to have and, in fact, had homeowner's insurance to cover the wind damage and, if in the flood plains, were expected to have flood insurance. The entire rationale for Congress and the president to allow states hit by Katrina to receive unprecedented assistance for homeowners was that tens of thousands of houses outside the federally prescribed flood zones had been damaged or destroyed by the storm surge or rising water flooding, and virtually all of those homeowners didn't have flood insurance because they had relied on the federal government's telling them they didn't need flood insurance.

Our original request to Congress and the administration evolved over the course of the fall and we ultimately had to accept some conditions in order to get the appropriation approved. What Congress did for Mississippi homeowners was a first, and they were persuaded by the unique facts of our situation and by the herculean work of our delegation. We got everything that was possible to get.

And we in Mississippi abided by our agreement. Later, as it became clear we would not receive as many applications for the grants as we had anticipated, we worked with the Bush Administration (and later the Obama Administration) to spend the unused funds on additional housing programs.

Not every homeowner who received a grant used it to rebuild or replace his or her home on the Coast, but the vast majority did. The fact that we had some who got the money, in the nature of insurance proceeds, and didn't rebuild is not surprising or even negative, as you couldn't fairly expect elderly people with no family on the Coast to go through a big construction project. Some moved to where their children lived or became renters or moved into assisted living.

This was the compensation plan we submitted to HUD on March 1. And while we were given a green light for that plan on April 1, the thirty-day comment period generated intense debate within the Bush Administration. Environmental advocates opposed the plan because of the exemptions. Many mortgage bankers opposed the plan because we did not stipulate that grant recipients had to use the money to pay off any existing mortgage. Others within the administration opposed it because it was different and could not guarantee the money would be used to build housing. In spite of it all, we didn't back down, and Secretary Jackson approved our plan. As I once had told the *Clarion-Ledger*'s Sid Salter, "People are depending on us to help them get back on their feet as best and as soon as possible."

While I had been busy helping secure approval of the plan, Terri Hudson and Donna Sanford had to organize an entire operation dedicated to receiving applications for the grants, processing those applications, verifying each applicant's eligibility, and then distributing the money. It was an unprecedented logistical and personnel challenge. They brought in a Maryland-based accounting firm, the Reznick Group, to help create and staff all of the local offices we used to accept and process applications. They also turned to Howard McMillan, a retired local bank president, who offered great counsel about many financial and technical aspects of the program.

Ironically, the large number of vacant buildings left by Katrina made it easy to find places to house the local offices we would use in each county to receive the applications—an old Piccadilly Cafeteria, a storefront in an outlet mall, and a damaged high school gym were just some of the places we found for office space—and in terms of staffing the offices, we benefited from the pool of well-trained and then-available casino employees waiting for their old jobs to reopen. Donna Sanford remembers getting a call from a friend on the Coast who was an administrator at the Hard Rock Casino. Her friend had heard about Sanford's role with the housing program, and she wanted to know if Sanford would need any staff since the Hard Rock was trying to find work for its employees as the company repaired the casino. As Sanford said in an interview for this book, "They were a great group of people because they had customer service training, and they had already been cleared through background checks." At one point, we had more than three hundred people working in the local offices to process application forms.

As a result we were able to organize the intake operations pretty quickly, and we took our first application for a homeowner's assistance grant on April 15, only two weeks after our program was approved. We then began to operate on two tracks. First, once our plan had been approved, it had to be published and subjected to a public comment phase and thoroughly vetted before it would become final and funds would be made available. That happened in early July, but not before the National Mortgage Bankers Association emerged again with its objections. They continued to oppose what we were trying to do because of our insistence that people be allowed to use the money to rebuild rather than pay off old mortgages.

By this time we had received more than 16,500 applications and were beginning to learn a few things about giving money away, or trying to give it away. Because we wanted to make sure we were providing grants to people who owned their houses at the time of landfall in the prescribed areas of the Gulf Coast counties, we contracted with local lawyers who looked to the legal titles of those properties for proof of ownership. For many of the people eligible to receive these funds, getting a clear title became an obstacle, mostly because old homes had passed through many generations without ever resolving underlying estate issues as they affected the ownership rights to the homestead.

Early in the summer, as we were working through all the requests, the federal government finally gave us approval to actually spend the money. While the pressure to turn loose of the money was enormous, I wanted to make sure Mississippi could ultimately report to Congress that we had been good stewards of the taxpayers' money and that this money was spent in the way I had told them it would be spent and without any hint of fraud. We worked closely with the auditors at HUD and used a special appropriation to the Mississippi State Auditor's office to fund a special fraud investigation office. For these reasons, we embarked on a pilot program during the summer to release a few of the grants, follow them through the process, make sure the recipients honored their end of the agreement, and ensure everything worked as advertised. We essentially pre-audited the program to completely ensure its integrity. By August we started releasing the funds, and by December more than 6,200 grants had been paid. The extra pre-audit testing cost us a few weeks, but applicants knew issuance of grants was just around the corner. And I thought we owed it to the taxpayers to protect them. Our program was later praised by several federal auditing agencies when reviews disclosed that the incidence of assistance to people who were ineligible was less than one-tenth of 1 percent.

I believe it was the careful way in which we managed the housing program that caused the Bush Administration and later the Obama Administration to allow us more than once to expand our programs. While on the face of it this was contrary to our understanding with Congress, the Bush Administration requested it and agreed to clear this amended version with congressional leaders. This amended program allowed an individual whose income was below the median area income for the Coast to apply for grants to repair, rebuild, or build a new home if their home was destroyed by storm surge. The need for one of the programs arose because so many low-income families had been living in mortgage-free homes. Since mortgage payments include insurance premiums, many homeowners without mortgages didn't realize they were no longer included in the flood insurance program.

The first grant program (called HAP 1) built or rebuilt 21,379 homes at a cost of about $1.5 billion, while the subsequent program (called HAP 2) raised the number of houses repaired, rebuilt, or built with homeowner assistance grants to about 27,700 at a cost a little over $2 billion.

Another very successful housing initiative was what we called the small rental program, which provided loans and even grants for private property owners to build (or rebuild) up to four apartments for rental at a single location. If the owner kept the monthly rate at or below the government's calculated affordable rent for low- and moderate-income rentals for five years, the balance of the loan would be forgiven. This program generated four thousand rental units at affordable rents, which the Coast needed because the rental versus home ownership ratio before Katrina was unusually high in the area.

By the end of my term as governor, under all of the various housing programs we operated using special disaster funds (many of which were expanded in later years with additional congressional appropriations), Mississippi families had built or rebuilt close to fifty-seven thousand units of housing, including more public housing units than existed before Katrina. Because we did it right from the very first allocation, we were over the years able to double our investment in new and rehabilitated housing.

Managing this enormous housing program reinforced for me the need to always be ready to make decisions, knowing some of them will be wrong. Leadership means recognizing a wrong decision—for example, an initiative might not be working out as you expected—and changing it to achieve a better result. For example, one early rule required the homeowner to show us proof of insurance at the time of landfall, and that proof was an actual policy or verification of coverage by the insurance company. The big companies like State Farm, Allstate, Nationwide, Mississippi Farm Bureau, and others were very helpful in obtaining those policies for the homeowners. They responded quickly, wanting their customers to get a grant and get back on their feet. But a handful of small companies that had not written many policies in the state simply ignored requests to verify the homeowner's claim of coverage. The failure of these insurers to cooperate made this requirement an unfair one for some grant applicants, so I changed the requirement and allowed the applicants whose insurers wouldn't respond to sign affidavits attesting to the existence of a policy.

Other Recovery Programs

Once the housing programs were up and running, we moved during the summer of 2006 to support another program that facilitated home ownership. After Camille, Mississippi had established a special insurance program to keep property and casualty insurance as affordable as possible, particularly on the Coast. The Windpool Insurance Program was administered by a private nonprofit board and was not funded by the state or taxpayers but through assessments on all the property insurers regulated by the State. Essentially, it purchased reinsurance to back up the standard policies in order to keep rates lower. Katrina blew through the reinsurance limits by hundreds of millions of dollars.

Looking forward, the insurance companies had to pay to honor their own claims, which ultimately totaled $12 billion, and they were eventually required to pay large assessments to make up for their share of Windpool losses. All of this meant property and casualty companies would dramatically increase their premiums or quit writing insurance in Mississippi. Either would be a disastrous result if we wanted people to rebuild in our coastal communities.

The Legislature in the special session recognized these insurance companies would be hit with hundreds of millions of assessments, and it provided for a recoupment scheme that would allow them to recover their Katrina assessments over five years by raising premiums. This was designed to keep the companies in the state, writing policies. But combined with actual losses, it meant premiums for property insurance would skyrocket.

To mitigate against these huge increases, we assigned some $80 million of federal disaster assistance money to the Windpool program to keep rates lower, so people would not decide to give up on the Gulf Coast because of insurance costs.

Nearly $670 million was spent to build another recommendation of the Barksdale Commission: a new water, sewer, and wastewater treatment system primarily north of the incorporated municipalities on the Coast, extending into Stone and Pearl River Counties.

The commission recognized that many families who wanted to stay in the coastal communities would want to rebuild farther away from the Gulf to be better protected from future hurricanes. As obvious as it was that many would think they needed to move inland, there was a major impediment: grossly insufficient water and sewer infrastructure.

Indeed, in Jackson County the residential developments north of the cities had already reached a point that septic tanks for new houses were an environmental threat. In the coastal plain of South Mississippi, water drains from north to south, so a significant influx of population north of the towns on the Coast would create or exacerbate environmental problems that would only get worse and worse. The commission's solution was a five-county water, sewer, and sewage treatment network designed and then contracted out, constructed, and today operated by local utility boards established by the Legislature in 2006.

Another recommendation of the Barksdale Commission did not fare as well, though the Coast members of the commission thought it was a very high priority. That involved moving the CSX railroad from its raised bed to an area north of Interstate 10 and building a new thoroughfare on the railbed. As I discussed in chapter 6, the need for this arose out of the fact that south of I-10 there were and are only two four-lane streets that run east and west, Highway 90 (or Beach Boulevard) and Pass Road. In Gulfport and Biloxi, the two largest cities, this has at least two very negative effects: (1) During a time of crisis, as Hurricane Katrina's evacuation demonstrated, it is extremely difficult and distressingly slow to move east or west to get to the limited number of northbound roads that cross Biloxi Bay or are west of it; and (2) Highway 90 is congested by regional as well as commuter and commercial traffic that diminishes the flow of tourist traffic and makes the beach experience less enjoyable.

The solution to both these problems was a controlled-access expressway running from east to west in Harrison County. To obtain right-of-way for such an expressway would be wildly expensive in a fully developed, compact urban area like these two cities, not to mention that it would take decades of eminent domain litigation. Hence, it had long been desired but never attempted. But with Katrina the CSX railroad's line had been breached in numerous areas of all three coastal counties. The rail right-of-way, on which this line sits, runs from the Alabama line to the Louisiana line, but in Harrison County it resides on a long, elevated stretch a few blocks off the beach through Biloxi and Gulfport. If CSX agreed to move its line north of I-10 to be protected from future hurricanes, as some were advocating, CSX could choose to sell the Mississippi Coast right-of-way to the state for conversion to a route for an expressway for automobiles and trucks.

This was the Barksdale Commission recommendation we took to Congress, proposing $900 million of disaster assistance funds be reserved to purchase this right-of-way from the CSX and build the expressway. By early 2006, when we felt confident CSX would go along with us, opposition began to surface in Congress, especially in the Senate led by Senator Tom Coburn of Oklahoma, a fine conservative and a friend, who made clear he would not support our request.

Early in the spring of 2006 we were making progress. We defeated Coburn's amendment to a new emergency supplemental appropriation bill for the states affected by Katrina and Rita that would have prohibited using any federal disaster funds for the CSX project. We prevailed by only one vote, which was cast by Senate Republican Leader Bill Frist of Tennessee. Coburn and others had come to the incorrect conclusion that this was a big windfall and a cozy deal for CSX. In fact, CSX preferred to rebuild in place, as they ultimately did. Regardless, we decided to drop the project in order to avoid increasing resistance to other federal assistance programs we needed. The project was just the kind of ambitious and expensive initiative envisioned by the Barksdale Commission that could transform the Coast. It would have been a boon for Coast tourism and for traffic flows, especially during evacuations for hurricanes, but its cost and complexity led me to believe it was "a bridge too far." Thad Cochran and our allies were relieved we let it drop.

Other programs funded by the 2005 emergency appropriation included the more than $320 million for our K–12 schools; an additional $115 million made available to our universities and community colleges, plus several private colleges; and more than $95 million for job training and temporary job support. Through a social services block grant program, Mississippi received $128 million that primarily went to counseling for survivors and reconstruction of health and mental health facilities as well as provision of direct care. We received an additional $25 million directly to the Mississippi Department of Mental Health for additional provision of services. I remember well a call in the late fall from Mike Leavitt, secretary of Health and Human Services at the time and former governor of Utah, in which he told me to expect a major increase in mental health problems among the affected population. Leavitt was good enough to provide a big infusion of money to meet those increased needs.

The Department of Justice provided a grant of close to $58 million to replace equipment—from automobiles to computers to weapons— for our local law enforcement agencies and to add gear for emergency response. Local prosecutors in the southernmost eighteen counties also received supplemental funding.

At one of my early presentations before congressional committees, I was asked what was the one thing a state needed most to protect lives during a megadisaster. Without hesitation I said, "A survivable, interoperable wireless communications system." Everyone at the hearing agreed. In fact, Mississippi planned to use part of its regular FEMA grant funds (known as the Hazard Mitigation Grant Program) to which it was entitled under the Stafford Act to build just such a system.

But when we requested to use nearly $140 million of the more than $400 million of the FEMA Hazard Mitigation Grant funds the state had coming to it, FEMA said building a survivable, interoperable wireless communications system was not a permitted use of such monies. This was the kind of FEMA decision that drove me crazy. Nothing would better mitigate the hazards of a hurricane than a system that allowed federal, state and local agencies of all types—military and civilian—to communicate with each other, yet FEMA wouldn't allow the "hazard mitigation" money to be used for such a purpose.

Finally Senator Cochran moved the needed funds from the FEMA Hazard Mitigation account to another FEMA account, at which point FEMA's leadership allowed us to create what is today the only statewide survivable, interoperable 3G wireless communication system in the United States.

But as you can imagine, not every idea or plan has turned out like we hoped.

The Port of Gulfport

That brings us to the Port of Gulfport, an initiative for which I had great hope and promise, which has yet to be realized, and for which I have received considerable criticism. So I will address it head-on.

The port is owned and operated by the state, with a board of commissioners, a majority of them at the time chosen by the governor and two by the local governments. Since it was built in the 1960s, the port, with a channel depth of only thirty-six feet, has been a sleepy hub mainly for bananas. The larger of the two piers is the West Pier, which extends some six thousand feet out into the Gulf from just west of and below the Gulfport Central Business District. The East Pier, a good deal smaller, extends from the shoreline to the east between the ship channel and Jones Park. The West Pier had three regular shipping customers in 2005, Crowley, Chiquita, and Dole, the latter two of which primarily brought in bananas packed into containers from Central and South America. The pier is low, with an elevation of only ten feet or so, which is adequate for the ships that can use the channel. Crowley brought in on average three ships a week, compared to only one each week for Chiquita and Dole. The East Pier primarily handled exports of lumber, other wood products, and chickens, the largest agricultural product of our state. It also had a large refrigerated capacity. The Gulfport Yacht Club and a small Coast Guard station also were located on the East Pier.

A separate issue, though tied to the port, also landed me in hot water with some of my friends on the Coast. While both piers of the port have rail service operated by Kansas City Southern, most incoming cargoes are transported out by truck, especially the banana cargoes of Chiquita and Dole. The trucks exit the port at Highway 90 along the beach and then most turn onto Highway 49 and head north to either connect with Interstate 10 or continue on to Jackson or Memphis. On the days ships are unloading cargo, the large number of trucks can create huge traffic problems. For example, there are thirteen traffic lights between the port entrance at Highway 90 and

Interstate 10. To alleviate this congestion, the federal Department of Transportation together with our state transportation commission developed a plan for what is locally called the Canal Road project—building a new elevated connector between the port and Interstate 10. It would be known as Interstate 310, and funds to begin the construction had been obtained several years before by Senator Trent Lott.

Before Katrina, Gulfport was the third-largest container port on the Gulf of Mexico, and while many on the Coast were satisfied with Gulfport as a small banana port, Katrina made a lot of us rethink that. The port was decimated. All the buildings were either flattened or made unusable by a storm surge that was more than ten feet above the elevation of the piers. The port would have to be totally rebuilt, so the obvious question was whether to build it back as it was or to significantly increase its throughput, which would require several changes: deepening the channel into the port so larger vessels carrying bigger cargoes could pass through; upgrading the railroad that serves the port to increase the amount of freight that can enter and leave it; building I-310 so the greatly increased truck traffic would not snarl other traffic movement; elevating the West Pier in particular, both to serve larger vessels but also to survive another storm surge; improving the loading and unloading capacity so the port could handle the larger ships carrying maritime cargoes today; and adding land by filling in around the south and west sides of the West Pier to allow more space for surface transportation and for storage.

This was very ambitious, and I believed then and believe today that making these improvements could be a game-changer for the Gulf Coast economy. The first clue that some wanted a return of the port as it was became obvious when it was difficult to get a plan from the port for its future, and, when one was finally forthcoming, it was a rehash of a several-year-old plan that would have done little to increase the economic impact of the port. I finally had the Mississippi Development Authority, which has oversight over the port, engage a national consulting engineering firm to create a new comprehensive plan. While it may not have been perfect, the state adopted it and held presentations for local leaders, residents of neighboring areas, port workers, and the media. The Longshoreman's Union endorsed it, as did the newly created Gulf Coast Business Council.

Advocates for certain groups opposed it primarily, it seemed to me, because they wanted most of the money we had set aside for the port diverted to housing, despite the fact the funding for the port had been included in our original proposal to Congress.

Some of the improvements at the port have taken place since Katrina, particularly on the East Pier, with the rebuilt Coast Guard Station and a wonderful remaking of Jones Park, just to the east of the port. Millions of dollars have been spent to upgrade the rail tracks, which now allow freight trains to "double stack"—that is, to stack two containers on top of each other on flatbed rail cars instead of one, thereby doubling the freight a train can transport. Nearly as important, the improvements increased the allowed speeds of trains on this track from ten to fifty miles an hour. Both the federal government and KCS railroad were great partners on this needed project, and I particularly thank former U.S. Secretary of Transportation Ray LaHood.

Regrettably the other two major projects that would have made the port's plan work have not been accomplished. The Interstate 310 project has remained mired in litigation. More significantly, the state has been unable to get a permit from the U.S. Corps of Engineers to deepen the thirty-six-foot channel to at least forty-two and preferably forty-five feet in order to accommodate larger ships. For years Congress even refused to allow any studies to assess whether deeper channels were needed at certain ports. A study of Gulfport's channel depth begun before Katrina had never been resumed, and a moratorium on new ones stopped us cold.

Even with the impending opening of the greatly expanded Panama Canal, which will accommodate much larger ships than before, the federal government's policy has not changed. At a time when many Washington politicians, from the president on down, talk about the need for transportation infrastructure, what actually gets done is embarrassing. Making the channels deeper at Charleston and Savannah each took more than fifteen years to accomplish, largely because of permitting delays. The State of Florida finally used its own funds to deepen the channels at Jacksonville and Miami because the federal government wouldn't act. Yet for years our leaders have known the Panama Canal was being greatly expanded, and cargoes coming through it from the Pacific will change the maritime needs of our country's East Coast and Gulf of Mexico ports, particularly for deeper channels to handle larger ships. Other countries on the Gulf of Mexico and Caribbean Sea have increased their maritime capacities to try to attract these vessels. The United States has failed to do so. It will be a terrific shame if the Singapore of the western hemisphere after the Panama Canal expansion is complete turns out to be Mariel, Cuba!

Time will tell if Mississippi's state port can reach its potential. If it does, it won't just be the Coast that benefits. The confluence of three major freight railroads near Hattiesburg presents an inland opportunity for handling increased container traffic not just from Gulfport but also landing at both New Orleans and Mobile. The significance of this terminus is that containers from each of these three ports can be quickly carried there by rail, where they would be unloaded at cross-docks and sorted for reloading onto trains headed to the final destinations for the freight. With the scarcity of warehouse space near the waterfronts of ports like these three, a nearby inland sorting center would prove to be a very efficient way to handle freight. When we were planning the not-yet-executed plans for our Port at Gulfport, we were visited by the developers of the intermodal center in Joliet, Illinois, where such an operation produced a billion dollar investment and some eight thousand jobs. That can happen at Hattiesburg in years to come, if the port is properly redeveloped.

The port wasn't the only fish that got away, but it was the biggest. It is a project on which I will continue to work.

Governor's Office of Recovery and Renewal

I have used the last two chapters to discuss some of the many programs and projects we developed and funded to help spur the rebuilding of South Mississippi. What became clear to all of us at the end of 2005, knowing we would be getting billions of dollars from the special congressional appropriation bill and knowing FEMA would be spending a like amount of money on eligible construction projects, was that we needed to create a separate office to coordinate this work. It became known as the Governor's Office of Recovery and Renewal. Its first director was Gavin Smith, whom you met in chapter 6 in my description of the work of the Barksdale Commission. Smith came to us from North Carolina and put his academic experience in disaster recovery to great use in Mississippi. Brian Sanderson became his deputy and ultimate successor, and the two of them did much to define the nature and extent of our recovery efforts and keep them on track in the coming months and years.

This office became a one-stop shop for any and all questions anyone might have about spending federal money, getting reimbursed for damaged facilities, applying for grants, complying with the hundreds of federal disaster rules, and literally anything else that was needed to help us rebuild. For example, our ability to rebuild houses and commercial buildings on the Coast was directly tied to the new flood zone maps that FEMA issued, new building codes the counties and cities adopted to conform to the new maps, and the requirements insurance companies imposed on new construction to conform to both FEMA regulations and building codes. It was a hugely complicated set of issues that directly impacted the speed with which we could recover. I don't know that anyone is completely satisfied with what was finally approved, but resolving the details was very important.

The amount of paperwork required to comply with federal regulations quickly overwhelmed local officials, and Gavin, his staff, and Horne CPA became the chief reasons we could ultimately work our way through the forms and get the funding into the rebuilding pipeline.

As I move into the lessons I learned, I am reminded how fortunate Mississippi was to have the kind of committed and dedicated state employees who took charge of our recovery. One of the most common refrains we heard in conducting interviews with some of them ten years later was that they lost track of time, the days merged into each other since there was no time off, no vacations. These men and women worked every day for months on end to help their state and its citizenry. I'm proud to have been their Governor.

CHAPTER 10

Lessons Learned

A Personal Reflection

ANY LEADER—GOVERNOR, MAYOR, CEO of a private business, military officer, or president of the United States—can learn many lessons from dealing with a crisis, especially a megadisaster like Hurricane Katrina. I certainly did, and one reason I wrote this book is to lay out the most important of those lessons learned, or, in many cases, lessons confirmed.

1. There is no substitute for preparation; for no government is big enough to take care of every problem for everybody all the time.

As we experienced during Katrina, even if the plan that has been established and trained for cannot be executed as planned, having a plan, teaching it to all levels, and exercising it will prepare your team and make everyone far more agile and able to make necessary adjustments when a disaster strikes.

Even though Katrina overwhelmed our state, thrust us into unimagined situations, and presented challenges we never dreamed of, hardly anyone in a leadership capacity panicked. I believe that was a product of continuous planning and sufficient practice that allowed our local officials, agency heads, and, especially, first responders to adapt to the unexpected and unprecedented destruction.

Military leaders often note that the plan goes out the window when the battle starts, but American soldiers have a history of being agile and creative in combat, consistent with their training. Planning and training for disasters is a bit like training for war, and when things are a lot worse than expected, preparation, planning, and training are still critical to a successful response. Our first responders, managers, and top leaders knew better how to deal with the unexpected because they had trained to a plan.

Interestingly, we thought we were planning for a worst-case scenario because we based our plan on Hurricane Camille, the powerful storm of 1969 with its two hundred mile-per-hour winds and more than a hundred tornadoes. Camille was considered the worst possible hurricane, the gold standard, until Katrina's vastness and its record storm surge obliterated the Coast and did unprecedented damage for some two hundred miles northward.

In interviewing people for this book, we found the planning and training today for the next hurricane have become much more sophisticated and comprehensive. Our communications systems are far more survivable, the capacity to provide critical supplies during the first crucial days is far superior and controlled by the state, and the plan recognizes that storm damage can be much greater than anticipated.

Yet a fundamental lesson of Katrina is that no government is big enough to take care of every problem for everybody all the time—and we never want a government that big!

Therefore, the importance of preparation as the first key lesson of Katrina is not just a lesson for government; it is absolutely essential for private businesses and for families.

Larger businesses are more likely than small ones to have disaster plans, but small businesses need to prepare, have a plan, make sure all employees know their roles, and, if possible, practice. Those employees who would have key roles in a catastrophe must be trained and, if possible, practice the needed skills. It doesn't have to be elaborate, but preparation saves lives and protects property.

In some ways hurricanes are easier to prepare for because there is normally a lead time of more than a day, sometimes a week. Rising rivers often allow several days for preparations for floods too.

Tornadoes, explosions, chemical leaks, and criminal or terrorist attacks don't give much if any lead time. But they can and must still be prepared for. Clear understanding and, better still, practice for how to protect lives and property will make a difference.

The final element of this lesson is self-preparation for families. Such preparation protects those families and their neighbors.

At a minimum, heads of households should decide on a disaster plan and explain it to the entire family. Essential supplies should be stored in a special place and be easily packed to move with the family during an evacuation or relocation to a safe room, whether in a basement or an internal room or closet. Necessary medicines, baby supplies (if applicable), three days of water, food that won't go bad for a while, flashlight(s) and a battery-powered radio all can be packed into a small bag or two. Adults should know where a gun is in the house and how to use it. Any gun should have a lock and be locked.

In a hurricane, the safest plan is to evacuate. Most of the approximately 170 people killed on the Mississippi Gulf Coast by Katrina would not have died if they had evacuated. If your plan is to evacuate, allow time to secure your outdoor furniture and other property to protect your neighbors' property. Have an evacuation plan that includes how you will transport yourself or who will transport you; where you will go and the route you will follow to get there; and where you will stay. In hurricanes and certain types of floods, evacuation is the safest option. Inform someone as to where you will evacuate.

But even if you can't evacuate, have a plan that puts you in the safest place you can go. It may be as simple as getting out of a mobile home in a tornado or going to an internal room in a house or business. In the Tuscaloosa tornado, a number of customers of a fast food restaurant survived in the freezer of the restaurant. They were blessed that the employees of the restaurant had been trained to get everyone into the freezer, for the restaurant was severely damaged.

Preparation saves lives, protects property, and keeps the damage to your business as small as possible. And disaster preparedness has to include business disasters, but that is the subject of a different book.

2. Someone has to be in charge.

This should seem obvious to most people, but in government it is not always automatic that there is a clear, single leader. Unlike business or the military, the head of government may have many people who do not report to or work for him or her. This is even more pronounced in a state like Mississippi, where we have a constitutionally weak governor.

All governors face the fact that local officials do not work for them; mayors and county officials are elected independently of the governor and are not part of state government. In my state, that is compounded by the fact that many state departments and agencies are run by directors who are not appointed by and do not report to the governor. Indeed, 79 percent of the state general fund budget my first year as governor was spent by departments and agencies the directors of which did not report to me.

Beyond that, every legislator was independently elected, and none of them reported to me.

And none of the federal officials involved in the Katrina response and rebuilding reported to me.

I was truly blessed when local officials on the Coast, many of whom were Democrats, recognized someone had to be in charge, and logically it had to be the governor. Almost immediately the city and county officials in the affected areas started working closely with MEMA and our team. As time went on they were deeply involved with the commission, MDA, and with our efforts to develop a special disaster assistance package for the state.

Whereas Louisiana governor Kathleen Blanco had to contend with strong resistance from New Orleans mayor Ray Nagin and other local elected officials who wanted to control the recovery effort in their areas, I had the support of our local officials.

We have talked previously about the great work done by our congressional delegation, especially about how they worked so well together. They also worked well with my team. Senator Thad Cochran led by making plain he would look to the governor to learn what Mississippi needed and would support us in getting it. The other members generally followed suit.

Trent Lott, Chip Pickering, and Gene Taylor, all of whom lived in extremely hard-hit areas, were much more outspoken in their criticism of the federal effort, but they were great in their support of our plan for special federal disaster assistance. Indeed, Lott and Pickering were stars in producing great results for our people on the Senate Finance and House Energy and Commerce Committees.

While the federal employees and administration officials never worked for me, they were great allies who worked with us. Don Powell, the president's advisor on Katrina, was very helpful and became a friend. Alphonso Jackson and Scott Keller at HUD were incredible supporters, and so were many others in the White House, at FEMA, and at many other federal agencies. In the Obama Administration, the secretaries of HUD, Sean Donovan, and Transportation, Ray LaHood, were strong allies as well. I'm grateful to them all.

The FEMA people on the ground in Mississippi became tightly integrated into the unified command and operated hand in hand with my team. Bill Carwile, an American superstar, set that up, and folks like Nick Russo and Sid Melton, who followed him, were like family to us. Marsha considers Russo and Melton among the greatest heroes of Katrina. They fought to help the folks in South Mississippi who needed it most. And they weren't afraid to lean forward to get the job done.

Legislators aren't executives, and the Legislature took bold action to help. I'll always admire House Speaker Billy McCoy for his courage on the onshore casino legislation.

Still the design of Mississippi government under our 1890 constitution was for a weak governor and a dominant legislature; however, having a constitutionally weak governor doesn't mean the governor has to have a weak constitution!

Cochran helped us get around the weak governor "problem" by putting the vast amount of money the state had discretion to spend directly under the governor via the CDBG and SSBG programs.

The state budget money freed up by Lott and Pickering's success in getting the state extra Medicaid funds had to be appropriated by the Legislature with the governor's participation. Use of CDBG and SSBG funds, however, was exclusively controlled by the governor, subject only to federal approval.

All these permutations came together to give me the authority needed to actually lead the recovery, rebuilding, and renewal. I will always be grateful to the other elected officials for recognizing and supporting the fact that someone had to be in charge, and the governor was the obvious choice.

There is an old political adage that giving away power is an unnatural act! That's quite true, but these politicians did it.

They did it because they knew our state and our people needed one person in charge. They knew governing by committee or the legislative process would never get the results that were needed and deserved by the strong, resilient, self-reliant people of the Coast and South Mississippi.

3. **It is critical in the megadisaster for the leader to be visible, present, and active: People need you, and they need to know they can trust you.**

Some famous military historian said, "The leader must ride to the sound of the cannon." If it is true that trained soldiers need to see their leaders, it is even more important for those caught in an unprecedented catastrophe to know that a strong, caring leader is at the scene, assessing the situation, bringing in resources, and providing support. And in the case of a megadisaster, the leader needs to be present to back up first responders, local officials, and the other "troops" on the ground who are part of his or her command.

After a megadisaster, especially one that results in the gross devastation such as that caused by Katrina, it is not only critical that the leader be seen, it is also absolutely essential the leader be open, honest, and tell the truth.

People in politics who are successful know it is not only wrong to lie; they know it also is harmful, and not just to their political careers. That harm is multiplied many times over in the wake of a great calamity. During the frightening catastrophe is the worst possible time to make untrue statements. That is the time people need to be able to believe in and rely on their leader the most. When it becomes clear the leader has misled the people, or failed to tell the truth, or even asserted a fact or facts that he or she does not know is truth, the leader is undermining the public's confidence in him or her and, therefore, in the state and its efforts.

When the goal is to kindle hope and confidence among the citizens of the devastated area that their communities can and will come back as good places to live, those residents have to feel as though they can believe every word the leader says. Anything less invites utter failure in recovering from the disaster and rebuilding the communities.

Don't be tempted to sugar coat the bad news or gild the lily on positive developments. Tell it like it is; the public needs to know the truth, and they can handle it.

When I was a White House staffer, former Secretary of State Henry Kissinger told a group of us, "If there is bad news in government or politics, get it out fast. Unlike fine wine, bad news does not get better with age."

Be sure you have good information when you give it to the public and the media. If you don't know the facts of a situation, admit it, and tell the media you will find out the facts and get back to them. The public needs confidence they can believe you, that you won't hold back on them, much less lie to them.

In some military or business situations, there is a reason not to tell everything you know because you don't want to reveal secrets to the enemy or the competition. That is perfectly proper in those situations, but unlike war or business, the leader in a natural disaster owes the citizenry all the relevant facts available that could affect the public's safety and recovery.

So get the bad news out as fast as you can confirm its accuracy. The public will learn you are trustworthy.

But the opposite is true as well.

If the leader doesn't tell the truth, it will come out sooner or later. The leader's credibility will be damaged or even shattered when it is revealed that he or she covered up or deceived the citizens. And that credibility, which is one of the greatest assets of any leader, is incredibly hard to recover or rebuild.

While telling the truth is a moral issue, an issue of character, it is also an issue of leadership.

Just as the public will lose confidence in a leader they feel they cannot believe, not telling the truth will be just as damaging to the confidence of your own team in you as the leader.

Your team must have total confidence in you, if they are going to serve you and the organization as well as they can. And if you don't tell the truth, your team will know it first.

So even if you set aside the debilitating effect not telling the truth has on the public's confidence in its leader, you must recognize the platoon leader, the team captain, the CEO, and every other kind of leader must tell the truth to have the confidence of those he or she leads. How could it be any different for the person who leads huge organizations or the public at large?

In the megadisaster the leader must be present, visible, active, and open in communication. And the communication must always be true, even if the message is "We don't know yet."

4. Make decisions, and know you'll make some bad ones; when you recognize bad decisions, change them.

The megadisaster almost by definition means the leader will be making it up as he or she goes along. It is tempting to be cautious and put off decision making. After all, in unchartered territory it may seem prudent to take things slowly. My experience, however, is that avoiding or delaying a decision is, in fact, a decision—a decision to let matters take their own course.

Regrettably, the normal course in the megadisaster is usually a course in the wrong direction, a course that doesn't push resources into the areas where they are most needed, doesn't inform those in harm's way, doesn't build hope and confidence. Failure to make decisions disadvantages those who are your partners and forces other decisions down the chain of command, sometimes resulting in conflicting policies in various geographical areas or among many different groups of employees.

The leader gets paid to assess the information available, weigh the options, and decide the most effective way to solve or reduce the problem or to gain maximum advantage in producing positive results. In the megadisaster, the options have more to do with protecting lives and property, reducing risk, ensuring the most effective use of resources, and keeping the strong commitment of your team and the lasting hope and confidence of your people. If you don't make decisions, others will start making them in your stead. If someone else ought to be making the decisions, you shouldn't be the leader.

Don't get me wrong: as we will discuss later in this chapter, an important trait of the successful leader is to delegate authority as well as responsibility. Good decision making is to tell the appropriate people on your team that they have the authority to make decisions in order to fulfill their responsibilities. Delegation is a good type of decision making.

Katrina taught me that being afraid of making a bad decision is no reason to fail to make a decision when one is needed. During Katrina's aftermath we were in unchartered waters despite decades of planning and training to a plan. The storm's devastation had so far exceeded our worst fears that we were making it up as we were going along. There were no precedents, and there were no "experts" who had ever dealt with a natural disaster on this scale.

I had no choice but to make the best decisions I could. There was no question I'd make some bad decisions. Indeed, it reminded me of an old piece of advice and instruction I'd given managers who'd worked for me in politics and government: If you think you know what to do, do it. If you mess up, we'll clean up, but don't wait on me if you think you know what to do.

Let's face it: If a person makes enough decisions, he or she will make some bad decisions. Don't let that stop you from making decisions because anybody who never makes bad decisions makes few or no decisions.

The worst problem with making a bad decision is not correcting it. Some politicians find it awfully hard to admit they made a mistake or a wrong decision. You have to get over that.

I made a number of bad decisions in the Katrina recovery and rebuilding, but I made a whole lot of decisions. I'm not ashamed that some decisions had to be adjusted or even reversed. I'm proud that our team recognized we weren't getting the best results and we fixed the problem. At the end of the day the leader must see that the original decision didn't produce the best possible outcome, and must have the courage to admit it and do something about it.

As usual, good staff—having a good team—is critical in both recognizing the problem and helping find the better answer. Of course, that requires a team that is not afraid to tell the boss he or she made the wrong decision. Smart, good leaders have sense enough and confidence enough to not only allow but to expect that of their team.

Make decisions, but have the humility to know you'll make the wrong decision sometimes, if you make enough decisions. Be a strong enough leader to adjust or reverse those bad decisions, but don't quit making decisions.

5. There is no substitute for having a strong team around you.

Throughout my entire career I have been blessed with having great people work for me and with me. I like to think I have been a boss who brings out the best in people, or maybe the good Lord has simply taken care of me!

My mother was a legal secretary, and I hung around the family law firm a good bit in my childhood and youth. I not only loved my mother, but I respected her as a parent and also as a worker—a smart, strong, capable colleague to the lawyers and the other secretaries in the office.

So when I ran the Mississippi Republican Party in the early 1970s and practiced law later in the decade, I couldn't help but appreciate the smart young women who worked for me. I gave them responsibility and authority to help redesign processes and policies. I had some very talented young guys who would work at the state headquarters for a year of two, but the women would stay much longer and made great contributions.

At the family law firm, the young legal secretaries who worked with me were exceptional: very smart, totally dedicated, great teammates.

When I went to the Reagan White House, my staff were simply phenomenal; many have had great careers since. My days of working with them and for Ronald Reagan were heady stuff for a boy from Yazoo City, Mississippi.

Many of the people I worked with then were critical six years later in my election as chairman of the Republican National Committee and were part of the amazing team that led to the Republican Revolution of 1993–94. Don Fierce, Sanford McAllister, and Larrilyn Bertocchio had been close associates or staff members at the White House, and Ed Rogers went from the White House to our firm, now called BGR Group. Rogers and our other partner, Lanny Griffith, a fellow Mississippian, not only ran the firm when I left—first to be RNC chairman and then governor—they also greatly strengthened it in my absence.

As governor of Mississippi, I was blessed with a fantastic staff full of self-starters, active thinkers, and tireless young people who grew into great public servants. And Katrina brought out the very best in all of them.

I relate my history with staff here because I appreciate them so much. I can't give them enough credit for the success we had in the Katrina story. Plus, they deserve to be praised. As my sainted mother used to say, only three kinds of people like to be appreciated: men, women, and children.

Every time I had a good staff—which was every time I had a staff—I learned to trust them. Leaders put together strong effective staffs and then let the staff do their jobs. If you don't trust your staff and don't let them do their jobs—solve the problems that should be solved at their levels, make the decisions that they should make, get the credit they deserve—either you have the wrong staff or you're not the boss they need.

Let the staff produce for you. A great leader has a great staff and trusts that staff to meet its responsibilities by giving it authority commensurate with that responsibility—and then gives the staff full credit.

President Reagan had a plaque on the credenza behind his desk in the Oval Office. It said, "There is no limit to what a man can do or where he can go if he does not mind who gets the credit." Once I asked the president about the plaque, and he told me, "When you're the top leader and things are going well, you get more credit than you can even appreciate. The leader's job is to spread the credit around. To give everybody who helped a share of the credit. That way, they are more likely to help again."

Of course Reagan's famous plaque wasn't directed at the staff, but that same sentiment applies to the staff. Leaders should make sure the staff know they are needed and appreciated. When in the throes of Katrina, staffers worked unbearable hours for weeks on end; you'd better believe I made sure they knew how valuable they were and how grateful Marsha and I were.

I've never known any leader in politics or government who made it by himself or herself. No one. Yet I've known too many who weren't able to recognize how important their staffs were to their success. I hope nobody can ever say that about me.

6. Americans are the most generous people in the world, and it is not just the rich who are generous.

Never underestimate the generosity and the goodness of the vast majority of Americans; that generosity was on full display after Katrina. The greatest natural disaster in American history appropriately produced the greatest outpouring of generosity in American history. Millions of citizens contributed to charities and churches for the benefit of hurricane victims. Employers, whether small businesses or huge corporations, also gave generously for the benefit of the victims. Voters expected but didn't have to demand unprecedented disaster assistance from the federal government because the elected officials in both Washington and every state capitol were also committed to helping the people of the Gulf Coast region recover.

This book gives you an understanding of the heroic efforts of corporations like Mississippi Power and Entergy in throwing everything they had and more at getting their customers back on their feet by restoring electric service in record time. Other companies were also pulling out all stops, such as Chevron's giving fuel to first responders, or Hancock Bank's making unsecured loans to anyone who asked for one and had a local address.

But these companies continued to go above and beyond. Chevron gave millions of dollars to rebuild every private preschool in the coastal counties after the company learned these schools were not eligible for federal assistance under the Stafford Act. Pharmaceutical companies, none of which are located or have facilities in the affected areas of Mississippi, gave millions of dollars of prescription drugs and other medical supplies to the state, and we made them available to medical providers in the worst-hit areas.

The examples of corporate philanthropy go on and on.

There were also extremely generous gifts from individuals and families, starting with Mississippian John Grisham's $5 million contribution a few days after the storm. Mississippian Jim Barksdale gave more than a million dollars, and many, many more Mississippians made large, generous donations to charities, churches, and our Mississippi Hurricane Recovery Fund.

There were also people from elsewhere who were incredibly generous. I remember Betsy DeVos, wife of Dick DeVos, the chairman of Amway, coming to meet with me in the Governor's Office. Betsy had been chairman of the Michigan GOP when I was RNC chairman. Betsy brought $700,000 in checks from Amway and family members as well as from the family of Jay Van Andel, who had founded Amway with Betsy's father-in-law, Rich DeVos. George Argyros, a California entrepreneur, gave a million dollars for the Gulf Coast campus of the University of Southern Mississippi.

So many incredibly generous people gave our recovery effort millions of dollars.

Importantly, people gave something more valuable than money: they gave their time. You can make more money; you can't make more time. An obvious example of giving incredibly valuable time was the Mississippi Rising benefit show. Sam Haskell and Lanny Griffith, two Mississippians who had made hugely successful careers away from their state, pulled together a wonderful array of stars: Morgan Freeman, Faith Hill, B.B. King, Ray Romano, Samuel L. Jackson, Gerald McRaney, Delta Burke, and so many more. Their time was incredibly valuable in the entertainment marketplace, worth millions of dollars. In their case, the value of giving away one's time is literal and easy to see.

But everybody who volunteers his or her time is making a contribution of the most valuable thing in that person's life! Thus, we should understand how fantastically generous were the nearly one million volunteers who came to our state to help people whom in most instances, they didn't even know when they arrived in Mississippi.

I don't know whether those first two truckloads of Mennonite men I met in Gulfport the day after the storm were rich or poor, but I doubt they or many of the nearly one million volunteers who followed them were rich. Yet they were giving something more valuable than gold; they were giving their precious, limited time, of which they have no ability to ever make any more to replace it.

That is why I always remind folks that generosity is not practiced only by the rich. It may be true that you'll never meet a poor philanthropist, but we think of philanthropy as giving away money. Katrina proves you will meet many, many poor Americans who are spectacularly generous with the greatest thing they have: their time.

7. A crisis brings out the best in most people.

When Jeppie, Wiley, and I were growing up, our mama taught us that great crises or catastrophes bring out the best in most people. When the news media was fixated on New Orleans, one did not get that impression, but I saw it confirmed time and time again in Katrina's wake. We've just talked about the fantastic outpouring of generosity, both in philanthropy and in volunteerism, that arose out of this enormous catastrophe. It was literally unprecedented, but there were many more examples that were recurring to the point of being commonplace.

The steadfastness of the men and women of the Waveland Police Department after all of them lost their homes makes the point perfectly: All twenty-six were present and on duty that very night.

I think of those young Coasties, hanging off helicopters on lines as those helos flew through the dark night. Their bravery resulted in some 1,900 Mississippians being rescued by air.

Over and over our first responders—local, state, National Guard, Highway Patrol—worked ceaselessly, living under the most primitive conditions to save lives, protect property, and maintain order. And they were joined by peers from Alabama, Florida, Ohio, Rhode Island,

Indiana, Pennsylvania, Kansas, Georgia, and nearly every other state. They risked their lives while living in battlefield conditions.

We talk about people who came from everywhere, but we must not overlook the people who were there before the storm, some of whom rode it out and others who returned in the aftermath. These strong, resilient, self-reliant people worked tirelessly to help themselves and their families, but, like the family Marsha met in Kiln who had lived in a doublewide trailer before the storm, they also worked hard to help the little old lady across the road who was a shut-in. They were the first to say, "Give that to somebody who needs it worse than we do."

Generally, my mama was right about the human nature displayed by those who were slammed by Katrina: It did bring out the best in most of them. A leader should know to praise that kind of behavior. Not only do you want more of it, you want it to be recognized and valued. The leader wants it to be well known because it encourages people to return to rebuild their communities and because it stimulates others to recognize "those brave, generous, determined, good people are the kind of people we'd like to have working for our company." Indeed, many a CEO said exactly that to me in the weeks and months after Katrina.

Katrina or, better put, the response of Mississippians to Katrina and what she left in her wake did more to improve the image of Mississippi than anything else that has happened in my lifetime.

America and the world got to see these strong, principled people under the brightest possible glare of megadisaster, watched them arise from utter obliteration, observed their courage and character, and said to themselves, "These are the kind of people I'd like to live next to, go to church with, and have my kids go to school with. I have to rethink Mississippi."

And many companies and families did give Mississippi another look after Katrina and liked what they saw.

8. Let your friends help you.

Some leaders have a hard time seeking or even accepting help from others. Whether it's a result of ego or fear of looking weak or whatever, there is a tendency among some to avoid asking for help to take care of their problems. In a megadisaster, that kind of thinking has to be banished from the leader's thoughts. You will need all the help you can get and more, so a part of preparation is inventorying the outside assets or partners that can help you and your enterprise recover and rebuild.

We were blessed after Katrina that huge numbers of people and entities were able to help and wanted to do so. In lesser disasters there may not be as many resources or helpers available. That makes it all the more important to know who can help and how they can help.

Hurricane Katrina was the worst natural disaster in our country's history, America's Great Storm, and it was altogether fitting that it would produce the greatest outpouring of philanthropy and volunteerism in American history.

Don't think, though, we were just waiting for support to come to us. There were some Bob Rileys and Jeb Bushes who sent in critically important first responders on Day One without being asked, but we were asking our friends for help too. And they were terrific in their responses.

Former Pennsylvania governor Ed Rendell often introduces me by telling about my call to him a night or two after the storm, asking him to send a convoy of Pennsylvania National Guard down to Mississippi to help with security and search and rescue. He did, and they were among the more than ten thousand guardsmen and women who came to our state after Katrina.

Much of this book deals with our seeking special emergency assistance from the federal government, both from Congress and the Bush Administration. We spent enormous amounts of time and energy preparing our requests, and we not only asked for this special help, we fought for it. Much of the story of the Katrina recovery is about the constant, concentrated, all-consuming effort to get the

Coast and South Mississippi what was needed to recover, rebuild, and renew itself. It was our crusade, and we couldn't fail. Yet, critically, we were asking people who wanted to help.

Our never-easy job on the federal side was to show our friends what the best ways to help were and to show them how to provide that help in a responsible manner—that is, responsible in that it would be done properly but also with the political appearance of responsibility. Those who ultimately did so much to support us had to do so without being accused of being irresponsible or setting bad precedents.

Again, in the megadisaster, virtually everybody is your friend and wants to help. Witness the great support we received from Congressman Barney Frank. But you have to show these friends what the needs are and the best ways to meet those needs.

A good leader puts tremendous focus on what he or she asks for. In designing a package with an effective method of execution, you should believe you'll only get one bite at the apple, so you must get it largely right the first time. You'll get to make adjustments, clean up some decisions, but you are unlikely to get to start over or make many large changes. Our team did a great job in assessing the real needs and comparing the existing Stafford Act program to see how they matched. Then they crafted an extraordinarily effective package of programs that met the crucial needs to bring the Coast and South Mississippi back better than it had been. And the team executed exceedingly well.

My point is to let your friends help you. You'll be amazed, as we were, with all the help from private, corporate, and charitable sources. It was phenomenal. So was the support from our sister states and the federal government. Even foreign governments such as Qatar and Kuwait helped us, so help comes from unexpected places too. Your friends want to help, but your job is to show them how and to make it as easy for them as possible.

And for the nearly one million volunteers, all they want is a chance to help someone who needs it and to receive a sincere "thank you."

They are why America is the greatest country in the history of the world.

9. The megadisaster requires leadership that creates followers among those who do not work for or report to the leader.

As you have noticed several times in this story and more than once in this chapter, the leader is called upon to lead people who don't report to or even work for him or her.

Some organizations may have a totally top-down structure, and everybody reports up a chain of command to one person. That certainly wasn't the case in our experience with the response to Hurricane Katrina, and time and again I found myself in horizontal relationships, trying to lead a person who didn't report to me and often was not connected to me in any kind of organization chart. They certainly didn't have to do what I said, but generally they did.

Part of the reasoning for this was discussed in the second section of this chapter. In a crisis, much less a megadisaster, someone has to be in charge. Rule by committee rarely works when situations require decisive action.

Our local officials realized there needed to be a leader, and their communities and citizens would be better off and have a greater chance for successful rebuilding if they accepted the governor as that leader.

Our team made this easier for the local leaders and their employees/contractors by including them from the very start; indeed, even before landfall. We planned together and practiced together. After the storm, we heard them out, considered their ideas, and, where appropriate, put their recommendations into effect. Our team, both state and federal, worked hand in hand with the locals' teams, sharing adversity and discomfort. We also gave them credit for successes, for it was rightly due them. They knew they were an essential and appreciated part of the unified command.

This was made easier by the fact that local and state leaders generally knew each other, and state and local departments and agencies
regularly work together on routine matters from education to human
services to law enforcement to economic development. Those pre-
existing relationships were a principal reason I so vigorously opposed
"federalization" of the post-Katrina response.

Still, the old adage holds true, for a politician to give up power
voluntarily is an unnatural act. Yet the recognition that a single
leader was needed in the wake of this megadisaster made these politicians do just that.

Leading the legislators would normally have been much more difficult than it turned out because in Mississippi the 1890 constitution
provided for a weak executive and a dominant legislature. The Legislature not only passes the state budget, but the Legislative Budget
Committee, composed of seven senators and seven House members,
prepares the initial budget for the full Legislature to consider. The governor is only allowed to submit to the Legislative Budget Committee
an "Executive Budget Recommendation."

Still, the Legislature accepted that a strong executive was needed
in the aftermath of the megadisaster, and while Democrats were in
the majority in both houses, they acceded to my being the leader.

A couple of factors came into play. I knew my way around Washington; indeed, my opponent in the campaign less than two years
previous had spent millions of dollars telling everybody I was "a
Washington lobbyist." Well, a Washington lobbyist was exactly what
Mississippi needed in this dark hour of crisis. It was obvious our state
had to have outside help; there was no way we could self-generate the
resources that would be needed to recover, restore, and rebuild.

People recognized my long relationship with national leaders from
President Bush on down. They thought no one would have a better
chance to gain the help from Washington than I.

The congressional delegation, especially Senator Cochran, helped
strengthen this perception. They were incredibly good partners who
consistently though not invariably accepted that I had more informa-

tion and a better perspective of both short- and long-term needs. More importantly, they allowed my team and me to develop the plans to acquire federal support for the Gulf States, to work side by side with them to get those plans passed into law and to implement the programs arising from the plans. They didn't have to accept or co-operate in giving the governor that much control, but they more than cooperated; they fought and won the battles to get our legislation enacted. They were all stars, and Thad Cochran was the brightest star of all.

A final factor in the Legislature's giving me much more authority and deference than ever before was that the greatest portion of the federal money over which the state had broad discretion in spending was in CDBG and SSBG funds and, under existing law, such federal funds were controlled by the governor, and the Legislature did not have the power to appropriate them. For that I thank Thad and the very smart staffers in his office and mine.

Our leadership situation with FEMA and other federal departments and agencies became strong very early. The FEMA people on the ground in Mississippi were extremely capable, and Bill Carwile, the FEMA supervisory lead for our state, was one of the first to recognize that FEMA's national logistical system had failed. He worked tirelessly for the people of Mississippi and put them first, even when his D.C. office didn't like it. His successors, Nick Russo and Sid Melton, were joined at the hip with Robert Latham at MEMA and his deputy and then successor, Mike Womack.

You've read in this book about the close relationships our team had with various federal departments: OMB, HUD, FEMA, USDOT, the Pentagon, and so on. Some of those relationships resulted from pre-existing friendships with folks like HUD Secretary Alphonso Jackson and Secretary of Education Margaret Spellings, but most did not. They arose out of working together to recover from the megadisaster and out of the respect for each other's teams that were quickly cemented.

A good example of horizontal leadership was the congressional leadership and the White House allowing our team to be the leader in developing the special disaster assistance package and in lobbying Congress to pass it.

Of course, part of that was attributable to Senator Cochran's decision that he would look to the Governor's Office to learn what Mississippi needed. Others followed suit, but this broad acceptance that our team would develop the programs and plan, and then get Congress and the administration to agree to them resulted from more than Cochran's imprimatur.

This acceptance that our office and team would be allowed to play this leadership role is unusual in my experience in Washington, in government generally, and in politics.

One reason this was allowed has to be the gigantic scale of Katrina's devastation: It was the worst natural disaster in American history, and nontraditional means were required to try to address the needs that arose from it. FEMA's failed logistics system and Louisiana's difficulties probably added to an opening for a different leadership model.

Whatever the reason, in this megadisaster I was permitted to play an unusual leadership role. I believe our team and I fulfilled that role effectively for the affected people of Mississippi, for the communities damaged by the storm and their leaders, for our state government, for the unprecedentedly generous volunteers and charities who gave so much, for our sister states, and for the federal government.

While our effort was certainly not perfect, it was highly successful in restoring, rebuilding, and renewing the communities on the Coast and across South Mississippi. Our effort kept our state government financially sound while civil order was never lost, even in the worst-hit communities.

And the reputation of our state actually was improved by the response of our people.

For government officials and political and business leaders, I call your attention to a couple of publications/papers on a concept called "meta-leadership," which focuses on leading those who don't report to you and don't have to take orders from you.

The first is a master's thesis by Col. Lee Wallace Smithson for the Naval Postgraduate School in Monterey, California. Colonel Smithson is an officer in the Mississippi National Guard, and the thesis is about the Katrina experience [https://calhoun.nps.edu/bitstream /handle/10945/44673/14Dec_Smithson_Lee.pdf?sequence=1].

The other is a Harvard University Kennedy School of Government paper by Leonard J. Marcus and colleagues entitled, "The Five Dimensions of Meta-Leadership" [http://npli.sph.harvard.edu/wp-content /uploads/sites/8/2013/04/Meta-leadership-Distribution.pdf].

In today's world, the ability to effectively lead those who do not have to follow you is a critical skill, particularly in a crisis situation. Increasingly, even in non-crisis times, that leadership capacity is becoming more necessary as business relationships become less vertical and more horizontal.

10. A strong, loving partner is a huge asset.

Being the leader when your people have been slammed by an unprecedented natural disaster like Katrina is emotionally draining, physically debilitating, intellectually demanding, and a whole lot more. It requires the leader and his or her team to do more than humanly possible, with the inevitable mistakes and oversights. It is life in the most glaring spotlight imaginable—no, it is worse than that!

It should be no surprise, then, that having a spouse who not only loves and supports you but actually bears an important part of the burden is a Godsend.

In Katrina, I was blessed to have such a partner: Marsha, my bride (then) of thirty-three years.

It is not an overstatement that Marsha became the face of the recovery effort—the face that said to people on the Coast, especially, that the state cared and was doing all it could to help them.

In the process, she became my eyes and ears, and for my team as well. She was on the Coast the night of the storm and for seventy of the next ninety days thereafter. Since she focused on those who had been disadvantaged before the storm and who were less likely to know how to help themselves, my team, including FEMA and MEMA, and I learned so much from her first-person reports.

Her efforts were very rewarding to her. Like hundreds of thousands of volunteers who came to Mississippi to help after Katrina, Marsha got more out of the experience herself than the good she felt like she did for those she was trying to help. It was a service based on her faith, her commitment to God, and her love for our people.

Because she knew so much about the situations and problems in the affected areas, we often spent most of our time together discussing those issues. In doing so we were working together in a tremendously rewarding way.

For much of our marriage I have traveled a lot, commuting to Jackson, running the South for the Ford campaign, working at the Reagan White House, and years as RNC chairman and as a Washington, D.C., lobbyist. We have been married forty-three years, but I joke that she still loves me because I've been gone thirty-eight!

She was my very effective partner as First Lady, but her Katrina role was far more than being First Lady. She was the face for the Mississippians in need.

And she was a bulwark for me.

Doing hard stuff is a lot easier if you have a strong, loving partner— one you can count on in every situation to help you do better, to buoy you up, to keep your ego in check, and to be your Gibraltar when things get tough or go wrong.

I was and am graced with such a partner. Partners such as she are great assets for leaders, especially in times of crisis.

Epilogue

EFORE MY SECOND TERM AS GOVERNOR ENDED, we took a look back at what had been done in the five years since Katrina devastated the Coast and impacted many other parts of Mississippi. I had made a promise to all Mississippians that the Coast, drawing on the resiliency and strength of its people, would come back bigger and better than ever. Here are some of the things we documented at that time.

Creative Collaborative Programs

- Governor's Commission on Recovery, Rebuilding, and Renewal combined ideas from local residents and leaders with expert knowledge from around the country to develop a recovery framework.
- We rethought disaster housing and designed the Mississippi Cottage as a better alternative to FEMA travel trailers; indeed, these cottages have proven their utility by providing temporary housing during subsequent disasters.
- Creation of the Homeowner Assistance Grant Program benefited nearly twenty-eight thousand households.

- A regional water and wastewater system is providing more effective services to residents who move inland to be safer from future hurricanes and protects the environment of the coastal communities.
- A statewide interoperable communication system is in operation to link emergency responders in times of crisis.

Governmental Sector, Private Industry, and Nonprofit Assistance Collaboration

- Housing needs were met. From the tens of thousands of FEMA units that housed nearly 100,000 Mississippians, fewer than 180 units were left.
- Public infrastructure was restored by using $3 billion obligated by FEMA in strategic alignment with other funding streams.
- State employment and job training efforts resulted in low unemployment rates on the Coast and bolstered the workforce to fuel coastal businesses.
- Every Mississippi school except one reopened within six weeks after Katrina.
- Medical and social services infrastructure were restored.
- Important restoration projects for the coastal environment, beaches, and forests were underway.

FEMA's Public Assistance Program

- Emergency Work

    - Debris removal: $717 million and more than 47 million cubic yards of debris removed, including nearly 400,000 cubic yards of marine debris
    - Emergency protective measures: $422 million

- Permanent Work

- Road systems and bridges: $91 million
- Water control facilities: $1 million
- Buildings, contents, and equipment: $650 million
- Utilities: $893 million
- Parks, recreational, and other facilities: $183 million
- State management administrative: $123 million

Hazard Mitigation Grant Program

- Provided $433 million to Mississippi for grants to local governments for measures that reduce the risk of loss of life and property from natural hazards.

Small Business Administration Disaster Assistance Program

- Home Physical Disaster Loans: $2 billion to 31,000 applicants to repair or replace damaged homes, and for homeowners and renters to replace personal property.
- Business Physical Disaster Loans: $545 million to 4,375 applicants for businesses of all sizes and to private nonprofit organizations to repair or replace damaged property and business assets.
- Economic Injury Disaster Loans: $19 million to 333 applicants for working capital for small businesses to cover normal operating expenses.

Disaster Unemployment Assistance

- Mississippi Department of Employment Security administered 34,600 claims for Disaster Unemployment Assistance

Crisis Counseling Assistance

- 300,000 individuals received counseling services to help relieve grieving, stress, or mental health problems caused by the natural disaster.

Mississippi Katrina Federal Funding

Supplemental Funding	
Community Development Block Grant (MDA)	$5,481,221,059
Federal Highway Administration Emergency Funds (MDOT)	$1,033,000,000
Medicaid (MDOM)	$643,668,933
K-12 Education (MDE)	$323,915,248
Alternative Housing Pilot Program (MEMA)	$281,318,612
Social Services Block Grant (DHS)	$128,398,427
Higher Education (IHL)	$114,745,515
National Emergency Grant (MDES)	$95,000,000
Law Enforcement (DPS)	$58,250,000
Historic Preservation (MDAH)	$27,500,000
Housing Choice Vouchers (PHAs)	$16,797,191
TOTAL	$8,203,814,985

Stafford Act Funding	
Public Assistance (FEMA)	$3,071,184,956
National Flood Insurance Program (FEMA)	$2,600,000,000
Homeowner and renter loans (SBA)	$2,066,425,900
Mission Assignments (FEMA)	$1,667,853,393
Individual Assistance (FEMA)	$1,284,714,374
Business loans (SBA)	$545,480,900
Hazard Mitigation Grant Program (MEMA)	$293,895,495
Comm Disaster loans (FEMA)	$270,621,714
Interoperable Communications (DHS-HMGP transfer)	$140,000,000
Crisis Counseling (MDMH)	$24,828,323
Working capital loans (SBA)	$19,182,800
TOTAL	$11,984,187,855

Federal Funds for Federal Activities	
Funding for military facilities, coastal restoration, U.S. Army Corps of Engineers, and USDA Rural Development	$4,406,576,453
TOTAL FEDERAL FUNDS	$24,594,579,293

Community Development Block Grant

Program	Allocation
Home Owner Assistance	$2,087,864,059
Regional Water and Wastewater	$641,075,000
Ratepayer/Windpool Mitigation	$440,000,000
Long Term Workforce Housing	$350,000,000
Small Rental Assistance	$232,500,000
Public Housing	$110,000,000
Elevation Grants	$70,500,000
Low Income Housing Tax Credit Assistance Fund	$30,000,000
Building/Code Inspectors	$9,500,000
HOUSING TOTAL	$3,971,439,059

Port of Gulfport Restoration	$570,000,000
Community Revitalization	$295,000,000
Economic Development	$247,182,000
Hancock County Long Term Recovery/Ground Zero	$200,000,000
Economic Development Employee Training Facilities	$20,000,000
Planning	$10,000,000
Tourism	$5,000,000
Fraud Investigation/Contractor Fraud	$5,000,000
State Administration	$157,600,000
BLOCK GRANT TOTAL	$5,481,221,059

The Mississippi Commission for Volunteer Service

Nonprofit and faith-based disaster response organizations and Ameri-Corps members:

- Provided 954,000 volunteers
- Served 10 million volunteer hours
- Donated $143 million in labor value
- Gave over $381 million in immediate emergency financial assistance
- Supplied $850,000 in relief, medical supplies, personal hygiene products, and household goods
- Leveraged over $17 million in recovery assistance for low-income residents
- Built 4,650 homes
- Rehabilitated 18,800 homes
- Provided over 376,000 individuals with pastoral, mental health, and emotional support services
- Completed 52,000 damage assessments
- Supported 2,412 community projects valued at $5.5 million
- Served more than 15 million meals, sandwiches, and snacks to volunteers and displaced residents
- Provided 208 shelters to house more than 284,000 people affected by Katrina
- Distributed over 178,800 cleaning kits and 235,000 food boxes
- Assisted over 106,000 families at Distribution Centers

AmeriCorps NCCC (National Civilian Community Corps)

- Served 2.7 million hours on over 1,040 relief and recovery projects on the Coast
- Donated services estimated at a value of $54 million

- Leveraged over 262,000 volunteers to refurbish over 10,500 homes and construct over 2,000 new homes
- Completed nearly 55,800 damage assessments
- Supported approximately 870 emergency response centers
- Distributed over 6,000 tons of food and served 1.6 million meals
- Refurbished 450 school rooms

Mississippi Center for Nonprofits

- Facilitated formation of the South Mississippi Alliance of Service Organizations to address infrastructure, partnerships, reduction of service duplication, and advocacy strategies
- Facilitated the creation of a technology-driven initiative to address the need for an information infrastructure and clearinghouse for nonprofits on the coast
- Held workshops for grant writing and governance
- Held three grant-writing blitzes that raised more than $500,000

Mississippi Department of Archives and History

- Within one month, identified 1,200 damaged but surviving historic properties scattered across 70 miles of coastline
- Volunteer teams completed damage assessments on hundreds of historic structures
- Saved many historic structures from demolition
- Received $24.7 million from Congress to assist citizens and communities in preserving and rehabilitating hurricane damaged historic buildings and sites
- Established the Mississippi Hurricane Relief Grant for Historic Preservation. Grants have gone mostly to owner occupied houses listed on the National Register of Historic Places and toward hundreds of affordable housing units

- Leveraged funds with FEMA, CDBG, and public and private sources to rehabilitate and rebuild historic places, including:

  - Beauvoir
  - Waveland Civic Center, formerly the Old Waveland School
  - Bay St. Louis Little Theatre, which relocated to a historic building
  - Historic Carnegie Library in Gulfport
  - Randolph School in Pass Christian
  - Old Hattiesburg High School
  - Gulfport City Hall
  - Hancock County Courthouse
  - 100 Man Association Building in Bay St. Louis
  - The Old Capitol Building in Jackson

MDAH Hurricane Recovery Grants for Historic Preservation

	Awarded	Projects Awarded	Projects Completed
Hancock County	$5,589,200	82	72
Harrison County	$10,828,584	121	94
Jackson County	$6,072,531	43	32
Other Counties	$2,234,686	17	11
TOTAL	$24,725,000	263	209

Housing

- Mid-2011 housing supply was estimated to be 100% of pre-Katrina totals compared to 96.2% of pre-Katrina population.
- Homeowner Assistance Program-Phase 1 (CDBG) provided $1.5 billion in one-time grant payments up to $150,000 for homeowners outside the established flood zones who suffered flood damage.
- Homeowner Assistance Program-Phase 2 (CDBG) targeted low- to moderate-income homeowners for grants up $100,000 for those who suffered flood damage due to insufficient insurance.

Homeowner Assistance Program

	Eligible Applications	Amount Awarded
HAP Phase 1	21,379	$1,534,728,683
HAP Phase 2	6,369	$468,707,770
TOTAL	27,748	$2,003,436,453

• Elevation Grant Program (CDBG)—Provided eligible applicants who were building in a flood plain a maximum grant of $30,000 to elevate above current levels, as required by FEMA; 932 grants have been paid totaling $23.9 million.

Public Infrastructure

• Mississippi Department of Transportation spent $1.1 billion on the following projects:

  • Rebuilt Highway 90
  • Rebuilt Bay of St. Louis Bridge
  • Rebuilt Biloxi Bay Bridge
  • Rebuilt parts of Interstate 10
  • Rebuilt Interstate 110

Public Facilities

• FEMA obligated $650 million to rebuild public facilities. These projects included:

  • 330 schools
  • 134 recreational facilities
  • 90 municipal buildings
  • 20 fire stations
  • 10 medical facilities
  • 4 police stations
  • 3 court buildings

Sources

In addition to the interviews and oral histories noted below, I relied on a number of secondary sources to double-check my memory as well as to expand on the stories I wanted to share and the points I wanted to make, especially the daily newspapers in Biloxi, Jackson, Laurel, Hattiesburg, and McComb and the books by James Patterson Smith and Douglas Brinkley. Following are the lists of interviews, oral histories, and print sources, I give particular citations for each chapter to support information I have included, especially if I have quoted from a source directly. The abbreviations in the chapter references refer to the secondary sources.

Interviews

Ryan Annison, taped interview, March 19, 2014
John Arledge, email exchanges
Henry Barbour, taped interview, July 28, 2014
Jim Barksdale, taped interview, November 18, 2014
Hank Bounds, taped interview, September 15, 2014
Butch Brown, taped interview, September 11, 2014
Jeb Bush, interview, April 8, 2015
Bill Carwile, taped interview, October 14, 2014
Mike Chaney, taped interview, October 31, 2014

Mike Cooper, taped interview, February 10, 2015

Pete Correll, taped interview, November 12, 2014

Harold Cross, taped interview, April 3, 2014

John England, interview, February 9, 2015

Eddie Favre, taped interview, September 10, 2014

Craig Fugate, taped interview, February 2, 2015

Larry Gregory, taped interview, December 19, 2014

John Hairston, email exchanges

Sam Haskell, interview, January 15, 2015

Curt Hebert, taped interview, May 7, 2014

A. J. Holloway, taped interview, September 10, 2014

Terri Hudson, taped interview, July 14, 2014

Paul Hurst, interview, February 10, 2015

Mark Keenum, taped interview, May 13, 2014

Scott Keller, taped interview, January 15, 2015

Marsha Meeks Kelly, interview, December 17, 2014

Bobby Kerley, taped interview, July 15, 2014

Robert Latham, taped interview, March 28, 2014

Trent Lott, taped interview, August 22, 2014

Ricky Mathews, taped interview, April 25, 2014

Jim McIngvale, taped interview, June 16, 2014

Bobby Moak, interview, January 4, 2015

Sam Owens, taped interview, February 3, 2015

Wade Parham, taped interview, February 3, 2015

Jim Perry, taped interview, June 3, 2014

Chip Pickering, taped interview, May 9, 2014

Ellen Ratner, interview, February 12, 2015

William Richardson, interview, February 9, 2015

Brian Sanderson, taped interview, July 31, 2014

Donna Sanford, taped interview, July 11, 2014

Albert Santa Cruz, taped interview, April 9, 2014

George Schloegel, taped interview, September 10, 2014

Billy Skellie, taped interview, September 30, 2014

Les Spivey, taped interview, June 2, 2014

Joe Spraggins, taped interview, January 7, 2015

Jerry St. Pé, taped interview, September 30, 2014

Anthony Topazi, email exchanges
Mike Womack, taped interview, April 25, 2014

Oral Histories

Provided by the Katrina Research Center at the University of Southern Mississippi

Henry Arledge, transcript of taped interview, May 31, 2007
George Dale, transcript of taped interview, July 7, 2006
Johnny DuPree, transcript of taped interview, August 1, 2006
A. J. Holloway, transcript of taped interview, January 18, 2007
Kay Kell, transcript of taped interview, January 11, 2007
Brian Martin, transcript of taped interview, December 31, 2007
Ricky Mathews, transcript of taped interview, August 25, 2006
Reilly Morse, transcript of taped interview, March 12, 2008
George Schloegel, transcript of taped interview, August 14, 2008
Gavin Smith, transcript of taped interview, January 10, 2007
Gene Taylor, transcript of taped interview, February 21, 2008
Brent Warr, transcript of taped interview, June 20, 2008

Books

DB—Douglas Brinkley, *The Great Deluge: Hurricane Katrina, New Orleans, and the Mississippi Gulf Coast*. New York: William Morrow, 2006.

DIS—Christopher Cooper and Robert Block, *Disaster: Hurricane Katrina and the Failure of Homeland Security*. New York: Henry Holt, 2006.

JPS—James Patterson Smith, *Hurricane Katrina: The Mississippi Story*. Jackson: University Press of Mississippi, 2012.

KOCH—Kathleen Koch, *Rising from Katrina: How My Mississippi Hometown Lost It All and Found What Mattered*. Winston-Salem, NC: John F. Blair, 2010.

PLAN—Gavin Smith, *Planning for Post-Disaster Recovery: A Review of the United States Disaster Assistance Framework*. Fairfax, VA: Public Entity Risk Institute and Island Press, 2011.

Federal Government Publications

ARMY—James A. Wombwell, *Army Support during the Hurricane Katrina Disaster*, U.S. Army Combined Arms Center, Combat Studies Institute Press, Fort Leavenworth, Kansas (November 2014).

BUSH—Public Papers of the Presidents of the United States, George W. Bush, Book II, July 1 to December 31, 2005, United States Government Printing Office.

CBO—*The Federal Government's Spending and Tax Actions in Response to the 2005 Gulf Coast Hurricanes*, Congressional Budget Office (August 1, 2007).

CRS—*Emergency Supplemental Appropriations for Hurricane Katrina Relief*, Congressional Research Service (August 22, 2006).

FAIL—*A Failure of Initiative: Final Report of the Select Bipartisan Committee to Investigate the Preparation for and Response to Hurricane Katrina* (2006).

FR—*Federal Response to Hurricane Katrina: Lessons Learned* (2006).

NHC—Richard D. Knabb, Jamie R. Rhome, and Daniel P. Brown, *Hurricane Katrina: Tropical Cyclone Report*, National Hurricane Center (December 20, 2005, and updated on August 10, 2006, and September 14, 2011).

NOAA—*Hurricane Katrina: Climatological Perspective*, NOAA's National Climate Data Center, Technical Report 2005-01 (October 2005).

State Government Publications

BB—*After Katrina: Building Back Better Than Ever*, A Report to the Hon. Haley Barbour, Governor of the State of Mississippi from the Governor's Commission on Recovery, Rebuilding, and Renewal (December 31, 2005).

CAMILLE—Governor's Emergency Council, *The Mississippi Gulf Coast Comprehensive Development after Camille* (1970).

FYAK—*Five Years after Katrina: Progress Report on Recovery, Rebuilding, and Renewal* (Office of Governor Haley Barbour, August 2010).

HJ—Mississippi House Journal.

LAWS—Laws of the Mississippi Legislature.

MDOT—*After Katrina: Rebuilding Lives and Infrastructure*, Mississippi Department of Transportation, Wayne Brown, Commissioner Southern District (November 2007).

SJ—Mississippi Senate Journal.

Newspapers and TV Transcripts

CL—*Clarion-Ledger*, newspaper
CNN—CNN Reports: Katrina, State of Emergency (2005).
CQ—*Congressional Quarterly*, journal.
CQT—*Congressional Quarterly Today*, journal.
NYT—*New York Times*, newspaper.
POST—*Washington Post*, newspaper.
RC—*Roll Call*, newspaper.
SH—*Sun Herald*, newspaper.

Miscellaneous Publications

"Entergy Response to Hurricanes Katrina & Rita," and "Inside Entergy Commemorative Edition," Entergy Corporation.
"Hurricane Katrina Slams Gulf Coast," *Guard Detail: A Chronicle of the Mississippi Army and Air National Guard*, May–September 2005.
Robert R. Latham, Jr., "Hurricane Katrina: Mississippi Operations," Mississippi Emergency Management Agency.
Jim McIngvale, "Hurricane Katrina . . . The Winds Stopped, the Challenge Continues," Northrop Grumman Corporation, April 27, 2006.
Brig. Gen. Joe Spraggins, "Harrison County Lessons Learned," Harrison County Emergency Management Office.
"State of the State Annual Report: Mississippi Gaming 2014," Mississippi Gaming and Hospitality Association.
"Our Story 2006," Mississippi Commission for Volunteer Service.
Lee Wallace Smithson, "Meta-Leadership in a Mega Disaster: A Case Study of Governor Haley Barbour's Leadership during Hurricane Katrina," master's thesis, Naval Postgraduate School, Monterey, CA, 2014.
Leonard Marcus, Barry Dorn, Eric McNulty, Joseph Henderson, and Isaac Ashkenazi, "Crisis Preparedness and Response: The Meta-Leadership Model." In *The McGraw-Hill Homeland Security Handbook: The Definitive Guide for Law Enforcement, EMT, and All Other Security Professionals*, ed. David Kamien. New York: McGraw-Hill, 2012.

Chapter 1

Key interviews included Ryan Annison, Butch Brown, Bill Carwile, Harold Cross, Eddie Favre, Bobby Kerley, Robert Latham, Ricky Mathews, Albert Santa Cruz, Billy Skellie, Joe Spraggins, and Mike Womack.

The description of Hurricane Camille is taken from JPS.

This description of Hurricane Katrina is taken from JPS, NHC, and NOAA reports.

"Meteorologists Believe" comes from Melissa M. Scallan, "Katrina Could Be in Gulf on Saturday," SH, August 25, 2005.

Information about issuing executive orders comes from JPS, FYAK, and FAIL.

Specific data on National Guard deployments comes from information provided by Harold Cross.

"as of now, landfall would be west" comes from "Coast Counties Appear Squarely in the Path," SH, August 27, 2005.

"Based on a survey" is from "Coast Counties Appear Squarely in the Path," SH, August 27, 2005.

"Fear the Worst" comes from Joshua Norman and Melissa Scallan, "Fearing the Worst: Category 5," SH, August 28, 2005. See also Tracy Dash, "Another Camille," SH, August 29, 2005.

"This is a tremendously dangerous storm" comes from Jack Mazurak, "Residents urged to prepare now," CL, August 28, 2005.

Information about evacuation orders comes from FAIL and from interviews.

Information for Saturday's prediction comes from "Coast Counties Appear Squarely in the Path," SH, August 27, 2005; NHC; and JPS. A NOAA report indicated the National Hurricane Center issued a Hurricane Warning for the Gulf Coast from Morgan City, Louisiana, to the Alabama/Florida border at 22:00 CDT on August 27.

Information on contraflow comes from JPS and interviews.

The Max Mayfield Saturday night call comes from interviews; also DIS, "At the NIC in Miami, one of Max Mayfield's colleagues suggested that he might want to make a round of calls to politicians in Louisiana and Mississippi, to give them a nudge, to inject them with a little urgency." Author talked about "Hurricane Pam exercise." Mayfield said almost apologetically, "I just thought it would be good to let them know."

Information on buoys comes from DB, JPS, and NOAA.

Information on regional/national FEMA calls comes from FAIL and DB.

Chapter 2

Key interviews included Ryan Annison, Butch Brown, Bill Carwile, Mike Chaney, Harold Cross, Eddie Favre, Bobby Kerley, Robert Latham, Ricky Mathews, Billy Skellie, Joe Spraggins, and Mike Womack.

Information about the status of Katrina comes from the NHC report, the NOAA report, and FAIL. JPS: Studies conducted by the Navy made clear that hurricane-force winds reached the coast four hours ahead of the storm surge. The Navy's analysis showed that from Waveland to Ocean Springs, hurricane-force winds arrived between 5 a.m. and 6 a.m. Category 3 winds of 111–130 mph pounded Gulfport and Biloxi from 9 a.m. onward. The maximum storm surge was not seen until almost two hours later, just before 11 a.m.

Information about shelters comes from FAIL and interviews.

Information about early reports of Katrina damage come from FAIL, FYAK, newspaper reports, and interviews.

"Looting is the equivalent of grave robbing" comes from CL, August 30, 2005.

"The water came in, blew off manhole covers" comes from FAIL.

"Right now, downtown [Gulfport] looks like Nagasaki" comes from Jerry Mitchell, "Flooding, Wreckage, Death Sweep Miss," CL, August 30, 2005.

"It's not like people can get up [today]" comes from Jack Mazurak, "Limbs, Debris, Litter City Streets," CL, August 30, 2005.

Information about Katrina's path through Mississippi come from JPS, NHC, and NOAA.

Information about the destruction come from FR, NOAA, NHC, JPS, FYAK, and FAIL.

Chapter 3

Key interviews included Ryan Annison, Butch Brown, Bill Carwile, Harold Cross, Eddie Favre, Craig Fugate, Marsha Meeks Kelly, Bobby Kerley, Robert

Latham, Ricky Mathews, Jim McIngvale, William Richardson, George Schloegel, Billy Skellie, Joe Spraggins, and Mike Womack.

Chapter 4

Key interviews included Ryan Annison, Butch Brown, Bill Carwile, Pete Correll, Harold Cross, Eddie Favre, Sam Haskell, Marsha Meeks Kelly, Bobby Kerley, Robert Latham, Ricky Mathews, Ellen Ratner, Albert Santa Cruz, George Schloegel, Billy Skellie, Joe Spraggins, and Mike Womack.

Chapter 5

Key interviews included Larry Gregory, Paul Hurst, Ricky Mathews, Bobby Moak, Jim Perry, and Jerry St. Pé.

The various legislative votes and times and dates related to the special session were taken from the relevant Senate and House Journals.

Information about casino employment and tax revenues came from materials provided by Larry Gregory.

"Casino Plan Stalls" comes from Geoff Pender, Melissa Scallan and Tom Wilemon, "Casino Plan Stalls in Senate," SH, October 1, 2005.

"Moments Before" comes from Geoff Pender and Tom Wilemon, "Senate Puts Casino Bill on Hold," SH, October 5, 2005.

"House leaders left claiming" comes from Geoff Pender, "Onshore Wins Standoff," SH, October 8, 2005.

Pettus's column was Emily W. Pettus, "Gaming Vote Cost Barbour Political Capital," CL, October 11, 2005.

Bills Passed by the 2005 Special Session, taken from 2005 State Legislation/Special Session/Chapter Laws

1 – special legislation for MDA for a certain project
2 – exempts certain schools from accountability standards
3 – authorizes local schools to take any and all actions to recover damaged timber and prevent further loss on sixteenth section lands
4 – allows a local government to change its seat of government because of a natural disaster

5 – authorizes state superintendent of education to appoint a financial advisor for certain school systems

6 – authorizes local governments in certain counties to compensate and/or grant leave to employees unable to work as a result of Katrina

7 – local and private bill for a public utility district in Harrison County

8 – extends statute of limitations in certain cases as a result of Katrina

9 – establishes within the office of the governor the office of disaster assistance coordination

10 – authorizes extensions of tax returns

11 – (HB 46)–revises the terms of "cruise vessel" and "vessel" to include a structure onshore

12 – authorizes the State Bond Commission to secure a line of credit up to $500 million to cover state government expenses

13 – provides a one-year waiver of out-of-state tuition for state universities and community colleges

14 – establishes the Mississippi Disaster Small Business Bridge Loan Act; authorizes the State Bond Commission to secure a $25 million loan to finance the program

15 – (HB 44)–tidelands legislation

16 – (HB 45)–on-land gaming legislation

17 – extends the time period within which money borrowed by a school district in anticipation of revenue can be repaid

18 – revises the terms under which local agencies may apply for certain disaster assistance funding

19 – authorizes additional transfers among major budget categories for state agencies

20 – authorizes counties and municipalities to donate supplies, labor, and equipment in disaster counties

21 – waives penalties related to payment of local counties in disaster areas

22 – exempts from state income taxes disaster payments

23 – authorizes certain school districts to borrow money beyond current statutory caps to respond to disaster situations

24 – requires all state agencies to obtain business property insurance in order to receive FEMA reimbursements

25 – special session appropriation

Chapter 6

Key interviews included Ryan Annison, Henry Barbour, Jim Barksdale, Butch Brown, A. J. Holloway, Ricky Mathews, Brian Sanderson, George Schloegel, and Gavin Smith.

In addition to the interviews, this narrative was generally informed by the report issued by the Barksdale Commission: *After Katrina: Building Back Better Than Ever*, issued on December 31, 2005; a series the SH ran from May 7 to May 18, 2006, examining the work of the commission; and materials provided by Henry Barbour, who served as executive director of the commission.

"I am utterly confident" comes from Emily Wagster Pettus, *Associated Press*, "Mammoth Rebuilding Effort from Katrina Alters Mississippi Politics," September 12, 2005.

The tent meeting coverage comes from Geoff Pender, "You Need to Develop Blueprint for Future," SH, September 21, 2005.

Sid Salter, Haley Barbour interview, CL, September 14, 2005.

Quotes from the opening of the Charrette comes from "Vision Quest Begins," SH, October 13, 2005.

The Barksdale Commission report (BB) contains the names of all committee members and the detailed recommendations: www.mississippirenewal.com/documents/Governors_Commission _Report.pdf. The commissioners were the following:

Jim Barksdale, Chairman	Hank Bounds, Jackson
Derrick Johnson, Vice Chairman	Felicia Dunn Burkes, Harrison
Ricky Mathews, Vice Chairman	Fred Carl, Leflore
Jerry St. Pé Vice Chairman	David Cole, Itawamba
Joe Sanderson, Vice Chairman	Mark Cumbest, Jackson
Anthony Topazi, Vice Chairman	Maurice Dantin, Marion
William Winter, Outside Counsel	Tommy Dulaney, Lauderdale
Chris Anderson, Jackson	Donald Evans, Harrison
Reuben Anderson, Hinds	Robbie Fisher, Hinds
Chuck Benvenutti, Hancock	Paul Franke, Harrison
James Black, Harrison	Robert Gagné, Hancock
Gerald Blessey, Harrison	Richard Gollott, Harrison

Clark Griffith, Harrison
Jill Holleman, Stone
Brooks Holstein, Harrison
Warren Hood, Jr., Forrest
James Huff, Smith
Robert Kane, Hancock
Kay Kell, Jackson
Suzy McDonald, Pearl River
Duncan McKenzie, Harrison
Pat Nichols, Harrison
John Palmer, Hinds
Bill Parsons, Hancock
Diann Payne, Jackson

Ron Peresich, Harrison
Charles Pickering, Jones
D'Auby Schiel, Harrison
George Schloegel, Harrison
Robert St. John, Forrest
Chevis Swetman, Harrison
Reginald Sykes, Harrison
Phil Teel, Jackson
Shelby Thames, Forrest
Richard Thoms, Newton
Phillip West, Adams
Dayton Whites, George
Glade Woods, Pearl River

Chapter 7

Key interviews included Ryan Annison, John England, Curt Hebert, Mark Keenum, Trent Lott, Jim Perry, Chip Pickering, and Les Spivey.

Information about the early FEMA appropriations comes from the *Congressional Record* for the dates in question (the Senate met on September 1 and approved a motion and a resolution, which essentially held that if the House were to pass the appropriations bill on September 2—the first time the House leadership could convene that chamber—then the bill would be deemed to pass the Senate, which would not be officially in session on September 2); PL 109-61 and PL 109-62.

Sid Salter, Haley Barbour interview, CL, September 14, 2005.

Representative McCrery's legislation was PL 109-73.

Louisiana's $250 billion plan comes from NYT, September 23, 2005.

The Medicaid provision was attached to PL 109-171, the Deficit Reduction Act of 2005, which appropriated $2 billion for Medicaid matching payments for Louisiana and Mississippi.

Details of Bush's request, including the CDBG allocation, come from Ana Radelat, "$35.4B Aid Bill to Be Pushed," CL, December 3, 2005; and JPS.

Details of Barbour's plan come from CL, November 1, 2005; FYAK; SH, November 8, 2005; SH, November 9, 2005; and JPS.

"I am disappointed" comes from Geoff Pender, "Barbour Unhappy with Bush's Katrina Plan," SH, November 8, 2005.

"I am prepared" and the longer quote come from RC, December 7, 2005.

Information about congressional testimony comes from Karen Nelson, "Now It's Coast's Turn to Testify," SH, December 7, 2005; and JPS.

Barbour "Delay is our enemy" comes from Joshua Cogswell, "Barbour Vexed by Congress' Inaction," CL, November 30, 2005.

Vacation editorial comes from "Congress Should Not Take a Holiday Until It Passes Relief for Katrina Victims," SH, November 18, 2005.

The "Appeal to the President" appeared on the front page of SH, December 4, 2005.

The "panic mode" quote comes from Geoff Pender, "Time Is Slipping Away," SH, December 11, 2005.

"Taking the starch out" comes from Ana Radelat, "Barbour: Recovery Stalled," CL, December 8, 2005; see also CQT, December 9, 2005.

Passage of GO Zone legislation in early December comes from Tony Pugh, "Barbour Beseeches Congress," SH, December 8, 2005.

Lott's "dusted off" comment is from CQT, December 9, 2005.

White House $24 million offer comes from Geoff Pender, "Cochran May Hold the Key," SH, December 14, 2005.

"By middle of December making progress" comes from Geoff Pender, "Aid Package on Track," SH, December 15, 2005.

Parts of the Barbour meeting with Speaker Hastert appear in JPS and NYT, February 26, 2006.

"We have a deal" comes from Geoff Pender, "Katrina Deal Reached," SH, December 18, 2005.

Information about the Sen. Ted Stevens push in the Senate comes from POST, December 20, 2005, and December 21, 2005; and CQT, December 21, 2005.

The special appropriations legislation was part of PL 109-148.

Giving Cochran credit comes from CQT, December 21, 2005.

The GO Zone legislation was part of PL 109-135.

The Medicaid legislation was part of PL 109-171; see also Ana Radelat, "Senate Oks $29B for Aid," CL, December 22, 2005; and "Katrina: Medicaid Funds Represent Real Help," editorial in CL, December 27, 2005.

Chapter 8

Key interviews included Hank Bounds, Butch Brown, Larry Gregory, and Ricky Mathews. Materials were also provided by Brown, Bounds, and Gregory.

The Christmas card verse from the Bible is found at Jeremiah 31:17, New Living Translation.

"Racket of Slot Machines" comes from Tom Wilemon, "IP Opens to Big Crowd," SH, December 23, 2005.

"Let the good times roll" comes from Quincy C. Collins, "Isle Reopens as Land Casino," SH, December 27, 2005.

Mississippi law restricts a student to the school district that encompasses his or her residence.

Barbour's appearance before the Legislature is from Laura Hipp, "Barbour Touts Relief Grants," CL, January 5, 2006.

Chapter 9

Key interviews included Terri Hudson, Scott Keller, Donna Sanford, Brian Sanderson, and Gavin Smith. Materials were provided by Hudson.

"FEMA had paid out" comes from SH, February 26, 2006.

"100,000 people in 34,000 FEMA trailers" comes from Bob Dart, "Senate Hears about Storms," SH, February 3, 2006.

"While the appropriation bill signed by President Bush": The initial allocation to Mississippi from the federal appropriation bill about $5 billion with a second appropriation made later. Our initial action plan submitted to HUD was for just over $3 billion, which included the compensation grant, elevation grants, assistance to local permit offices and the grant to the State Auditor's Office for investigation unit. It was anticipated that $2 billion would be expended for compensation grants.

"People are depending on us" comes from Sid Salter, Haley Barbour interview, CL, September 14, 2005.

"Indeed, we subsequently were told Louisiana": Louisiana used compensation grants but initially tied the funds to percentage of completion of the construction, and they were instructed by HUD to restructure their program because their method invoked environmental requirements. This setback, the complexity of the grant calculation they created, and their slow start with taking applications put Louisiana's progress behind ours.

For information about mortgage bankers see Joshua Cogswell, "Banker Association Objects," CL, June 23, 2006.

Epilogue

This information came from FYAK.

Index